HOUSE CALLS *and*
HITCHING POSTS

Accept my talents, great or small,
Choose thou the path for me,
Where I shall labor joyously
In service, Lord, for thee.

– a verse from Dr. Lehman's favorite hymn,
"Teach Me Thy Truth"

House Calls and Hitching Posts

Stories from Dr. Elton Lehman's career among the Amish

as told to Dorcas Sharp Hoover

Good Books

Intercourse, PA 17534
800/762-7171
www.GoodBooks.com

With gratitude to
the many patients who entrusted their medical care to me
for two generations;
and to Dorcas Sharp Hoover, without whose tireless efforts
there would be no book;
and to Phyllis, my wife, and our children,
Dr. Randy and Brenda Benner, Dr. Brent and Dr. Claudia Lehman,
and Bev Lehman, for their support.
– Dr. Elton D. Lehman

Credits
The two large photographs and the photo of the doctor's bag on the front cover, the two photographs on the back cover, and the photograph on the spine are all by Chris Russell/ *Columbus Dispatch.*

The inset photograph on the front cover above the title is by Karen Schiely/*Akron Beacon Journal.*

"Teach me thy truth" in *Hymnal: A Worship Book,* copyright 1992, by Brethren Press, Faith and Life Press, and Mennonite Publishing House: Scottdale, PA 15683. Used by permission.

The photograph on the title page is by Chris Russell/*Columbus Dispatch.*

Design by Dawn J. Ranck

HOUSE CALLS AND HITCHING POSTS
Copyright © 2004 by Good Books, Intercourse, PA 17534
International Standard Book Number: 978-1-56148-502-4 (paperback)
International Standard Book Number: 978-1-56148-438-6 (hardcover)
Library of Congress Catalog Card Number: 2004002356

Library of Congress Cataloging-in-Publication Data

Lehman, Elton.
    House calls and hitching posts : stories from Dr. Elton Lehman's career among the Amish / as told to Dorcas Sharp Hoover.
    p. cm.
ISBN-13: 978-1-56148-438-6   ISBN-10: 1-56148-438-5
1. Lehman, Elton. 2. Physicians–Ohio–Holmes County–Biography. 3. Medicine, Rural–Ohio– Holmes County–Anecdotes. 4. Amish–Medical care–Ohio–Holmes County– Anecdotes. I. Hoover, Dorcas. II. Title.
    R154.L366A3 2004
    610'.92–dc22   2004002356

TABLE OF CONTENTS

Elton, middle, and brother Merlin, right, with their pony on the Sylvester and Martha Lehman farm in Kidron. Individual on the left is unknown.

The Sylvester and Martha Lehman family in 1953, with their 12 children from left to right. Back row: Ruth (Lehman) Bontrager, Florine (Lehman) Yoder, Beth (Lehman) Wiebe, Doris (Lehman) Sommer, Merlin Lehman, Elton Lehman. Middle row: Jenelle (Lehman) Gould, Don Lehman, Larrry Lehman, Dave Lehman. Front row: Sylvester, Geraldine (Lehman) Mumaw, Martha, Carol (Lehman) Burkholder.

Dr. Lehman at his graduation from Midwestern University-Chicago College of Osteopathic Medicine, with his fiancé Phyllis Schloneger in June 1963.

Dr. Elton and Phyllis Lehman at their wedding on June 15, 1963.

Dr. Lehman hangs his shingle in July 1964 at the square in Mount Eaton.

The Mount Eaton Care Center.

Pencil sketch by Susan Weirich

Lehman family photo

This pencil sketch of Barb Hostetler hangs in the Mount Eaton Care Center. Barb opened her home to women in labor and assisted Dr. Lehman with many deliveries. She died August 6, 2003.

Five thousand pennies for 5,000 deliveries in June 1993. Lehman would deliver more than 6,300 babies in his career before "retiring."

Awards Received by Dr. Elton Lehman

- Outstanding Mentor Award, 1991—Ohio University College of Osteopathic Medicine
- Outstanding Achievement Award, 1994—Chicago College of Osteopathic Medicine Alumni Association
- Country Doctor of the Year Award, 1998—Staff Care, Inc.
- Alumnus of the Year Award, 1998—Eastern Mennonite University
- Family Physician of the Year Award, 1998—The Ohio State Society of the American College of Osteopathic Family Physicians
- Shining Light Award, 1998—Mental Health and Recovery Board of Wayne & Holmes counties
- Citizen of the Year Award, 1998—*Wooster (Ohio) Daily Record*
- Distinguished Rural Health Provider, 2000—Ohio Department of Health
- Distinguished Service Award, 2002—Ohio Osteopathic Association
- Distinguished Service Award, 2004—American College of Osteopathic Family Physicians

Elton and Phyllis Lehman with children Brenda (standing), Brent, and Bev in 1979.

The Lehman family in 1987. Standing left to right are Bev, Elton, Phyllis, Brenda, and Brent.

Dr. Lehman thanks children, Bev, Brent, and Brenda at the Country Doctor of the Year celebration on April 24, 1998.

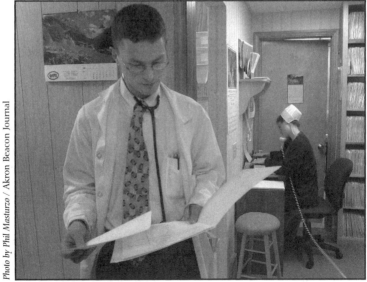

Dr. Brent Lehman reviews a patient's charts at the Mount Eaton Medical Center.

Dr. Elton Lehman in his pharmacy, 2003.

INTRODUCTION

When my husband Jerry and I first met Dr. Lehman, his calm, thoughtful manner and commitment to integrity impressed us immediately. We knew we could trust this country doctor to deliver our children, even if it meant driving nearly an hour to his small-town clinic.

Dr. Lehman went on to deliver four of our six children in the peaceful birthing center he designed for his Amish patients. At each delivery, my husband asked the doctor about his adventures, and "Doc" proceeded to entertain us with another account, keeping us between laughter and tears.

"Doc, you need to write a book," my husband always said. Dr. Lehman would glance up with a look of startled horror on his face. Quickly, he'd slip back into his shy reserve and dash off a row of notes on his clipboard. "Oh, no," he'd say, heading for the door. "I'm not a writer."

Then one afternoon Doc called me at home. "Folks have been telling me I need to record my experiences," he said, "but I'm not a writer. Would you consider writing my story for me?"

Later, as Jerry and I listened to Dr. Lehman share his stories in the living room of our log cabin home, we recognized the inspirational value in the stories from this community servant. He embodied the biblical concept that in dying to self, we truly live. My husband and I decided we were willing to make sacrifices of our own to bring these stories to others.

Dr. Lehman's patients have selflessly shared their hearts, thoughts, and memories with us so I could share them with you. I have tried to protect their privacy by changing their names, with the exception of the characters in "Five Small White Crosses" and "The Mysterious Case of Little Boy Blue," which received wide media coverage. As a rule, I used the actual names of Dr. Lehman's staff, his relatives, pastor, historical figures, acquaintances, colleagues, and his Mennonite patients. I also used actual names in "The Pie Takes the Prize," with the exception of "Harry" at the beginning of that chapter.

In my efforts to protect Dr. Lehman's patients—many who, by religious conviction, wish to humbly stay out of the limelight— I have taken a writer's liberty to make minor changes to insignificant details in the accounts, while being tenaciously loyal to the basic facts. In order for the book to read as a story, the factual account is recorded in historical narrative—using conversations based on facts. In a few rare incidents, it was necessary for several events to be placed within the same story. Where there were conflicting accounts from the countless interviews, I have chosen to use the perspective of the person closest to the incident in question. All the events recorded in the book are, in fact, true. If there are errors, the author acknowledges they are hers.

Since neither 911 emergency services nor squads were available to the Mount Eaton community in the mid '60s when Dr. Lehman began his practice, he occasionally found it necessary in those early years to transport patients to the hospital in his personal vehicle. Med school professors had advised against using a personal vehicle to transport patients, but the little village of Mount Eaton, Ohio, with its large Amish population, defied convention!

Finally, this book could not have been published without the gracious assistance and support of patients, friends, relatives, and colleagues to whom I am indebted. Though I regret I am unable to mention each by name, I cannot forget to express my appreciation to:

- Dr. Elton Lehman, Phyllis Lehman, and children Brenda, Brent, and Beverly for sharing their lives
- Dr. Lehman's patients and the capable office and Care Center staff for sharing their stories
- The late and legendary Barb Hostetler
- Dr. Wain Eberly, who invited Dr. Lehman to Mount Eaton
- Dr. Nolan Byler for contributing stories and checking for errors
- The late Louise Stoltzfus, who first began this project
- Celia Lehman, who carefully researched several chapters
- Paul M. Schrock, former director of Herald Press and Dr. Lehman's EMU classmate, who graciously advised and guided the project
- Myrrl Byler, the teacher who encouraged me to write
- Merle and Phyllis Good and Delphine Martin of Good Books for their expertise in refining the book
- My uncle Dr. David R. Miller, Dr. Lehman's classmate, who reviewed the medical terminology
- Supportive colleagues and patients of Dr. Lehman, as well as friends and relatives of the Lehmans and the Hoovers
- My husband, Jerry Hoover, and our children, Jerry Allen, Justin, Judith, Joshua, Janae, and Janelle, for their patient support
- My parents, Urie and Delilah Sharp, college classmates of Dr. Lehman, for their encouragement and support
- Our precious Lord—the ultimate example of selfless service—for his grace and guidance through this project

For the glory of God,
Dorcas Sharp Hoover
March 2004

1.

THE SCENT OF TROUBLE

With a puzzled look on her youthful face, the receptionist studied the young man entering the office. It wasn't his
straw hat or suspenders that held the stares of the secretary
and patients in the waiting room. It was the rusty coffee can
concealing the newcomer's hand. A pungent odor filled the
room, and the Amish patients eyed each other knowingly.
Kerosene. The scent of trouble.

Another emergency, the receptionist thought, studying the
conspicuous can as she answered the ringing phone. "Mount
Eaton Clinic, Dr. Lehman's office." Nancy brushed back strands
of brown hair escaping the barrettes that secured her hair into
a bun. Her eyes kept returning to the hand held into the
kerosene-filled can.

"So, you would like Dr. Lehman to stop by your house
tonight to check the traction on your daughter's broken leg?"
Nancy asked, eying the coffee can. "Can you hold, please,
while I check with the doctor?" A moment later Nancy confirmed the house call.

Right again, Rebecca, she thought, replacing the telephone
receiver as the young Amishman set the can on the counter in

front of her. You always said Mount Eaton Clinic is like the community emergency room here in the north end of Amish Country, and you're right again. One never can tell what emergency will burst through those doors!

"Let's see your hand," Nancy gripped her pen and leaned expectantly toward the can.

The youth lifted a mutilated hand from the container, revealing white circles of naked bone and red, tattered tissue where fingers should have been. Nancy froze in horror as the patient fished dripping, dismembered fingers from the can. "Put them back! Put them back!" she recoiled in horror.

"*Ach mei zeit!*" the patients in the waiting room chorused. "*Ei yi yi!*"

"I should have known better," the receptionist muttered while nearly colliding with a nurse in the hall. "Alice! Get Doc! We've got an emergency!"

No one in the paneled waiting room spoke. *The Farm and Ranch, Sugarcreek Budget,* and *Guideposts* lay ignored in patients' laps as every eye followed the young man with his odorous can until the door shut behind him.[1]

After a long moment, a lanky patient seated in the corner thoughtfully rubbed his smooth-shaven chin. "Poor guy's wasting his time here. The doctor will send a case like that straight to the emergency room. He should have gone there directly," the man sniffed. "No doctor would treat a hand like that in the office."

"Then you don't know Doc Lehman," said a balding patriarch stroking his long, gray beard. He set his gold-rimmed glasses higher on the bridge of his nose and appraised the outspoken man in the corner. Obviously, this *Englischer* was a newcomer to the area.

"Let me tell you something," the elderly man proposed quietly, leaning forward on his cane. "Dr. Lehman goes out of his way to accommodate patients like us Amish folk who don't have insurance to pay hospital bills nor cars to take us to the emergency room. Why, some time back, I had a cyst almost as big as an egg and Doc cut it out here at the office."

"We're talking about *surgery*," the *Englischer* persisted impatiently. "I've never known a general practitioner yet who'd do that type of extensive repair right in the office. That's a job for a surgeon in an emergency room."

"Well then Lehman ain't no general practitioner," quipped a plump, graying woman tugging at her bonnet ties. "I don't know what kind of doctor he is, but we call him a country doctor. Why, my Lester got his hand chewed up in a corn picker, and Doc sewed him up again just as nice and neat as you please."

"*Yah*, that's Doc, all right," a young woman shyly agreed as she patted a sleeping infant lying on her lap. She carefully smoothed the wrinkles in the apron that nearly brushed her black shoestrings. "Our neighbor got her hand all chopped up in a steak cuber. Doc fixed her hand up real nice. Put 96 stitches in it. He worked on it three hours and now you'd hardly know it was ever hurt."

"Ninety-six stitches!" the man in the corner whistled. "Here in this building? I never heard of a doctor caring for those kinds of emergencies in the office. I'll believe it when I see it."

Still weak from seeing the dismembered fingers, Nancy couldn't help but smile at the patients' conversation. They talked as though their doctor could repair any injury they'd encounter. No matter how severely mangled, they expected their "Doc" could sew them up and send them on their way again. Nancy recalled a few emergencies that Dr. Lehman needed to transfer to the hospital: the child whose throat was slit in a dog attack, the young hunter who accidentally shot himself in the abdomen, and the man with the chainsaw wound on his head.

Back in one of the four treatment rooms, Alice offered a chair to the youth with his hand in the coffee can and observed him closely for signs of fainting. A moment later, Dr. Lehman swept into the room.

"What do we have here?" he asked, adjusting his glasses and gently lifting the mutilated hand from the can.

"*Ach yammah.* I ran it through the saw at the mill. Too *schuslich,* I guess," the patient answered, studying Dr. Lehman's dark hair, ruddy cheeks, and solid build.

"Well, one has to look at the bright side," the doctor replied with the trace of a smile. "From now on it won't take as long to trim your fingernails!"

"Ha! Never thought about that!" Joe chuckled. "That just shows that there's something good in everything that happens."

While Dr. Lehman assessed the damage, Rebecca carefully arranged a syringe, forceps, bone-snips, suture driver, and a stack of gauze on a sterile towel next to a bottle of Zephrin. She set a waste can on the floor beneath the end of the examining table.

First of all, he needs something for pain, Dr. Lehman thought, examining the wound. "Tylenol with codeine, Rebecca," he instructed, noting the patient's restrained emotion so characteristic of the Amish folk.

"So I see you brought the fingers with you," the doctor observed, examining the contents of the coffee can. "Do you want them reattached?"

"You mean you could sew them on again?"

"I don't have the facilities to do that here to give you proper use of your fingers again. You'll have to go to the hospital if you want them reattached, but it could be done."

The patient shook his head. "*Ach,* that could cost me an arm and a leg. That would be *dummheit,* giving an arm and a leg to fix a couple of fingers!"

"In that case," Dr. Lehman replied, "I'll have to trim your bone back to the next joint. That will give us a flap of skin to bring up over the exposed end of the finger, and then I'll stitch it up. I can do that here, but you'll have to understand it is not the most pleasant procedure."

"*Yah*, that's okay. Just go for it."

While Joe soaked his hand in Dreft laundry detergent to disinfect the mutilated fingers, the doctor and nurses quickly tended to several other patients. The doctor extracted a kernel of corn from a youngster's ear and examined a toddler scheduled for a measles, mumps, and rubella vaccine. The child lay quietly on the examining table, her large eyes watching the doctor hold the stethoscope to her chest. "She's growing nicely," he observed. "It doesn't seem that long since I delivered her."

"I know it," the mother agreed, stroking the toddler's hand reassuringly. "They grow so fast. I just want to treasure every day."

I couldn't ask for more ideal patients, Dr. Lehman thought. Such pleasant, respectful folks. He never imagined that this child would die half a dozen years later when a car plowed into a group of 10 Amish children walking home from a birthday party. The accident would draw national media attention.

Out front at the receptionist's desk, Nancy slid open the window partitioning her cubicle from the waiting room. "Doc will be busy with the emergency for an hour or so," she announced. "If any of you want to reschedule your appointment, I'll be glad to work you in at a later date. But for those who want to wait, Dr. Lehman will see you over his lunch hour."

A few rescheduled their appointments while others chose to sit and chat. The patients accepted these kinds of delays as part of a country practice, and they were glad Dr. Lehman was willing to treat their emergencies.

"What about you, Mr. Keener, do you want to set up a new appointment?" the receptionist asked the lean, clean-shaven stranger.

"No, I'll wait."

"You could run over to the restaurant and pick up a sandwich in the meantime, if you want," she suggested.

Mr. Keener gazed thoughtfully out the window at the horses standing patiently at the hitching post across the road. Then he turned back to the waiting receptionist. "No thanks. I want to be here when that guy comes out so I can see for myself if the doctor treats such a case."

"Does Doc have any openings tomorrow?" a middle-aged woman asked.

"The doctor's not in on Thursday. Is Friday at 2:15 okay?"

"That's fine, but what does Doc do on his day off, anyhow? Go fishing?"

"Oh no. He goes over to Country Lawn Nursing Home and makes rounds, checking on the residents there at Navarre."

"Hmm. Always busy helping others. Well, it's good that man didn't cut off his fingers tomorrow when Doc's not around."

"That's for sure. But I suppose something will happen tomorrow, too. It seems the worst cases turn up when the doctor's out."

"*Ach* my! Surely not worse than this case today?"

"Oh yes," Nancy relayed casually as she addressed an envelope. "We had a man bring in his little boy who was blue-looking. He found the little fellow in a water trough." The ringing phone cut Nancy short, so she handed the patient the appointment reminder card and reached for the telephone.

Down the hall, Joe's nostrils tingled with the clean scent of the Dreft bubbles bursting as water swirled around his throbbing fingers. "Don't know why I need to soak them in this soapy water," the boy muttered. "Why, the kerosene killed all the germs."

His eyes swept the room while he waited. He took in the brown-paneled walls, high window, metal cabinet, jar of wooden tongue depressors, gauze pads, small sink, and large goose-necked lamp at the end of the examining table. An Enfamil calendar hung on the wall along with a Norman Rockwell painting of a portly doctor placing his stethoscope on the chest of a young patient's doll.

The door opened and Dr. Lehman strode purposefully into the room. "Okay, Joe," he said, lifting the dismembered hand from the Dreft solution. "Let's take another look." The doctor silently studied the finger stubs for a moment then gently poured Zephrin over them. He brushed specks of sawdust, grease, and dirt from the tissue and laid the hand on a sterile towel.

"This will sting a little," the doctor warned. He took the syringe the nurse handed him and jabbed the needle into the base of an injured finger. "And another little sting," he said injecting the needle into another side of the finger.

"Can you feel this?" Dr. Lehman asked, tapping the forceps against the finger.

"Can't feel a thing."

"What about this," Dr. Lehman asked, snipping at a bit of tissue.

"Nothing."

"Let me know if you feel any pain," Dr. Lehman said as he began dissecting the tissue, muscle, and tendon from the skin and bone. The doctor snipped painstakingly around a finger until only a hollow sleeve of skin remained over the bone above the joint. Gently, he rolled the sleeve of skin well below the knuckle. In gloved hands, he picked up the bonesnips—a tool resembling a pair of pliers with sharp, broad blades similar to a small hedge trimmer. He straightened his shoulders and inhaled deeply. Carefully, he aligned the snips, clamped the handles together, and a piece of bone plopped onto the towel.

Dr. Lehman dissected remaining bits of tissue from the sleeve of skin and crafted a flap to cover the bleeding stump. After dousing the finger with more Zephrin, the nurse draped a sterile towel over the hand to keep the suture clean. Only a stub of the index finger poked through a hole in the towel. Dr. Lehman folded the flap of skin he had meticulously scraped and shaped over the naked bone stub, and prepared to stitch the flap in place.

Joe watched intently as Dr. Lehman clamped a suture holder onto the end of a curved needle. The doctor pierced through one skin layer and the adjacent tissue. Then he released the suture holder, fastened the instrument to the pointed end of the needle protruding from the skin, and pulled the suture through the skin layers.

"It's my way of quilting," the doctor remarked when he glanced up to see the patient's fascination.

"Does your *frau* know you can sew like that?" Joe wondered. "If I could sew that *gut*, Mom would make me mend the holes in my socks!"

"You'd better not tell my wife," Dr. Lehman winked, while continuing to stitch the flap down over the stub. "I'm busy enough without having to darn my socks yet, too!"

Feeling queasy, Joe focused on the doctor's face to distract himself from the activity on his finger. He wondered how the doctor keeps each hair in place, and how he has such red cheeks when he always works inside.

"How old are you anyhow, Doc?"

"How old do you think I am?"

"*Ach*, I'd say you gotta be at least 75."

"Why is that?" the doctor asked, wondering what made the youth guess a number much higher than his actual age.

"Well, you're my doctor. And you were Dad's doctor and *Grohs Dawdi's* doctor, too. You're the only doctor I ever knew. You've been around forever!"

Dr. Lehman laughed heartily with the nurse and proceeded to stitch the finger without bothering to correct the young man's guess. "Did you ever hear the story of the man who cut off his ear?" Dr. Lehman asked to distract the patient.

"No, can't say that I did. What happened?"

"Well, somehow this fellow accidentally got his ear cut off. All his fellow workers quickly got down on their hands and knees to sift through the sawdust for the missing ear. Finally, someone held up the ear and announced, 'I found it! Here it is!' The man took one look at the ear and said, 'That's not mine.' The other men asked, 'What do you mean that's not your ear?' The fellow replied, 'It's not my ear. I can tell because my ear had a pencil behind it!'"

Joe could not help but chuckle, the tense lines on his face melting as he smiled.

With Joe's first finger neatly sutured and bandaged, Dr. Lehman began to debride the middle finger by removing tissue and muscle to create the hollow sleeve of skin. As Dr. Lehman picked up the bone-snips, the door opened a crack.

"Excuse me, Doc," Nancy called, "but I just spoke with a caller whose daughter has the symptoms of appendicitis. It'll take her half an hour to get here. We'll try to watch for her and let you know when they drive in. I know you like to watch the way a person walks when you diagnose a suspected appendicitis case."

"Busy day, Doc?" Joe wondered.

"Hectic. I delivered two babies during the night and then this morning I made an emergency house call for a cancer patient."

"You need another couple of hands, Doc," the patient observed.

"You got that right," Dr. Lehman said as Alice wrapped the mended fingers in Telfa dressings, gauze, and tape.

A moment later, Joe walked up to the receptionist's window waving his thoroughly bandaged finger stubs. "You like this better?"

"Much better!" Nancy smiled, handing him a packet of Tylenol with codeine tablets. "That's much better."

"I left the fingers in the coffee can for you," Joe's eyes twinkled. "I told Doc as busy as your office is, you could use some extra fingers around here, so you just keep them."

A smile crossed the face of the elderly Amishman in the waiting room. He watched the surprised *Englischer* study the bandaged hand. When their eyes met, the Amishman winked.

"Must be an unusual doctor," the stranger acknowledged with a shrug.

"Very," said the Amishman stroking his beard. "He can tell lots of stories. For instance, that 'Little Boy Blue' story in the *Reader's Digest* some time ago was Dr. Lehman's patient. The sheriff working on the case called Doc asking him for footprints and—"

"Mr. Keener!" The nurse called from the doorway. "You can come on back now."

"Why do you do it, Doc?" Mr. Keener asked when Dr. Lehman walked into the examining room. "You skipped your lunch to accommodate that patient. You wouldn't have had to go out of your way like that."

"That's a good question," Dr. Lehman responded, trying to decide how to express his philosophy of life. "When I first started my practice—"

A nurse knocked briefly before slipping into the room.

"I'm sorry to interrupt, but I wanted you to know that a child was just brought in who drank kerosene and is going to need his stomach pumped."

Mr. Keener rolled his eyes. "First you have a patient that *soaks* his wounds in kerosene, and then you have one that *drinks* the stuff. What next?"

"That's what we say," Dr. Lehman smiled as he completed the exam. "I can assure you that there's never a dull moment around here! And to think, I almost turned down the invitation to come to Mount Eaton to practice medicine."

Dr. Lehman remembered the first day he drove into Mount Eaton almost a quarter century before. He could still see his new wife seated beside him as they breezed through the countryside on that lovely summer day.

2.

A Country Boy Come Home

Like a vast, downy quilt, luxuriant patches of gold and green velvety fields spread out before the young doctor and his bride. The intern scanned the farmsteads nestled among the patchwork as if they held answers to the questions that weighted his heart. Is this the place? Elton kept asking himself as he guided the '63 Mercury Comet through the valleys threaded with an occasional stream. Is this where I belong?

He breathed in deeply the scent of freshly-mown hay as if trying to inhale the restful stillness pervading the countryside. The young intern's gaze followed a horse-drawn carriage winding past fields lined with fences and dotted with grazing cattle. Will I have any Amish patients? he wondered as the buggy disappeared behind a distant knoll.

Coasting into a little village, the couple glanced at the sign announcing, "Welcome to Mount Eaton." Neither of them dreamed that 34 years later, a new sign would stand in its place: "Welcome to Mount Eaton, Home of Elton Lehman, D.O., 1998 Country Doctor of the Year." Never!

As a general practitioner, the young doctor imagined delivering a few babies each year in the nearby hospital delivery room. He certainly never thought of delivering a baby in his Jeep at a stoplight, or delivering twins by the light of a kerosene lantern in an Amish bedroom. He could see himself stitching lacerations—but gunshot wounds? The thought never crossed his mind. Neither did the fact that a rare blood factor would be discovered among his patients.

On that first morning drive back into Mount Eaton, Dr. Lehman could not foresee waking up to the explosion of metal and fire when a carload of drunks slammed into his patients' car outside his bedroom window. Nor could he visualize riding in a buggy, or on the back of a dump truck, or on a fire truck to reach patients during a snowstorm. As the young doctor and his wife drove into Mount Eaton that balmy summer day in 1964, they had little indication of the adventures to come.

Elton's glance at the establishments of the two–traffic–light village assured him that Mount Eaton offered everything essential for existence, from grocery, hardware, and dry–goods stores to a gas station and bank. In the town square was a funeral home. Yes, Mount Eaton seemed to have everything a person would need, and more, he thought.

"What do you think, Phyllis?" Elton asked.

"Feels kind of quaint and peaceful, doesn't it? I wonder where the house is that your brother Merlin said is for sale."

"It should be right here." Elton glanced at the directions his brother had given. "Intersection of 250 and 241, left side. This is the junction."

And there it was. Just ahead on the left, a white, Victorian two–story house graced the village square. Gingerbread trim fringed the eaves and bordered the top of a wide porch. Phyllis drank in every detail, from the stately windows to the wraparound porch, as her husband parked the Mercury along the sidewalk.

Elton's eyes followed the steps to the porch and a pair of doors that opened off it. Merlin had said the door at the top of the steps led into a living room, while the entrance at the end of the porch opened into rooms designed as a doctor's office.

The couple exchanged a look of mutual delight. Neither spoke; they simply knew. The house was more than they had dreamed.

Entering the living room, the Lehmans found high ceilings and tall windows, giving the place an airy atmosphere. A sunny nook in the living room overlooked the town square. The office rooms along the right side of the house were not overly large, but they were adequate for the beginning of a small-town practice.

Behind the living room lay a small bedroom overlooking the tiny front yard and the main road just beyond. A small kitchen, dining room, and bath completed the main floor. An enclosed staircase led to a second-floor apartment that could be rented for additional income, they were told.

Every room was papered in a shade of purple and the house practically sat on the road, but the Victorian dwelling with the gingerbread trim was a fine place for a new doctor to begin a practice.

"Can't you see a sign in the yard: E. D. Lehman, Osteopathic Physician, General Practice?" Phyllis gestured to the patch of lawn as the two walked down the porch steps. "And buggy horses tethered to the hitching post, and patients lined up in the waiting room?"

Elton sighed and walked slowly toward the car. "Phyllis, it's a great dream. But we might as well be realistic. How are we going to pay for the house? You know as well as I do that we don't have a penny to put down on the place and not even one asset to secure a loan. All we have is a $10,000 medical school debt."

Phyllis' eyes traced her husband's dark, purposeful eyes and the strong build he inherited from generations of Swiss farmers. "If God wants you to practice here in Mount Eaton, he'll open the doors," she said, a confidence lighting her eyes and face.

I've seen that expression before, Elton smiled. She looked that way the night of our first date when we went to Isaly's Ice Cream Parlor after listening to William Detweiler preach at Stoner Height's tent revivals. She didn't know how to give me directions to her house from Isaly's, but she thought I'd get her home somehow.

"Well, Phyllis," the troubled lines on the doctor's dignified face relaxed a bit as he found her hand, "you've got faith—in me and in God. I sure don't know how he'll do it, but if God wants us to serve in Mount Eaton, he'll make a way."

Calmness settled over the young couple as they drove away from the Victorian home. "We might not know what the future holds," Elton said softly, "but God does. He's got it all planned."

Elton braked at the intersection and glanced at his watch. "You know what? We'd have time to stop and see Mother before we head back to Cuyahoga Falls. Kidron's only five miles away."

"Fine with me," Phyllis nodded. "I always enjoy a drive through Amish Country. It's so peaceful and relaxing. I'm actually not ready to head back to the city yet."

As the car followed Route 250 west down the hill and out of Mount Eaton, a team of draft horses plodded down the road ahead, pulling a wagon heaped with hay. A pair of boys wearing suspenders lay sprawled on the top of the mounded hay, chins propped in their hands, bare feet waving in the air.

Behind white farmhouses and dark red barns, the silver blades of an occasional windmill whirled against a sky free of electric wires. Here and there, teams of draft horses moved through the lush alfalfa fields, pulling a sickle bar or drawing a wagon trailed by a hay loader.

Dr. Lehman cranked down his window and let the fresh country air rush over his face. He was still short of breath from the viral pneumonia that had kept him hospitalized the last weeks of his internship. The young man filled his weakened lungs with pure, hay-scented air. The serene stillness from the rolling hills, peaceful streams, farmsteads, and grazing cattle flowed gently into his soul.

"Mount Eaton . . . Mount Eaton," Phyllis mused, surveying the rolling countryside. "I can understand the Mount part, with the village sitting up on a hill above the rest of the area, but Eaton? Where did that come from, I wonder?"

Elton scratched his head, remembering. "Seems to me I heard a story once about some immigrants moving into the community in the 1800s and stealing chickens. When the thieves were caught eating the stolen fowl, the area became known as Mount Eatin.' At least that's what I've been told.

"They say those same immigrants carried along the body of a child who had died of cholera along the way," he continued. "The disease spread. Some folks say around 10 percent of the village's population died from cholera that year, including James Galbraith, Mount Eaton's founder."

"Wow. Quite a history for a little village." Phyllis studied a barefoot girl kneeling next to a flowerbed, and a woman with a long plain dress and a white *kapp* gathering diapers off a clothesline. "Well, Mount Eaton seems like a good place to live now, especially surrounded by all these Amish farms. It is absolutely quiet and peaceful here. And that house with the gingerbread trim has character. What if we put the house and office together? Then you wouldn't have to drive to the office for every little emergency."

"It's ideal," Elton agreed. "Absolutely ideal. But I'm imagining one thing that would make the set-up even better."

"What's that?"

"Would you possibly consider being the receptionist and nurse when I open the office?"

"Oh, Elton, I couldn't do that! I'm a teacher, not a nurse!"

"You'd learn. I'd teach you what you need to know, and you'd be fantastic with the youngsters. And until I build up a practice, we really can't afford to pay a nurse. Besides," his voice grew soft, "there is no one I'd rather work with than you."

"I would really enjoy it if you think I could do it."

"I know you could, Phyllis. And more than that, your desire to learn, your character, and your pleasant ways mean more than a degree."

"It *would* be a treat to be together every day," Phyllis remarked wistfully, remembering how seldom they'd seen each other during their courtship. While she studied music education at Goshen College, toured with the collegiate choir, and then taught at Honeyville School near the Goshen, Indiana, community, Elton was studying at Chicago College of Osteopathic Medicine (CCOM) in Illinois. School vacations didn't provide the couple with many hours together either, because Phyllis spent one summer helping missionaries in Puerto Rico, and Elton traveled to Alaska another summer.

Even after they were married, they still had little stress-free time together. In the space of one month's time, Elton graduated from CCOM and wrote the State Board Medical Exam, the two were married and honeymooned in Pennsylvania, and then Elton began his internship. The newlywed doctor was assigned to night duty in the emergency room for the first month of his internship and as night house physician the following month. Phyllis began teaching that fall, and then their schedules seldom meshed. It sounded like a treat to work side by side in this new adventure.

"I'm willing to try it," Phyllis declared finally, watching several Amish children pedal their bikes down the country road.

A frisky steed trotted briskly toward them, pulling an open carriage behind. The bearded driver dipped his straw hat in their direction as the Lehmans approached. The bright-faced young woman clung to her infant with one hand and to the strings of her bonnet with the other.

Will any of these people be my patients someday? Elton wondered as they passed black buggies and farm wagons returning from the Kidron Livestock Auction. Would they accept me as their doctor?

Gently, the hills leveled into wide-open fields. Dr. Lehman's Swiss ancestors chose to settle in the area, partly because the rolling countryside reminded them of their homeland near the Jura Mountains. In the beginning, they called the community Sonnenburg in memory of their European homeland. When the village built a post office and needed an official town name, Elton's grandfather, William Lehman, and several others wanted to name the village Cheese Factory Town. But they reached a compromise, agreeing to name the tiny town Kidron, because of the small brook flowing through the valley, like the biblical stream near Jerusalem.

Heading north on Kidron Road, the Mercury passed a cart of laughing boys clinging to their straw hats and hanging onto the reigns of their lively horse.

"Hey!" Elton laughed. "My brothers and I used to drive a little cart like that on this very road, hauling milk cans to the cheese factory!"

Phyllis studied the spacious fields, well-kept barns, and farmhouses with manicured yards and brilliant flowerbeds.

"There's Kidron Floor and Paint, Cousin Bessie and Willis Nussbaum's business," Elton pointed. "That's where I worked during college vacations to help pay my way through school. And on the left is Gerber Poultry."

Phyllis smiled. She had seen them all before. Elton always got excited when he drove into Kidron. It still felt like home.

"Ah yes, and Kidron Electric. I went to church with the Neuenschwanders who run that business. Good solid Swiss folks. Now here on the left is the Kidron Auction barn and on the square is Lehman Hardware."

The Comet slowed as it passed the long white buildings of the Kidron Livestock Auction, with endless rows of buggies, wagons, and carts lining the hitching posts. Bearded men in straw hats and dark shirts milled about the buildings. The neighing horses, bawl-ing cattle, and pungent animal scents of the auction signaled the old Lehman homeplace, which lay just around the corner.

And there it stood—the old red barn with the lofty gable win-dow, which six-year-old Elton peered out of one day to discov-er that the world was larger than the Kidron Village Square. Now he absorbed the once-familiar scenes and inhaled the tangy barnyard scent.

A hundred memories flashed past the doctor's eyes as he drove in the lane behind the auction barn toward the brown house bordered by colorful flowerbeds. Instantly, he saw his mother with flowers, his 11 siblings, and his parents around a long dinner table, laughing. He recalled Mother's voice filling the house with hymns, Father's prayers, their family devotions, Mother reading missionary biographies and nature books and Bible stories, all of them milking cows. The old homeplace filled him with nearly forgotten stories and pictures.

And there on the porch stood Mother, sweet and grace-ful in her simple dress with a white net headcovering on her graying hair. Between bites of fresh strawberry pie and sips of iced garden tea, Elton told his mother about the struggle he and Phyllis faced in determining where God wanted them to serve.

Sitting on the familiar airy porch, Elton began to sort out his muddled thinking. He was moved by children dying in distant villages for lack of pennies-worth of medicine. But he couldn't deny this local invitation and the needs of this community. Elton believed God's hand had gently guided him from his boyhood to this moment.

His mother's love for plants and the nature stories she read stirred his interest in nature from the beginning. He loved growing up on the farm, surrounded with endless places to explore.

At Sonnenberg Mennonite School, Alvin Jantzi, Elton's biology teacher, nurtured his love for nature with fascinating field trips and spell-binding lectures. Choosing a major at Eastern Mennonite University (EMU)[2] wasn't difficult. Elton picked biology, hoping to teach, do research, or perhaps enter the medical field.

EMU emphasized Christ's call to serve, witness, and minister, and in that atmosphere Elton decided to go to medical school. Often, as the sun set, he stood at his dorm window gazing across the Shenandoah Valley to the Massanutten Mountains beyond, imagining himself as a doctor in one of Mother's missionary stories.

When Father died suddenly of a stroke 10 days before the end of Elton's freshman year at CCOM, his dream began to crumble. But the young man's family refused to let his vision die. Elton's brother Merlin and uncle Silas Lehman helped to pay his tuition bills. Cousin Bessie's husband Willis L. Nussbaum provided Elton with summer jobs painting barns.

Now Elton had survived med school and his year of internship was coming to an end. He had never thought much about coming back to Wayne County to practice. But the longer he contemplated Dr. Eberly's invitation to join the Mount Eaton practice, the more he thought God might be calling him to serve in what was fast becoming the largest Amish community in North America.

"Dr. Eberly asked you to help him?" Mother asked, looking at her son with a tinge of awe. It was still hard to think of her farmer boy as a doctor.

"Several of Eberly's six children are teenagers. He'd like to cut back and spend more time with his family. And he wants to be free to take medical mission trips and work on research projects. He's so swamped he says there's plenty of work to keep a couple doctors busy."

"You've decided not to go to Uniontown?"

"The only place available there is a house trailer."

"So are you feeling settled about Mount Eaton?"

Elton shrugged. His eyes met Phyllis'. "I always thought God was calling me to be a medical missionary, but now we're feeling more and more like God might want us in Mount Eaton."

"Well, Son, God will give you a peace about where you are meant to be, and he'll open the right doors, I'm sure. There's a ministry serving the Amish in this area. The plain folk need doctors that can understand them and meet their needs. I'll be praying for the two of you."

The young couple drove down the country road away from the farm, the sinking sun silhouetting the farms behind them.

"You know, Phyllis," Elton said thoughtfully, "doesn't God lead through the advice of parents—and through an inner peace?"

"And through principles in his Word, as well as circumstances," she added.

"So if they all agree, we can feel certain that we're doing what God wants. I guess all we're waiting on now is for the last circumstantial detail to fall in place."

But as the lights and the smokestacks of the city appeared on the horizon, dreams melted into reality and the Victorian house in the heart of Mount Eaton seemed to vanish in the rear-view mirror.

A short time later, the Bank of Mount Eaton's board members met to discuss an unusual request.

"Loaning money to a man and a woman who have no assets, and who have the nerve to apply for a loan that will double the debt load they already carry? Ridiculous!"

"Unheard of!"

"Doctors are a poor risk," another board member declared.

"Why, one of the last doctors who lived in that house couldn't make the payments and went up to the attic and shot himself. I couldn't advise loaning to a doctor."

"But the Lehman family has always been known to be reliable folk," Harvey Nussbaum, the owner of Mount Eaton Grain Elevator, countered. "I know Elton Lehman would pay off the loan and be an asset to the community to boot, if we gave him a chance. I wouldn't be a bit afraid to loan him the money myself if I had it."

Mr. Senff, the bank president, sat quietly for a while. "I'll take your word for it, Harvey," he suddenly announced. "I couldn't go against bank policy and lend him the entire $10,000, but what we can't loan him through the bank, I'll personally lend him out of my own pocket. I'd like to see the young man given a chance."

"You won't be sorry," Mr. Nussbaum promised.

"It sounds like God wants the country boy to be a country doctor," Elton smiled as he and Phyllis absorbed the news. Little did they realize that many years later, Dr. Lehman would gratefully return the favor by caring for Mr. Senff's elderly widow in her last hours, making sure everything medically possible was being done for her.

A ministry awaited Dr. Lehman. The plain people needed doctors who understood and respected their convictions for living simple, separated lives. If the young physician's first calls were any indication of the future, his life as a country doctor would be far more unconventional and exciting than he had ever imagined.

3.

Patients on the Floor

"Great and marvelous are thy works, Lord God. . . ." The notes of the piano music floated through the white Victorian house in Mount Eaton square and out the open windows. The last golden rays of sunset shone through the tall living room windows and illuminated Phyllis' music scores as her fingers flitted across the piano keys.

The door between the living room and office stood ajar. Dr. Lehman busily organized the instruments that had arrived in the mail that day. Carefully, he arranged the shiny scopes, thumb forceps, suture holders, hemostats, scissors, thermometers, scalpels, suture materials, tongue depressors, bandages, jars of gauze, and pill bottles.

My very own practice, he thought incredulously as he glanced around the treatment room. Everything is in order and ready—everything except the examining table, and that should be here any day. His eyes traveled from the hitching posts beyond the window to the chairs in the waiting room. Who will my first patients be? he wondered. And what problems will bring them to my office?

Later that evening, Elton glanced out the window as cousin

Bessie's husband Willis climbed the porch steps. Has my first patient arrived before my examining table? he wondered, noting his friend's bloodshot eye.

"Come in!" Elton invited, swinging open the porch door. "Looks like you've got a problem. What's up?"

"Oh, I was scraping some old paint at work and a flake got in my eye, and I haven't been able to get it out," Willis explained, dabbing at the tears trickling from the bloodshot eye. "It's been bothering me something awful, so Bessie suggested I come over and see you."

"I'll be glad to take a look at it." Dr. Lehman ushered Willis into the office. "I don't have my examining table yet, but—"

"Say, I'll lie anywhere, even on the floor. I know you're not really set up yet, so I don't mind a bit lying on the linoleum, if only you can get that miserable flake out of my eye."

"Phyllis!" Elton called. "I could use a hand. Could you please bring a pillow?"

The doctor knelt beside his first patient, who lay stretched out on the floor with his head resting on a pillow.

"I've got a little bottle on the shelf up there that says 'Ophthaine', Phyllis. Can you find it for me, please? By the way, the prefix o-p-h stands for eye," the doctor explained.

He inverted the bottle of numbing solution over the offending eye and squeezed out several drops.

"Saline eyewash. Thanks."

The liquid trickled out the corner of the patient's eye.

"Ophthalmoscope."

Elton squinted into the instrument and carefully searched the eye that had been rinsed with saline solution.

"The dye, Phyllis, and a needle."

He lowered the ophthalmoscope and explained, "Willis, I can see a foreign body in your eye. I'm going to try to flick it out with a needle, and then I'll put a dye solution in your eye that will expose any scratches the flake may have caused. Phyllis, please give him a few more numbing drops first. There. That'll do."

Elton flicked lightly with the needle and peered through the scope again. "It's gone. Phyllis, hand me some antibiotic drops, please. Since your eye is numb, Willis, we'll put a patch over it to protect it from irritation."

After neatly taping the patch in place, the doctor helped his patient off the floor. "You're all set."

"I can't tell you how much better that feels," Willis declared pulling out his wallet. What is your fee, Elton—uh, Dr. Lehman?"

"We'll be charging $3.50 for office calls, but since I don't have my examining table yet—"

"Here." Willis handed Phyllis three bills and two quarters. "Don't cut the rate for that. I should be paying you time–and–a–half for making you work after hours!"

"Don't mention it. You gave me summer jobs when I needed them, and I'm just glad to be of service to you if I can. I want my patients to know I'm available if they need me."

"In that case, you'll have a successful practice," Willis declared. "The Amish folks in the area can't just jump into a car and take their emergencies to a hospital. It will mean a lot to them if they know you'll be there when they need you. You'll need to learn to flex your practice to fit the Amish way of life, including de-livering babies in their homes."

"In their homes? In 1964? I don't think so. I've been taught there are proper places to deliver babies, Willis. The hospital de-livery room with fluorescent lighting, stainless steel, technology, and trained nurses is the best place for a child to enter the world. Not an Amish home with kerosene lamplight, no running water, or even a phone for emergencies. No, I'm afraid I won't be doing home deliveries."

"Well, Doc," Willis opened the door to leave, "you don't mind if I call you Doc, do you? Let me offer you some advice. The Amish consider the birth of a child a natural function and not an emergency requiring a hospital call. If you can adapt your practice to fit the lifestyle of the Amish, you'll have all the patients you can care for. Otherwise, well, there are always barns that need painting!" he ended with a chuckle.

The young physician studied his former employer thoughtfully. I suppose I can learn something from everyone I meet. I don't have all the answers, but *home births?*

Willis opened his mouth as if to continue, then closed it. Sighing, he began again. "I may as well tell you what some of the old-timers are saying around town. I've heard them say, 'That new Mount Eaton doctor and the young Apple Creek veterinarian aren't going to make it in this area. They'll fold up in a year or two.'" Willis looked the startled doctor in the eye. "But I don't believe a word of it!" the painter exploded. "Prove them wrong, Doc! But no matter what," he continued brightly, "you can count on always having one loyal patient."

"Hmm. I can learn something from everyone I meet," the young doctor murmured, thoughtfully watching his first patient walk down the porch steps.

"So, are you going to consider doing home deliveries?" Phyllis wondered as she tidied the office.

The doctor faced his wife. "There are proper places to deliver babies, but homes do not fit into that category." Phyllis smiled at the firm set of her husband's face. When he made up his mind, she knew better than to try changing it.

"You'll make a great nurse," Elton announced as Phyllis penciled $3.50 on the first line of the ledger.

"It'll be an interesting change from teaching, for sure," she replied, placing the eye drops and instruments on the shelves.

I wonder what emergencies this office will see in the next years, the doctor thought as he switched off the light in his new office. If the local folks brought their emergencies to the doctor's office as Willis inferred, serious, even life-threatening injuries could show up in this office over the coming years.

"Lord," he whispered, breathing a prayer that would be his daily petition for the remainder of his medical practice, "please, give me wisdom to help these people."

Within days the examining table arrived and patients began flowing into the office on the side of the Victorian house in the heart of town, especially when his colleague Dr. Eberly was making house calls or traveling out of town.

Doc, as his patients called him, gave baby shots, placed casts on broken arms, listened to lungs for signs of pneumonia, and sewed up lacerations from farm machinery wounds. Phyllis answered the phone, scheduled appointments, recorded payments, and handed her husband the instruments and bandages, giving assistance when needed. Once in a while, she transported sick or injured patients to the hospital.

As he went about his work, the doctor often reminded himself: I can learn something from every person I meet. Soon this became his motto. He didn't have all the answers, he knew. But he could learn something from everyone he met—or at least nearly everyone. Now and then, people seemed to challenge that theory, like the farmer with the kerosene remedy.

Soon after Dr. Lehman hung his shingle, he got a call from a Kidron farmer whose son had injured his hand in a farm-related accident.

"I know it's probably supper time at your house, but Dr. Eberly's out of town and my boy has a bad cut on his hand."

When Melvin Steiner and his son walked into the office, an overpowering odor accompanied them. The boy had been feeding the cows and tore his hand on a hay hook that he wasn't supposed to be using. The 12-year-old thought it would be easier to throw hay bales to the cows using the hook to pick up the bales instead of his hands. But the cow snatched the bale with its teeth, yanking the hook across the boy's hand and tearing his flesh.

I can understand a barn smell on the boy's clothing, the doctor thought. But this is more than a barn odor.

"What do I smell?" Dr. Lehman asked, looking up from the ugly gash he was examining.

"Kerosene," Melvin replied. "It's a good thing we always keep a jar of it in the cupboard. Otherwise, I'd be concerned about tetanus."

"But what does kerosene have to do with the cut?"

"Why, he soaked his hand in kerosene, of course. But Clarence, here, knew he wasn't supposed to be using the hay hook. 'Be sure your sins will find you out,' I told him, and he knows that now. But anyway, after he cut his hand, he slipped down to the shed and soaked it in kerosene. He was in a hurry and spilled it on his clothes, so that's what you smell. He thought he had to change clothes before he came, but I said there wasn't time, the way the blood gushed out of that wound the moment he took it out of the kerosene."

"You soaked the wound in *what?*"

"Why, in kerosene, of course! It helps the pain and slows the bleeding. Why, we always bathe our wounds in kerosene, don't you? Besides, it kills all the germs and you don't need a tetanus shot if you use kerosene. I'm sorry about the smell."

"I'm not worried about the smell. I'm concerned about all the contaminants introduced to the wound. What made you start using kerosene on your wounds?"

"Why, Doc, it's a good, old-fashioned Swiss remedy, my grandfather says. Your kin probably used it, too."

"But, Melvin, the germs! The contamination! I can't believe this!"

This boy's going to have a serious infection, I'm afraid, Dr. Lehman thought as he cleaned the wound and tried to rinse every trace of fuel from the laceration. Well, I guess this farmer will learn that there are better remedies than kerosene to use on wounds. And the only thing I'll learn from him is that some folks believe kerosene has healing properties!

Mr. Steiner watched as Dr. Lehman stirred Dreft laundry detergent into a bowl of warm water.

"What are you planning to wash?" he wondered.

"We'll be soaking the hand in Dreft to clean the wounds," Dr. Lehman replied.

"Oh, Doc, you don't have to worry about the infection. The kerosene took care of all the germs."

"Let's do it anyway," the doctor replied, inwardly cringing at every mention of the filthy fuel. Gently, he lowered the boy's hand into the warm, sudsy water.

"Now what are you going to do?" the farmer asked a few moments later as Dr. Lehman picked up a bottle of Zephrin.

"We are going to thoroughly disinfect the wound. We want it to heal without infection," he replied, pouring a generous amount of the liquid all over the mangled hand.

"The kerosene took care of all the germs," Mr. Steiner insisted and then shrugged and fell silent.

After numbing the site, the doctor carefully sutured the wounds with precise stitches and wrapped them in a sterile bandage, gauze, and white tape.

"I'd like to see him in a week," the doctor told Mr. Steiner.

"We are going to see a nasty infection when that farmer's son comes back," Dr. Lehman told his wife later. "Kerosene, indeed!"

A week later, the father brought his son back. Expectantly, Dr. Lehman peeled back the bandage on the injured arm.

"Hmmm," he muttered, adjusting his glasses and studying the wound again. "Well, I declare, Phyllis, take a look at this!"

The two stood and stared at the pink skin but found no trace of puss or redness. Instead, the lacerations were knitting nicely.

"Unbelievable. Absolutely incredible!"

The farmer didn't say a word, but a smile slid across his face. This young doctor was going to learn a few more things yet.

Kerosene might slow the bleeding, reduce pain, and fight off infections, the doctor reasoned when he saw the successful home remedy time after time. But soaking lacerations in kerosene contradicted everything he learned about sterile procedures for treating open wounds.

At CCOM, Dr. Lehman learned the latest medical trends. Regular office hours kept a practice running efficiently. House calls had disappeared with the horse and carriage. And sterile hospital delivery rooms were the safest place to deliver babies, now that hospitals were conveniently accessible to every American.

However, Dr. Lehman soon discovered that his professors apparently had not traveled to Wayne County, Ohio, nor had his patients attended CCOM. Many concepts he learned were better suited for a city practice. Horses and carriages were still part of everyday life in the hills around Mount Eaton, and so were house calls. Those who drove buggies had no ready access to the hospital 15 miles away.

Willis was right, Dr. Lehman discovered. All sorts of emergencies arrived at his office door any hour of the day or night. A youngster showed up on his porch one evening reeking of the manure he had been applying to the field using a horse-drawn spreader.

"My boy was just standing up to fold down his seat when the horse took off and sent him flying across the spreader. He crashed into the beater at the back of the machine. Cut him up pretty badly, too," the farmer explained.

"I'm sorry for the smell, Doc," he apologized as he helped his bandaged son out of the door later that night. "But the way it was bleeding, and all, we thought we better not take time to wash him up."

"I grew up on a farm myself, and the country odor doesn't bother me at all," Dr. Lehman assured the farmer.

Since many of his patients had no phone and a trip to town involved a major journey with a buggy, the doctor frequently received letters requesting appointments or health advice.

"Here's a letter for you," Phyllis told her husband one afternoon, handing him a scrap of notebook paper.

I was rather excited. I broke out with a rash on my shoulders and back and a few other places. I noticed a few more and some healing up. It is too

*cold for me to come over. If you think there is anything dangerous, could you
please come over or drop me a few lines? Had unusual headache yesterday.
You couldn't drive in our lane. There's too much snow.*

Mattie Schlabach

"You can't take the words of the Amish folk too literally," Dr.
Lehman cautioned Phyllis, remembering his own early phrasing
struggles as a bilingual child who had spoken a Swiss-German
dialect before English. "And you've got to be very specific in
your questions to them. Take the word 'excited,' for example.
Obviously, she means she's worried rather than happy about the
rash."

Soon Dr. Lehman realized that Willis was right about the
need for house calls. Because the community was not equipped
with an emergency medical squad and the 911 system did not
yet exist, folks called the doctor when emergencies arose. Where
eighteenth-century transportation still existed, it often made
more sense for the doctor to jump into the car and rush to the
patient's home than for the patient to hitch up the horse and
buggy and travel to the doctor's office.

One of Dr. Lehman's first house calls took place the morning
a severe thunderstorm passed through the community. A young
farmer had been struck by lightning in his barn, a neighbor
claimed, and the man wasn't responding. Could Doc please hurry out to the farm and check on the farmer?

When the bolt of lightning shot through the barn, the farmer
dropped his milk bucket and collapsed to the floor. A moment
later, he staggered to his feet and then collapsed again. He still
lay where he had fallen and he hadn't moved since, the worried
young wife explained to the doctor when he drove into the
farmyard.

Dr. Lehman walked into the barn and spotted the young man
sprawled on the concrete floor next to the cattle he had been
milking moments before. The doctor dropped his bag and knelt
beside the youthful farmer. He listened desperately for a heart-

beat, but not even the faintest throb traveled up the stethoscope.

The doctor forced himself to face the wife's anxious eyes. "I'm so sorry," he whispered. "But there's not a thing I can do for your husband. I'm afraid he's gone."

"God must have allowed it," the young widow resigned.

The faith she displayed was typical of the Amish folk, Dr. Lehman discovered as time went on. In the midst of tragedy, they demonstrate a deep, settled confidence that God permits whatever happens for a higher good. Their faith often provides an anchor as they quietly accept the catastrophes that touch their lives.

"Did he have life insurance?" Phyllis wondered when her husband shared the sad story later.

"Oh no," he replied. "The Amish and some of the more conservative Mennonites don't carry insurance because they feel it unequally yokes them with unbelievers and shows a lack of faith in God. If they incur large bills, the churches collect offerings to cover them. Take this widow, for example. Her church and relatives will help with the farm work and will support her financially. I'm discovering in my practice that since the Amish have no medical insurance, they don't run to the doctor with every little ailment. But when they do come, you know it's urgent."

"I believe that," Phyllis nodded, thinking of a farmer who had mangled his hands in a piece of farm machinery.

"Another aspect of doctoring among the Amish is this bioethical question," he continued. "Since they believe life events are determined by God, the Amish don't believe in taking costly measures to counteract or postpone what they consider was meant to be. Nature should take its course, they feel. Besides, we were not intended to live forever. Heaven is at the end of the road."

"So will they have surgery to remove cancer?" Phyllis questioned. "And what about hospitalizing premature babies?"

"Dr. Eberly says each person is different. You never know. Some cancer patients don't want surgery because they feel it wouldn't be right to spend so much money to change what God had allowed. Other times they surprise us and want the surgery."

"But Elton, what about home births? Can't a lot of things go wrong?"

"That's where I draw the line," he announced, spooning up the last syrupy bite of pie. "Home remedies and house calls might be inconvenient, but I can live with them. But home deliveries? I don't think so."

Shortly after Dr. Lehman set up practice, Dr. Eberly arranged to take a week-long vacation and asked Dr. Lehman to cover for him.

"Sure, enjoy the time with your family," Dr. Lehman encouraged. "We don't have much scheduled other than an invitation to Willis and Bessie Nussbaum's home one evening, but I suppose we can cancel it."

"There's no need to cancel any engagements. Just arrange for someone to answer the phone while you are out," Dr. Eberly advised. "I doubt anything will develop, but you never can tell," he quickly added.

"I don't suppose any babies are due that weekend?" Dr. Lehman asked as an afterthought.

"Uh, let me think. Yes, as a matter of fact, three women are due that week. And by the way, before I forget, they all have their babies at home."

"Oh? A home delivery?"

"It's not a problem. Actually, Elton, you'll find these home deliveries a breeze. Those sturdy farm wives have delivered children in their homes for centuries. The women are relaxed in their own familiar environments. Indeed, the home deliveries generally go smoother than those at the hospitals. Something to do with relaxation, I suppose."

"But, there won't be any nurses," Dr. Lehman objected.

"Take Phyllis with you. She can help. But, of course, if you'd rather not, I don't need to leave."

"No, no. I'll cover for you. I don't suppose any of your patients will go into labor while you're gone. But why don't they just go to the hospital, Wain? It would be so much more convenient."

"Really, Elton, birthing is an everyday occurrence on the farm. The Amish don't see any reason to traipse off to a hospital for something as normal as birthing when they are far more comfortable in their own bedrooms. To the Amish, birthing is a private affair. The arrival of a baby is a deep, dark secret that the children know nothing about until they discover their new sibling in the crib."

"But Wain, is it right for me to deliver a child in a home when I feel the baby would have a better chance of survival being born in a hospital?"

The senior doctor looked his young colleague in the eye. "Elton, we don't take chances. Any high risk situation—high blood pressure, breech, placenta previa, multiple births—they go directly to the hospital. Absolutely. But I see very few complications in the relaxed environment of the home. You'll find you cannot make decisions for your patients. We explain the facts, let them make the decision, and then give them the best medical care we can under the circumstances. That's all a part of practicing medicine, especially in an Amish community."

Before Dr. Lehman and Phyllis left for the New Year's Eve party, the doctor gave his sister Geraldine a few instructions and jotted down the Nussbaum's phone number. Then he and Phyllis headed for Willis and Bessie's home.

"So have you gotten your table or do your patients still lie on the floor?" Willis wondered as the couples chatted in the Nussbaum living room.

"I got the examining table, but I'll have to tell you, Willis. You aren't the only one who has lain on the floor in the office," Dr. Lehman said, settling back comfortably in his chair. "I walked into the room one day and found a man lying on the floor. I thought maybe he tripped or fainted or something, so I helped him up and asked him what was wrong. 'Your table is too short for me,' he said, 'so I laid on the floor.'

"'Look,' I told my patient, 'I've got a secret to show you,'" Dr. Lehman continued. "And you should have seen his eyes as I pulled out the extenders at the foot of the table! 'Now you don't have to lie on the floor,' I told him."

The laughter stopped short at the jangling phone. Phyllis' eyes met Elton's. Oh boy, here we go.

"For you, Doc," Willis said handing him the phone. "It's your sister."

"This man called and said the water broke," Geraldine related. "I thought it was a prank call. I was ready to tell him to call the plumber when I realized what he meant. So I guess you better head out to Andy S. Yoder's in Maysville."

"Thanks, Sis. I've got my bag in the car so we'll be on our way."

"A home delivery?" Willis appraised the doctor with raised eyebrows.

"Of course," the doctor responded with a shrug. "I'll run an I-V on her as a precaution, and we'll take the oxygen along."

"But there won't be any electricity. No running water, no phone. I thought you weren't going to get involved with home births."

"Well, I suppose we can learn something new from everyone we meet," Dr. Lehman replied with a smile, shutting the door behind him.

4.

CHECKY AND BECKY

The Mercury Comet wove down the country roads, like a needle threading the patchwork of fields and pastures beneath a starry, velvet sky.

"I don't know why I ever agreed to anything so foolish," Dr. Lehman grumbled to Phyllis. "Those folks don't even have a phone in the house, to say nothing of electricity. What if the patient hemorrhages or the baby doesn't breathe?"

"I suppose you'll pray."

"Absolutely! But prayer is never an antidote for sloppy medicine. We do the best we can in the circumstances we find ourselves. If something unforeseen develops, we pray with all we've got, absolutely. But prayer never replaces the best treatment we can give."

"So, what are you going to do if you run into an emergency in this home delivery?" Phyllis asked trying to decipher the road signs in the blackness beyond the window.

"Well, we've got a laryngoscope for resuscitation. We have oxygen and an I-V, plus injections for hemorrhaging. Actually," he laughed shakily, "about the only thing we don't have is a team to do a C-section! But then, there's not a great risk of needing that, because I'm sure Dr. Eberly checked for placenta previa or breech. But if I see we need to do an emergency C-section, I'll put her into the back seat of the car and we'll make a bee-line for Doctors Hospital in Massillon."

"You mean you wouldn't call an ambulance?"

"Ha, the closest thing we have to an ambulance around here is Desvoignes' hearse. And by the time we'd find a house that has a phone, wake the folks, call Mr. Desvoignes, have him locate a driver, and wait for them to show up, we could drive to the hospital and back again."

"I'd think the sight of a hearse coming in the lane would send the baby here fast!" Phyllis laughed.

"Or else shut down labor for a whole week," Dr. Lehman added. "But seriously, Phyllis, if a problem develops, I'll want to take my bag and instruments along, so pack them as fast as you can. In situations like that, every second counts."

Trying to think of every possible scenario, he added, "But if for some reason we need to find a phone, look for a farm that has an outdoor light. They won't be Amish and they'll have a phone. You could also look for little shanties along the road that resemble outhouses. They have pay phones inside for the Amish to use."

Neither spoke for a few moments, each enveloped in the suspense and uncertainty of the night ahead.

"What do the Amish have against electricity, anyway?" Phyllis asked, looking out into the expansive darkness blanketing the slumbering farms.

Dr. Lehman scratched his head thoughtfully for a moment. "They avoid telephones, electricity, cars, and technology as a way of living out what they believe is meant by some verses in the New Testament—like 'Be not conformed to this world.'"

"So that's why they drive buggies? To be separate from the world?"

"Well, sort of. It's part of expressing a simple lifestyle, and it helps preserve family togetherness. They want families to spend their free time together and not running here and there."

"Hmmm. Interesting."

"One patient told me that Leroy Beachy, a local Amish historian, was invited to speak to a nearby college faculty about the Amish," Dr. Lehman went on. "The moderator told Leroy that the staff was made up of Presbyterians, Episcopalians, Methodists, Baptists, and so forth. 'We're all Christians,' she said, 'and we know the Amish are Christians, too. We got to discussing the Amish at one of our faculty meetings and we were wondering how the Amish differ from other Christians.'

"Thinking for a moment, the Amishman asked the group of 52 college professors, 'How many of you own a television?' Fifty-two hands went up. 'How many of you think you would be better off without it?' Six or eight hands went up, and the historian waited a bit. The professors looked at each other and, one by one, 52 hands went up. 'Since you are better off without a television, how many of you will go home tonight and get rid of yours?' he asked. Not one hand went up.

"'And that,' the Amish historian went on to say, 'is the major difference between many people and the Amish. If the Amish feel something is detrimental they will get rid of it. And if they believe the Bible teaches a principle, they try to carry it out, no matter how inconvenient it may be or how different it may make them appear.' Obedience is central to the Amish faith," Doc finished. "They often cite the Bible verse that says it's not just those who say 'Lord! Lord!' who will enter the kingdom of heaven, but those who do what they are asked to do."

"Talk about quick thinking," Phyllis laughed. "But tell me, Elton, do you think their lifestyle of obedience, as you put it, flows from a love for God or out of obligation to the church?"

"I find a lot of variation among the Amish," Elton replied thoughtfully. "You can't say 'the Amish do this' or 'the Amish do that,' because there are many different kinds of Amish."

"So what's the difference between the various groups?" Phyllis questioned, drawing her coat around her.

"Well, to an outsider, some Amish seem more expressive spiritually and encourage their young folks to stay free of drinking, drugs, and immorality. Some, which appear to be more strict and more reclusive, seem to place a greater emphasis on joining the church and obeying its standards. Some of their youth 'sow their wild oats,' then eventually most of them sell their cars and settle down to join the church and get married."

Because of the large variety of Amish in Wayne and Tuscarawas counties, accurately classifying the groups posed a challenge. Amish congregations were as varied as the colors and designs of the marigolds and petunias in their flowerbeds. Yet nearly all the groups shared common roots in central Europe during the Reformation period. The first group of Amish migrated to North America more than 200 years ago, seeking greater religious freedom.

"Now the family we are heading for, what kind of Amish are they?" Phyllis wondered, noting the glow of a kerosene lamp winking from a window.

"I bet Andy and Katie are Swartzentruber Amish, since many of the Amish around Mount Eaton are from that group," he replied. "We'll be able to tell by the color of the barn. Swartzentruber barns are always painted a dark shade of maroon, and they have dirt lanes. You can soon tell."

A picket fence lined the lane, enclosing the rolling pastures. Pines and weeping willow trees sheltered the large, white, two-story house. Phyllis strained to see the color of the shadowy barn, but it was too dark to see.

As Andy held the screen door for Phyllis, she glanced at the army of muddy boots beside the doorway. The new baby would not be the first child in this home, she decided, glancing at the row of boots and assortment of chairs, boosters, benches, and high chairs surrounding the lengthy kitchen table.

"Come on back to the *kammah*. Katie's soon ready for you," the bearded farmer invited. His stocking feet padded across the wood floor as he led the way. Cloth suspenders stretched up over his broad shoulders, crossed the back of his blue shirt, and were stitched fast to the home-sewn denim-colored pants that buttoned at the waist.

In the bedroom, a kerosene lamp on an antique dresser cast a golden glow on the placid face on the pillow. Blonde strands escaped the white scarf covering her hair and tied at the back of her neck. Relief flickered in her blue eyes accented by the blue blocks that tumbled across the quilt.

"How's Katie?" the doctor greeted his patient, setting down his satchel and rolling up his sleeves.

"Oh, not too bad." The woman managed a feeble smile of relief at the doctor's appearance, and then grimaced with the onset of another contraction.

While the doctor suspended an I-V bag from the curtain rod and set up the oxygen tanks, Phyllis removed the obstetrics kit from the black satchel. She cleared off a dresser and unrolled a clean white towel, careful not to touch the sterile instruments tucked inside. Then she spread several layers of newspaper at the foot of the bed.

Dr. Lehman slipped his arms through the sleeves of a surgical gown that Phyllis held out for him. Quickly, she tied the laces at the back of his neck and opened a package of sterile gloves and held them open as he slipped his large hands into them.

Moments later, Phyllis handed her husband a bulb syringe as he supported a small, damp head of curly, dark hair.

The doctor caught the baby in his gloved hands. "A boy!"

"Cord clamps, Phyllis, scissors."

With awe, the schoolteacher-turned-nurse reached for the slippery, wriggling, howling bundle and held him in a clean towel while her husband clamped and cut the cord.

"Lay him down so I can examine him," the doctor said, gesturing toward the bed. "Now, I'll need my stethoscope. There are five things we check," he explained, reaching for the stethoscope his wife handed him. "Heartbeat, respiration, color, reflexes, and muscle tone."

"Boy, he sure has a healthy set of lungs," the doctor chuckled as he finished examining the shrieking infant. "Dry him, Phyllis, so he doesn't lose too much heat, and then wrap him in a blanket so he'll feel more secure," he suggested, turning to check on the mother. "Then maybe Andy can hold him a bit and show him to Katie while you give me a hand."

After drying off as much of the white, cheesy coating as she could, Phyllis wrapped the baby in a flannel blanket and handed him to his father. "Here you go, Daddy. Another farm hand for you."

The farmer took the baby in his strong, callused hands. "Look at those big feet," he crooned. "And those hands! He's going to be a big fella some day."

The mother's eyes followed the pair in weary relief, a faint smile playing on her lips.

"And now, Phyllis," the doctor suggested, "you'll need to bathe the child."

Incredulous, Phyllis stared at her husband. "You mean I'm supposed to wash that wiggly, slippery bundle?"

"Go ahead and try," the doctor encouraged.

"Water's heating on the stove," Andy offered. "And under the sink is the washbowl. Doc Mayer's wife used to put that bowl on the floor so the slippery *buppeli* wouldn't drop, but Dr. Eberly's nurse washes them in the sink."

"Tell her the *buppeli's* clothes are in the crib," Katie added, "and the towels and soap are by the sink."

"Well, *buppeli*," Phyllis murmured, cuddling the little bundle near. "We'll see what we can do, the two of us."

Holding the baby in the crook of her arm, Phyllis pumped

some water into the dish pan, added a little hot water from the tea kettle, and then pumped a little more water again until the bath water felt warm. Somehow, she managed to bathe the slippery infant. "Now I'm as wet as you!" she laughed as she dried the baby and dressed him in a diaper, gown, and flannel blanket that Katie had sewn on her treadle sewing machine.

"What a little sweetheart you are!" Phyllis cooed as the infant gazed up at her with large, round eyes and sucked on a tiny, red fist. Lovingly, she combed his thick, damp hair into a curl on the top of his head. This beats teaching school any day, she decided.

Dr. Lehman looked up from the papers he was signing as his wife carried the baby into the room and handed him to his mother. The husky farmer reached down his callused hands and caressed his son's damp head nestled in the mother's arms. "Another precious gift from God," the father murmured.

Suddenly, the doctor felt a stab of sympathy for the queasy fathers stashed in a remote hospital waiting room. He thought of the sedated mother surrounded by strangers under the glare of the delivery room lights, missing out on those first treasured moments of togetherness in the afterglow of birth.

It wasn't as bad as I thought, Dr. Lehman reflected. I'm not saying I wouldn't do it again if I absolutely had to.

And he did. Over and over again, he delivered babies in Amish homes. If they decided to come while Dr. Eberly was out of town, someone had to deliver them, after all.

It was at Jake and Lydia's house that Dr. Lehman encountered an unexpected dilemma. As the delighted couple exclaimed over their newborn, the doctor discovered his job was only half finished. Only Phyllis noticed the startled expression on her husband's face and saw his eyes shut momentarily. Sweat beaded on his forehead and his rosy cheeks reddened more deeply. For a fleeting moment, the young doctor couldn't help wondering what dear old Dr. Seaver Tarulis, his medical school professor and mentor, would say if he could peek into the room and observe the drama unfolding beneath the gas lantern.

We're off to the hospital! Phyllis thought, preparing to collect the instruments.

"Get me the bulb syringe!" the doctor cried. "We've got another baby coming!"

Jake collapsed into a chair, nearly dropping his new son as shrill cries of the second infant filled the room. *"Vas in die velt?"*

"I'd say God must have been watching over you," Dr. Lehman told the couple as he cut the tiny girl's cord. "Frequently we find that, with twins, at least one is breech and a C-section may need to be done. In fact, if I would have known you were having twins, I would have sent you to the hospital," he announced, laying the second infant on her mother's stomach and covering her with a blanket.

Phyllis bathed and dressed the little boy and brought him to his mother. Carefully, she washed, dried, and diapered his tiny sister, dressing her in a gown like her brother's. Then she picked up the tiny *kapp* lying beside the clothing the mother had laid out.

"I guess she wants this on you, too!" Phyllis smiled, putting the little white cap on the dark hair and tying a neat bow under the pudgy chin. Then she placed the little girl in Lydia's other arm and gazed from one tiny face to the other.

At the kitchen table, Dr. Lehman spread out the forms for the birth certificates as Phyllis gathered up the newspaper from the floor. "Have you decided on names yet?" The doctor looked up from the form he was filling out.

"Names? No way. We did not even think about having twins," the Amishman declared.

"Well, Dr. Mayer suggested to one couple that Pete and Repeat would make good names for twins."

"Pete and Repeat!" Jake stared at the doctor in horror. *"Unfahgleichlich!"*

"The couple thought about those suggestions for a while," Dr. Lehman continued casually, "and they decided that they liked the name Pete but not Repeat."

The tension that gripped the young father at this unexpected turn of events melted into hearty laughter when he realized the doctor was merely joking.

"I think we can come up with something better than those names," he chuckled.

"*Vas danksht*, Lydie?" Jake asked his wife, laying his large hand over hers. "What do you think?"

The two conversed quietly in Pennsylvania German for a moment, and the farmer thoughtfully stroked his beard.

Finally, Lydia nodded her head and Jake announced, "All right, Doc, it's Checky and Becky."

"I suppose you want Jacob and Rebecca written on the birth certificates?" the doctor asked.

"No, chust Checky and Becky. Them's the names."

As months passed, Dr. Lehman and Phyllis continued to deliver babies in Amish homes. Eighteen months after coming to Mount Eaton, they delivered a New Year baby in an Amish home. The delivery went well, and when it was over, Phyllis cleaned the instruments and packed them back into the bag while the doctor filled out the paperwork and the parents enjoyed their new baby.

"Be as quiet as you can," Dr. Lehman whispered to his wife, gesturing at the curtain partition to the side of the room. "Dr. Eberly says birthing is a top secret in these homes. None of the children sleeping on the other side of the curtain are supposed to have a clue about the arrival of a new sibling until the doctor leaves and they see the baby lying in the cradle."

As he finished filling out the forms, the room was still except for the hissing lantern and scratching pen.

Perhaps the glow of the glass lantern shining through the curtain woke the youngsters. When the doctor glanced up, he saw a pair of tousle-haired boys blinking curious, sleepy eyes at him from around the curtain. Uh-oh, he thought, this wasn't supposed to happen.

"Ver ist sella kall?" one whispered. "What's he doin' here?"

His brother studied the doctor, his papers, and black bag. Suddenly, his eyes lit up. "I know who that is! Why, it's the Watkins man!"

The doctor's and Phyllis' eyes twinkled with suppressed laughter.

"So, those Amish boys have finally figured out where babies come from!" the doctor laughed as they drove away into the night. "The Watkins man who sells spices and flavorings brings babies, too!"

5.

AGAINST BETTER KNOWLEDGE

"A specialist is a doctor who has trained patients to be sick during office hours."

Dr. Lehman chuckled as he laid the quote on his desk, wishing life would be that simple. Inevitably, patients were injured on a doctor's day off, babies were born in the middle of the night, and children became ill on holiday weekends.

"In a country practice, everyone needs to be flexible—from the doctor and staff to the patients and physician's family members," an experienced doctor advised. "It's either be flexible or be miserable. There are no other options."

But sometimes circumstances tested the limits of that flexibility. And *this* would be one of those times.

Glancing out the window, the doctor noticed a horse and buggy pull up in front of the porch. A plain-clad woman dipped her bonneted head and stepped nimbly from the buggy, pulling her black shawl around her.

Not only my schedule needs flexibility, but the philosophies I brought from med school need to adapt as well, the doctor thought. And few of those philosophies needed more adaptation than the approach to birthing. Visions of delivering infants in the sterile, stainless-steel environment of the hospital faded fast as the young doctor's practice grew.

Dr. Lehman glanced up to see Phyllis sweeping into the office, looking professional in her fresh, white dress as she flipped through the patient files for the day.

"Hi, Emma, you can come on back now," he heard his wife call cheerfully. "And how are you feeling today?"

"I'm doing just great," the woman smiled, smoothing her apron and flipping her *kapp* strings over her shoulder as she followed Phyllis. "Maybe too good," she added, eyeing the scales warily.

"Ah, stepping on the scales is the fun part, isn't it?" Phyllis commiserated, resting her hand on her own expanding waistline. "We had one lady who wanted to take out her false teeth before we weighed her," she laughed. "As if that would have changed her weight."

"Let's see, you are due in July, aren't you?" Phyllis questioned as her husband took the patient's vitals. "You're lucky. I have to go through the whole summer and wait until October. I suppose you have your babies at home?"

"Oh, no. I always have them at Bill Barb's place."

"Bill Barb? Who's that?"

"You mean you never heard of Barb? Oh my! She's the dearest soul. Her husband's name is Bill. That's why we call her Bill Barb. She took her furniture out of her *sitzschtupp* and fixed it up for women to come there and have their babies."

"But what's the advantage of going to Barb's house? Why don't you just have your babies at home?" Phyllis wondered.

Emma laughed. "Oh, Mrs. Lehman, I can tell you haven't had children before. Out at Barb's, she takes care of the women and encourages them through labor. Then afterward, she and her girls clean up, wash the bedding, and serve the nicest meals. She even gives back rubs at night!" Emma's eyes sparkled as she gushed on about the joys of Barb's house. "And it's so quiet and peaceful out there. Why, a woman can relax and rest up for a couple of days before getting back to a house full of children."

"Ah, I see."

"Yes, and it's close. The menfolk can load the youngsters into the buggy and drive over to visit their wives after chores. I declare, once you've had a baby at Barb's you don't want to have one anywhere else. I sure hope Dr. Lehman will deliver at Barb's house."

The doctor's pen froze mid-word. Dr. Eberly had warned him this question would come up. Was there one paragraph in his med school texts that had prepared him for this? Surely, delivering babies at this Barb Hostetler's house couldn't be much different than deliveries in other Amish homes. Or could it? What if an emergency arose and he and Barb disagreed on the course of treatment? Who would the patient listen to?

"Well, Doc, I suppose *you've* met Barb already," Emma chattered on, oblivious to the doctor's discomfort with the subject.

"Actually, I haven't had an opportunity to meet her yet. Have you had much nausea or noticed any swelling?" he questioned.

"No, I haven't. But I do hope you have the opportunity to meet Barb," Emma persisted. "'Cause that's where I always have my babies."

Dr. Lehman scanned the woman's chart. "You've had twins?"

"That's right."

"I certainly would not deliver twins there, at least if I knew it ahead of time," he declared, adjusting the stethoscope. "I can only pick up one heartbeat this time, and the size of the baby seems right for your due date."

"By the way, what do you charge for deliveries?" Emma asked as Phyllis helped her sit up on the table.

"Eighty dollars for a hospital delivery, and $100 for home deliveries because I need to provide oxygen and the nurse. But

I've never delivered any babies at Barb Hostetler's place, and I hadn't decided if I should."

"Oh, Doc—"

Dr. Lehman read the pleading, hopeful expression on his patient's face. He sensed she would rather switch doctors than leave the midwife's care. This was her seventh delivery, he noted, and she seemed to be an ideal labor patient—full of common sense, discipline, and spunk. But then, if he delivered Emma's baby there, others would ask to go to Barb's, too. Should he start it?

"This Barb, how long has she been monitoring deliveries in her home?"

"Oh, I don't know, a long time. Maybe 15 years or more, but I couldn't say for sure."

"And where did she get her training?"

"Dr. Mayer trained her years ago."

Dr. Lehman closed his eyes and scratched his head. Dr. Mayer had been the Lehman family doctor and had delivered Elton in the farmhouse behind the Kidron Auction barn. If Dr. Mayer had trained Barb, and if she had worked with the experienced doctor, she should be quite capable.

A sharp rap on the door interrupted the doctor's deliberations. "Doc, there's a problem out here!"

The doctor yanked open the door. "What?"

Near the front door, he spotted a bearded man with a straw hat leaning on the back of a chair with one hand and holding a bloody towel to his knee with the other. A red stream trickled down the torn pant leg, coursed over the crusted work shoes, and pooled on the floor.

"Sorry about the floor, Doc."

"Don't worry about the floor," Dr. Lehman gestured for the injured man to sit on the chair. "Let's see what we have here."

As he lifted the red, dripping towel, blood gushed from the large, horseshoe-shaped laceration.

"*Yammahlich!*" a young woman gasped. "It's just frightful!"

"*Ach*, I don't know what got into the horse, anyhow," the wounded man shook his head in disgust. "He is a jumpy one, but he never kicked me before. I was just hitching him up. A fly must have bit him or something."

"That's a nasty laceration," the doctor remarked, reaching for the sterile white towel Phyllis handed him. "And when did this happen?"

"Oh, I suppose about an hour ago."

The doctor closed his eyes and thought for a minute. It would take a good hour to clean and repair the laceration. Several patients were waiting to be seen, but this wound needed immediate care. It was surely contaminated with countless barnyard germs, and the man was in pain, he could tell.

"Just take care of him, Doc," a mother bouncing a fussy infant encouraged. "We can wait."

"*Yah*, sure," the others agreed.

The taut lines on the injured man's face relaxed and he smiled gratefully at the other patients. "*Grohs dank!*"

"If any of you have shopping to do at Spector's, or any other business you could take care of in town rather than waiting here for the next hour, you are welcome to do that," the doctor announced, helping the injured man to the waiting room.

The women tied their black bonnet strings under their chins, took their children in hand, and headed down the sidewalk toward the dry-goods store.

By the time Dr. Lehman stitched the wounded knee and saw the other patients, most of his lunch hour had slipped away. The afternoon patients would soon be tying their horses to the hitching posts.

Phyllis nibbled on a sandwich and flipped through a stack of mail. Slitting the top of a hand-addressed envelope, she removed a neatly-folded Benadryl pill carton and a scrap of notebook paper.

Greetings as always,

Well, we are puzzled with these pills. I got a bee sting since last week. We think I'm elergic to a sting. So last Sunday my sister in church said she was once elergic to a sting and she got those benadryl pills from you and she thinks I need those. I am throwing again more up. Here is the box from the pills we got out at the store last week. I am kinda scared taking them. Thought maybe you could tell me if I could take em. Hope you can understand my unworthy lines. Would like to hear soon.

Sending best wishes,
Verna Miller

"Here's something you might want to look at," Phyllis remarked, handing the note to her husband.

Dr. Lehman studied the paper a moment. "Hmmm. Mrs. Miller is worried the pills are going to hurt the baby she is carrying. If it was an allergic reaction, she's probably fine now, but I'll see if I can find a moment to stop by her house and make sure she's okay."

"But we're having company tonight, and besides, I thought you wanted to weed the garden before they arrive."

"If my patients need me—" he began as he placed a bottle of Benadryl into his satchel.

"Elton, you *did* ask Dr. Eberly to cover for you tonight, didn't you? After all, I don't want to be stuck entertaining your friends."

"Why, no, I didn't. I don't really expect any calls, and Wain has a growing family. I hate to bother him more often than I really need to."

With a sigh, Phyllis trudged to the kitchen to check the pies baking in the oven and then headed back to the office for the afternoon.

When the last patient walked out the door, Phyllis completed the charts, put the office in order, and placed the instruments in the autoclave tray, added water, and started the sterilizer. Then she hurried to the tiny kitchen to fry the chicken for dinner. If only I could rest for 10 minutes, but I'll be stepping to get ready as it is, she thought wistfully.

Meanwhile, Dr. Lehman drove out to Verna Miller's home. As expected, he found she had recovered well from the allergic reaction to the bee sting. She was relieved to learn that the Benadryl would not hurt her baby.

Wow, Verna's got a fine-looking garden, the doctor observed as he drove out her lane. I sure hope I can get mine weeded before it rains and before the company arrives. I do like things looking tidy. The Swiss in me, I guess.

Several minutes later, Dr. Lehman attacked the weeds ambitiously with his hoe, waving to the farmers who called out a greeting from their farm wagons rattling up Route 241. As he chopped at the weeds, Dr. Lehman fought an inner battle. Should I start doing deliveries at the midwife's house or not? Do I or don't I?

Looks like I'll beat the rain, he thought, glancing up at the sky as a car pulled up in front of the office. A bearded man in a straw hat jumped from the passenger's seat and yanked open the rear car door.

"Got a problem, Doc. Sammy, here, ran his hand through a nail," the man called when he spotted the doctor in the garden.

"Let me take a look at what we have here." Dr. Lehman walked over to the car and gently peeled back the blood-soaked cloth, exposing a deep puncture in the boy's palm. "Aw, that's a nasty one. What happened?"

"Me and my brother were racing to the new *sei shiah* and I couldn't stop, so I held out my *hend* and I crashed into the *shiah* and *un naggle* was stickin' out and went in so far that I couldn't pull my *hand* off," the boy sniffled. "Then Dad heard me screamin' and came and yanked it out."

"That must have hurt awfully," Dr. Lehman sympathized. "Why don't you come inside and we'll get it fixed up."

"Phyllis! I need you a minute!" Dr. Lehman's voice carried to the dining room where Phyllis was setting the table.

He gently examined the wound and addressed the boy's father. "Let's see, you're Emma Miller's husband, Henry, I believe."

"Yep; Henry Miller. My wife was in today."

"That's right. I didn't expect to see any of the Millers again so soon. Phyllis, mix a little Dreft laundry detergent in a bowl of water, please."

After the child soaked his hand in the warm, milky solution for a few moments, the doctor dried the hand and examined it again.

"Zephrin, Phyllis."

After pouring disinfectant over the wound, he swabbed it dry, covered it with a bandage, and wrapped the hand with gauze and white tape. "Well, that's all we can do for a puncture wound, other than giving a tetanus shot. His chart says he's not up to date on his tetanus shots so he really should have one."

"Yeah, I suppose. Don't want the boy to end up as sick as Monroe Miller was some time back."

"Tetanus is a nasty thing. You don't want to get it," the doctor agreed. He rolled up the youngster's sleeve and swabbed the arm with a cotton ball saturated with alcohol. With a quick flick of the doctor's wrist, the needle pierced the skin. The boy flinched slightly and then sighed as the needle eased back out.

Dr. Lehman placed a Band-Aid over the bead of blood on the boy's arm. "I'll give him some tablets for pain," he told Henry. "His hand's going to be pretty sore for a day or two. Be sure to keep the wound clean. I suggest you put a little hydrogen peroxide on it once a day when you change bandages for the next couple days."

"By the way," Henry said, paying the $3.50 for the office call and fee for the shot. "Emma's sure hopin' you'll come out to Barb's for her."

"I'm still thinking about it," Dr. Lehman replied, opening the door for the patients. "I didn't get a chance to answer her question after that emergency came into the office today. But tell her I'll let her know next week what I've decided."

"Watch out for nails!" Dr. Lehman called to the boy climbing down the stairs.

"Well, Doc, sorry about the garden," Henry called, holding out his hand to catch the raindrops.

"No problem, Henry. The weeds can wait, but a boy with a punctured hand can't." The doctor shut the office door behind him and strode into the living room to greet the guests that had arrived while he was bandaging the hand.

An irresistible aroma of fried chicken floated through the house. China dishes on the lace-covered dining room table sparkled in the candlelight.

"Now that you're ready, we can eat," Phyllis called when she spotted her husband. Somehow she had managed to finish setting the table, Dr. Lehman noticed as he greeted the guests.

"So, you all arrived before I did, and I just came from the next room," the doctor laughed, unruffled by the interruptions of the day. While Phyllis set the platter of fried chicken on the table along with buttered mashed potatoes, fresh green beans, steaming gravy, dinner rolls, and a crisp lettuce salad, the doctor helped his guests find seats.

Ah, what a wonderful way to end a busy day—sharing a tasty meal with friends, he thought, glancing at the faces glowing in the flickering candlelight.

After a prayer of thanks and blessing, the conversation began to flow as Phyllis served the heaping platters.

"Oh, Phyllis, I'll bet you just love being married to a doctor!" one woman purred. "How idyllic—working together in an office in your own house. What a charming life!"

Phyllis managed to avoid her husband's laughing eyes and smiled politely. "It sure has its advantages."

"Is there any news of Daniel Gerber?" a guest asked as the conversation turned toward Dr. Lehman's relative from Kidron who was abducted by the Viet Cong several years earlier while in Vietnam as a hospital worker and conscientious objector.

"There are occasional rumors he's been seen," someone offered, "but nothing concrete."

As Dr. Lehman cut into the tender chicken leg on his plate, the shrill ring of the telephone sliced through the conversation. Phyllis' fork froze in midair. She held her breath and listened tensely as Elton answered the phone.

"Sure, I'll be right over," she heard him say. Her fork crashed to the plate and her heart seemed to slither down to her toes.

Not tonight! Please, not tonight! she thought desperately. These are Elton's friends! I don't want to entertain them alone all evening!

Elton's eyes met Phyllis' for a fleeting moment and read disappointment in them. He cast a longing look at the chicken, knowing it would be cold and crusty when he returned. The potatoes would be stiff and the salad wilted. And, very likely, his friends would all have gone home.

After the door closed behind Dr. Lehman, no one spoke for a few moments. Only the occasional scraping of a plate or the hissing candle flame broke the silence. Several guests made a few half-hearted attempts at conversation, but the atmosphere went flat. Silently, a few guests helped Phyllis wash the dishes while the rest paged aimlessly through old newspapers in the living room. Then they quietly left.

I worked so hard to have everything just perfect! Phyllis fumed. The room grew dark as she snuffed out the flames of the tapers. Is this the way things are going to go for the rest of our lives? Phone calls . . . change of plans . . . interrupted dinners . . . disturbed nights. . . . What an idyllic, charming life, indeed!

Pressure built up inside her like steam inside a tea kettle with no vent. They weren't even my friends to begin with! Why couldn't he get Eberly to cover for him, anyhow? Angry tears spilled down her cheeks as she ripped off a sheet of tin-foil, smashed it over the plate, and shoved it into the oven.

As the oven door slammed shut, the thought of her husband's untouched plate and how hungry he must be sent a stab of pity through her heart. Elton probably wasn't enjoying the evening, either. He hadn't wanted to leave any more than she wanted him to, but he felt he had no other choice. He was needed.

With a sigh, Phyllis sat down at the piano as raindrops trickled down the windows. She didn't feel much like playing, but she remembered her own advice: "If you don't play for a day, your instructor will know it. If you don't play for two days, you will know it. And if you miss three days, the whole world will know it."

Her fingers skimmed across the keys and her body swayed gently with the soft, flowing chords of music. As always, the therapy of playing music lifted her spirits. Her thoughts turned to the day they had purchased the piano—the day President John F. Kennedy was shot.

"Things could be worse," she told herself, thinking of Jackie Kennedy, who now spent every evening without her husband. "Things could be much worse."

And what was that little saying she had read recently? That it was better to have 10 percent of a 100 percent man, than 100 percent of a 10 percent man. Wasn't that the truth!

The porch creaked under the doctor's footsteps and Phyllis hurried to pull his supper from the oven. As she placed the wilted salad, stiff potatoes, and crusty, shriveled chicken pieces on the table, she asked, "Well, a boy or a girl tonight?"

"Neither," he said quietly, avoiding her eyes.

"What?"

"The baby didn't come yet. I'll have to go back in a few hours."

"*Elton Lehman*! You missed the whole evening and then you didn't even deliver a baby?"

Neither spoke for a few minutes. What was there to say? Finally, he looked up. "I made my decision. If you see Emma Miller, tell her if there are no complications, I'll deliver her baby at Barb's house. While I sat in that hot bedroom waiting and waiting for something to happen, and thinking of you all here at home, I decided this was ridiculous. If that midwife wants to watch the women until they are ready to deliver, and then give me a call, she could save me a lot of grief—at least if she knows what she's doing. And that, we'll find out."

Phyllis sighed and some of the tension in her heart melted.

"And another thing," he continued decisively, "I think we can afford to hire a nurse now. You've been great, but you'll need to get ready for the little one soon."

"I suppose," his wife agreed, "but there's really not a whole lot to do to get ready for the baby. I don't have a nursery to prepare."

"Poor child," Elton sighed. "We don't even have space for a crib. Do you think the baby could sleep in a basket for six months? By April, the new clinic should be finished; then you can use one of the offices for a nursery. I guess the baby will learn early on that in the Lehman household, everyone has to . . . "

"Be flexible or be miserable!"

6.

BARB'S HOUSE

D r. Lehman gazed across rolling fields, observing the dark red barns and neat farmhouses fringed with flower beds and punctuated by poles holding hand-crafted bird houses. Here and there, a string of dark shirts and dresses hung from a line strung beneath a porch roof. Mountains of logs surrounded a sawmill, and a creek meandered through a pasture. At the end of an occasional dirt lane, hand-painted signs advertised brown eggs, hickory rockers, potatoes, hand-made baskets, or cedar chests for sale. Almost every sign bore the small postscript announcing: "No Sunday sales."

What will this Barb be like? Dr. Lehman wondered, not noticing the white, one-room schoolhouse with a bell in the cupola, swings dangling idly in the yard, or the pair of outhouses behind the school.

Cruising down the hill on that summer day in 1966, he scarcely noticed the small bridge he crossed, but three decades later, a tragic accident would claim five of his young patients, and he would never cross that bridge without turning to look at the small, white crosses marking the accident site. But today, thoughts of the Amish midwife tumbled in his mind, and the bridge flashed past without a second glance.

What have I gotten myself into now? he fretted as he turned off onto a country road. What if this Barb is pushy or difficult to work with?

Beyond the hills, a distant fire engine wailed and a whiff of smoke filtered through the window. "A barn fire," patients told him at the office that morning. "It was struck by lightning."

Barn fires always involved significant loss, the doctor knew. He recalled the large barn on his uncle Eli's farm filled with animals, feed, equipment, straw, and hay. Fires reduced all this to a heap of blackened, smoking rubble.

Braking, Dr. Lehman studied the spacious, white farmhouse set into a grove of trees and shadowed by a neatly-painted white barn. Well, this must be the place, he decided, pulling into the driveway. The barn's white, so the Hostetlers are not Swartzentruber Amish, he noted. Slowly, he guided the car up the driveway bordered by brilliant flower gardens.

Beyond the beads of rain trickling down the car windows, the doctor noticed orderly rows of corn bordering the far side of the weedless vegetable garden. Rows of petunias fringed the front of the garden while apple trees sheltered it from the road. Henry's sorrel stamped restlessly at the hitching post.

He parked his Mercury Comet on the lane between the house and garden and checked his odometer—10 miles. Clutching his black satchel, he picked his way around the puddles in the driveway as lightning flashed across the black clouds.

Looking up, the doctor knew immediately that the woman holding the door was Barb. The strings of her prayer cap were tied loosely beneath her chin and a gray apron covered the plain, dark dress that nearly reached her ankles. Instantly, the doctor read an unusual alertness in the soft, pleasant face and warm eyes behind the wire-rimmed glasses. So much for visions of a stooped, old woman! A crash of thunder shook the house and a fresh torrent unleashed itself over the doctor's head.

"Well, forevermore! What a storm to be out in, anyhow!" Barb welcomed the doctor with a gracious smile.

As the midwife hung his dripping raincoat from a metal hook on the wall, the doctor noted the gleaming linoleum floors, polished heating stove, gas lamp, and wooden table and chairs. On the spotless, ivory-colored walls hung a calendar depicting a stream rushing over a mill's waterwheel. A clean, fresh scent mingled with the aroma of homemade bread and a faint whiff of kerosene.

"Emma's about ready to go," Barb announced, leading the way to the next room. The midwife parted the curtains on the far doorway. In the glow of the gas lantern, Dr. Lehman recognized his patient on the bed in the little room. Henry's wet, brown hair was plastered to his head and his shirt clung to his shoulders as he stood at his wife's side, letting her grip his work-callused hand. He looked up and broke into a relieved smile.

"Hey, Doc's here!"

"How's Henry?" The doctor set down his black satchel. "You had quite a jog through the rain to reach a phone this morning."

"You better believe I did. Half a mile one way and through a muddy field at that. And it was lightning all around me. Emma better appreciate it!" The Amishman's eyes twinkled as he spoke.

"And how's Emma?"

"Okay," she sighed, forcing a brief smile before focusing back on the peaceful woodland stream pictured on the wall calendar.

"It won't be long," Dr. Lehman promised, spreading out the sterile obstetrics kit on the clean white towel and pulling on his scrubs and gloves.

He surveyed the storm-darkened window and single gas lantern. "Do you have a flashlight, Barb?"

"Sure, right here."

"Great. Henry, can you hold it for me?"

While the patient's husband held the flashlight, Barb sponged Emma's flushed face with a cool, damp cloth.

"This . . . *buppeli* will never come," the mother moaned, digging her fingernails into the mattress.

"The *buppeli* will come," the midwife assured her, wiping the forehead again. "They always do," she soothed. "You are doing just fine. It's almost over."

A high-pitched cry filled the room as a wet, wriggling, chubby baby slid into the doctor's gloved hands.

"A girl!" he announced triumphantly, suctioning mucous from the tiny nose. He handed the infant to Barb, then clamped and cut the cord. After assessing the baby's breathing, heart beat, muscle tone, reflexes, and color, he handed her to the midwife, who weighed and bathed the infant while the doctor cared for the mother.

Deftly, Barb slipped one of her hand-made gowns over the diapered newborn, wrapped her snugly in a homemade blanket, and handed the infant to Emma. "Here's your little dolly!"

Dr. Lehman worked quietly in the afterglow of birth, as the couple shared relief that labor was over and awe for their newborn child.

"How's your son's hand?" Dr. Lehman asked as he collected his instruments.

"Oh, the way he uses it, you'd never know he hurt it," Henry replied, stroking his damp beard. "But I'll tell you, he had a lot of pain the first day or two. I spent half that first night beside his bed holding his hand."

"That was a painful injury," the doctor observed, placing his stethoscope in his satchel. He shut his black bag and gave Emma a few brief instructions on caring for herself and the baby the next several weeks. She wouldn't need much direction, he knew, since she was an experienced mother with seven other children.

Dr. Lehman extended his hand toward the Amishman. "Enjoy the little one, and tell that boy to watch out for nails!"

"We'll do that," Henry laughed. "Don't worry none about nail troubles. In fact, I don't think that boy will ever be a carpenter. He wants nothing to do with nails!"

"You can do your paperwork at this table," Barb gestured as she led the way into the outer room furnished with a rocking chair, wooden changing table, and small cribs flanking the wood stove.

"Well, aren't these cute little cribs," Dr. Lehman observed, examining the beautifully-crafted wooden beds with casters and ornate spindles.

"Oh, Bill made those," Barb explained. "And he made a special low one to put by my bed in case I need to keep tabs on a baby during the night."

"So, he doesn't mind all this intrusion into your home and family life?"

"*Ach*, no. All he asks is that I'm up to see him off to work."

"And what do we have here?" Dr. Lehman asked, walking over to examine a crib with closed quart jars of water lining the perimeter.

"Come and see!" Barb invited as she scrubbed her hands in the wash bowl. Peering over the edge of the crib, the doctor was startled to see a tiny infant whose arms were no thicker than his fingers.

"A three-and-a-half pounder," Barb explained, tenderly picking up the wee infant and wrapping the blanket neatly around it. "Your Mamma hitches up the horse and comes over to feed you every morning and evening, doesn't she, little one?" she smiled down at the baby gazing at her with thoughtful eyes, as if he comprehended everything she said.

Dr. Lehman knew the hospitals could do nothing more for the tiny infant than Barb was already doing, other than to administer antibiotics or oxygen, which the child didn't need. Someday, many hospitals would provide neonatal intensive care services, but most regional centers didn't in 1966.

"And what are the jars of water for?" he questioned.

"I put hot water in the jars, screw on the lids, and put them along the sides of the crib. They keep the little one as warm as toast," Barb explained as she dripped warm droplets of formula into the tiny mouth using a medicine dropper. "And I lay a hot water bottle next to him. We've no electricity for an incubator, you know."

"Ingenious. You Amish always come up with something, don't you?" Dr. Lehman remarked, sitting at the table and spreading out his papers in front of him. "I'm sure you run into all kinds of situations. What do you do when a woman starts to hemorrhage, for instance?"

"Well, Doc, I just do what Doc Mayer taught me, and we never have any problem. I tell you, Doc, we've never lost a mother. The Good Lord must be looking over this place is all I can say."

"But, Barb, sooner or later you are bound to need a doctor or ambulance immediately. Is there absolutely no way you could have a phone?"

"A *phone!*" Barb's hearty laughter ripped through the room. *Ei yi yi,* Doc, an Amish preacher with a phone! *O du yammah!* Nope, Doc. Not a chance."

Dr. Lehman put down his pen. "Barb, how on earth did you ever get into this?"

"Oh, forevermore," Barb shook her head and continued to feed the infant. "Never planned on this when I went to my neighbor's house some 25 years ago. *Mei zeit,* no. My neighbor was having her first baby. She was a bit older when she got married. Maybe she thought all that was past." Barb's eyes twinkled as she fingered the ties of her cap. "Well, my friend was a little scared about this birthing," she continued, "and she asked if I'd come over when her time came. I says, 'I don't know nothing about that stuff. I couldn't be any help.' Why, I wasn't much more than about 22 years old and just had a couple of our six children by that time. But she kept insisting, 'You've been through it, Barb! It would help so much just knowing you're here.'

"So I went. Everything went well. Dr. Mayer delivered the baby and his wife bathed it in the big dishpan she set on the floor." The midwife chuckled at the memory. "And then other women started asking, 'Won't you please come and be with me when my baby comes?' A doctor always delivered the babies, but they wanted me to support and coach them through the labor, I guess. And now you can see what I got myself in for!" Barb said, nestling the little one in his crib again, refilling the hot water bottle, and adjusting the blanket around him.

"Now excuse me just a minute here, Doc. I have several loaves of bread in the oven, and it's time to get them out," Barb said, breezing from the room, her long dress swishing as she went.

Quite a woman, quite a place, the doctor thought, glancing around the orderly room that had once been Barb's kitchen. Bill's parents had lived in the *Dawdi haus*, Barb had said. Then, after Bill's folks passed away, Barb and Bill moved into the apartment and converted their parlor and kitchen into the little birthing center.

The doctor's stomach rumbled as the toasty aroma of home-baked bread floated into the room. A moment later, the midwife returned carrying a tray with several cups of tea and two golden slices of pie smothered in whipped cream and oozing sweetness.

"I was canning peaches yesterday and saved some to make a couple pies," she announced with a smile. "I know how hungry doctors get. Especially around lunch time."

After setting the steaming cup and generous slice to the side of Dr. Lehman's papers, Barb carried the tray to Henry and Emma in the room behind the curtain.

Gratefully, the doctor speared a peach slice and swirled it through the thick cream. Never worked in a hospital yet that served homemade pie to their doctors after a delivery, he thought, savoring every bite of the scrumptious pie and flaky crust that melted in his mouth.

Barb set her cup of tea on the table and sat down across from the doctor. For a moment, she gazed thoughtfully at the rays of sunshine piercing through the dark clouds and the humming-birds sipping nectar from the feeder beyond the window.

Dr. Lehman scraped the last bit of crust and cream from the china plate with this fork. "Tell me, Barb, how did you start bringing them into your house? You have a family to care for, too."

Barb paused for a moment before answering. "Well, Doc, it seems to me one family had the measles, and I told the moth-er to come to my house when the baby was born so the baby wouldn't be exposed to the germs." She propped her chin on her hands thoughtfully. "Or maybe it was the time a family was remodeling their house, and I told them it would be eas-ier for them to come to my house than for me to go to theirs in the midst of all that mess. But anyways, other women start-ed asking to have their babies here. So I let my relatives and the church women come, but then, don't you know, soon oth-ers asked to come, too—Mennonite women, and even a few who weren't Mennonite or Amish.

"After one delivery, the mom said, 'You did a great job sup-porting and coaching. Now I know how to handle the women at the hospital when they're in labor.' And I said, 'What! You're a nurse at the hospital and you came to my house to have a baby?'" Barb shook her head. "And they just keep coming."

I can see why, the doctor thought, recalling her nurturing, encouraging support during the delivery. I can see why they come, and I know this won't be the last baby I deliver here. This woman has a way with the mothers that a lot of nurses could learn from. She didn't try to order me around but was supportive, showed common sense, and has a relaxed way that makes anyone feel at home. Even a doctor could learn from her. Yes, Barb's one unusual woman.

The next morning before his office opened, Dr. Lehman stopped back at the Hostetler home to check on Emma. As the doctor drove into the lane next to the sprawling white frame house, he noticed a tall, bearded man with slightly humped shoulders striding up the lane, a white covered bucket in his hand.

That must be Bill, Dr. Lehman realized. He's probably emptying the chamber pot in the hole he dug in the field.

To the side of the house, sheets and pillowcases fluttered on clotheslines. Inside the house, Barb bathed the Miller baby while her daughter served Emma a breakfast of eggs, toast, Cheerios, and hot Jell-O in charming china bowls and plates.

"Wow, Emma. Barb's treating you royally!" Dr. Lehman exclaimed, striding into the room.

"I know it, and she's spoiling me good!" the mother laughed. "And I'm going to miss her back rubs when I go home."

As Dr. Lehman continued to deliver babies at Barb's house, he observed that, somehow, Barb found time to do the things that mattered, even if it deprived herself of sleep. The house always sparkled, and every day she stirred up marvelous pies, breads, and wholesome meals. The workload had to be heavy, Dr. Lehman knew. When relatives died or her daughters married, the house had to be thoroughly cleaned and the furniture moved out to accommodate the crowds for the services. And then there were chickens to butcher and pies to bake.

More and more women arrived unannounced on Barb's doorstep any hour of the day or night. Barb could not turn them away, so Dr. Lehman and Dr. Eberly began giving Barb a list of names and due dates, so she would know who to expect and approximately when.

With all the deliveries and babies and mothers to care for, the midwife had more work than most people could handle. In addition, Barb had obligations as a bishop's wife. On one occasion, she served as a cook at a wedding and returned home at nearly 2 a.m. after cleaning up the dishes from serving the youth at midnight. Barb helped deliver the arriving baby as if she'd just had a full night's sleep. No one, not even Barb, could keep such a pace. So when Sarah knocked on Barb's door one evening, she was received as an answer to Barb's prayers.

That evening, the house seemed to overflow with mothers and crying babies. Piles of sheets and towels mounded on the basement floor, waiting to be fed through the wringer washer. Another baby had arrived around suppertime, and the rays of the lantern illuminated dishes piled high in the sink and on the counters. As Barb rocked a fussy infant, a light knock sounded on the back door. A slight wisp of a girl with her hair tightly pulled back under her prayer *kapp* stood on the steps holding a little suitcase.

"My sister had a baby here and her husband is going to take me to their house to be their *maut* when he comes to see her tonight," the girl explained. "I was wondering if I could wait here for him."

"Of course! *Kumm uscht rei* and find yourself a seat," Barb invited warmly, gesturing toward the living room. "I'll have to go back and help with a delivery, but you just make yourself comfortable."

Sarah visited with her sister for a few moments and cuddled the newborn. Then she settled into the hand-quilted cushions of a hickory rocker in Barb's living room and listened for the rattle of her brother-in-law's buggy wheels coming in the lane. Barb's house felt like home and looked like most other Amish houses. The kerosene lamp glowed warmly over the hickory rockers next to the wood stove with its tea kettle. Hand-made rag rugs warmed the floors and a scenery calendar hung on the wall alongside a wooden rack labeled "mail."

Glancing around, Sarah noticed the stacks of dirty dishes on the kitchen counter. Like most Amish girls, Sarah was not used to sitting around if there was work to do, so she rolled up her sleeves and washed the stacks of plates and kettles. By the time her brother-in-law was ready to leave, the pile of dishes had disappeared.

The following week, Sarah received a six-page letter from Barb inviting the girl to work for her.

I can promise you there will be more to do than scrubbing dishes, she wrote. *There is always something exciting happening around here. I desperately need help, and you seem to be a responsible worker.*

So Sarah came.

One of the first things we do in the morning, Sarah wrote her sister one evening, *is to empty chamber pots. Yuck! Bill used to do it, bless his heart. He'd take them out and dump them into a hole he had made with the post hole digger, and then he'd put a heavy lid on the hole.*

Then comes the fun part. One of us helps the mothers get ready for breakfast, and the other gets the trays ready. We always serve eggs, toast, a bowl of Cheerios, and a cup of hot Jell-O water. The ladies always look forward to their bowl of Cheerios, as it is too expensive for some of them to buy for their families.

After breakfast, the mothers nurse their babies and then take their showers. We change the sheets, put them through the washer, and hang them out. If the women get to go home that day, we don't change the sheets until they leave. We always put a clean crib sheet, blanket, gown, pamper, and shirt on a pile in the crib so it's all ready for the next baby.

For lunch we have some kind of potatoes, vegetable, meat, and a dessert. Bill don't like potatoes much. Today I dug a wee potato about the size of a pea, cooked it with the others, and served it to Bill. "Here," I says to Bill, "if you can't handle all of it, I'll help you." I thought Barb would fall off her chair, she laughed so hard.

In the evening there is always soup, toasted cheese sandwiches, a bowl of fruit, and a cookie or doughnut. There was a lady who hadn't eaten her doughnut one night. She said, "Will you please give me a bag? I want to take this doughnut home for my children to taste as we don't have money to buy them." And this was their fourteenth baby. So there was a lot of sharing with one doughnut.

Later, Sarah wrote, *Well, there were another set of twins today, Elsie and Eli. Dr. Lehman didn't know there were two. They were born between 5:00 and 6:00 in the morning, so we made breakfast for Doc Lehman. He says: "Since I delivered two babies, I should get a double breakfast." I said, "You may come back for lunch."*

When the Petersheims came after Doc had left, they were in such a hurry. The man ran to the neighbors to call Doc, but the baby was here before the father or the doctor got here.

This morning I am getting babies dressed to go home. One father who was a blacksmith says, "My goodness, it does take ya so long to get that baby ready. I already had three horses waiting on me when I left!" But that's the nicest job around here, dressing the schnuck buppelin. *The worst one is emptying chamber pots! No job is all pie.*

Barb was right. The house buzzed with activity. There were always babies to rock, towels to put through the wringer washer and hang out, sheets to iron, floors to mop, bushels of vegetables and fruit to can, and, yes, pecan pies to bake for the doctors and patients who seemed to have appetites of a buggy horse.

Barb sacrificed her time, family life, and privacy to serve the women of her community in the selfless manner that characterized her people. From quilting bees to barn raisings, the Amish helped each other.

And the barn that had burned to the ground the morning Henry and Emma's baby was born was standing again. Several weeks after the fire, Dr. Lehman passed the scene of the fire while heading out to a house call. The ashes and rubble had all been cleared away, and the stark skeleton of another barn was rising against the clear sky as a shout of "HEAVE OH HEEEEAVE!" filled the air. A team of muscular Amishmen strained against long, spiked poles, lifting the gigantic frame into place while others clung to long ropes to keep the frame from going farther than it should.

When the doctor passed again around noon en route to a delivery, the roof of the new barn swarmed with men in straw hats, their suspendered backs bending over the boards they nailed in place several stories above ground. The air rang with the pounding of a hundred hammers. Crews of men and boys lifted boards to those above, while still others worked on the inside of the barn in an incredible organizational feat that would produce a completed barn in less than a day. Barb's and Emma's husbands were among them, the doctor was sure.

Under shade trees near the farmhouse, long tables stretched across the yard. Women and girls, their white prayer *kapp* strings floating in the breeze, gracefully carried steaming platters, bowls, pitchers, baskets, and dozens of pies and cakes out of the farmhouse.

"Do unto others as you would have them do unto you," Dr. Lehman thought. If anyone carries out that Scripture, it's Barb and her people.

"There goes Dr. Lehman!" Barb's husband called as he saw the shiny Comet flash past.

"So, what does your wife think of the new doctor?" a young man asked above the pounding hammers.

"Barb says he knows what he's doing—he's careful, thorough, and a man of common sense. Not every doctor goes the extra mile to accommodate patients like Dr. Lehman does."

"*Yah*, I tell you, it's a blessing to have a doctor that'll do house calls when the children are too sick to take out, or when *Gross Mommi* gets pneumonia. I just hope the dog bites and stray bullets don't make him decide to quit making house calls."

7.

Dogs, Bullets, and Other House Call Hazards

Just where are all those spots John was talking about? Dr. Lehman scratched his head thoughtfully. I only see a few mosquito bites. Mentally, he replayed the phone call he received that Sunday afternoon.

"Our young'uns have got some red spots and they're awfully hot. Would you want to come and take a look at them? I'd sure hate to take them out with the way they are coughing, and all."

Red spots, fever, cough, Dr. Lehman checked off the symptoms. "Are the spots blistering?" he questioned.

"Blistering? You mean getting watery-like? No, they ain't blistering none. Just plain red spots."

Then it's not chicken pox.

"Is there any chance they may have been exposed to measles?" the doctor asked, dreading the answer.

"Oh yeah. We were at a wedding in Pennsylvania, and after we got home we found out that some children out that way broke out with the measles."

"How long ago was that?"

"Two weeks ago, I reckon."

"Two weeks." Dr. Lehman's voice carried the tone of a judge pronouncing a sentence. "Two weeks. I see. And how many of your children are sick?"

"Three of them, and a couple of the others is feeling poorly, too."

"And you say this is John Miller?"

"Yep. That's me, all right!"

Dr. Lehman had eaten a few bites of roast and potatoes, packed cough syrups and Motrin into his bag, and then headed over to John Miller's home. If he hurried, he could be back to attend Phyllis' choir program scheduled that afternoon.

Now where are all those red spots? Dr. Lehman asked himself again in the Miller living room. "I believe your children just have the flu. Nothing serious, and certainly not measles. I'll leave cough medicine for them and some Motrin to keep the fevers down, if you need it. Now, do you have any questions?"

"Yeah, I have one. Just how'd you know the children were sick?"

The doctor looked at the woman sharply. "Why, this is the John Miller home, isn't it?"

"Yes, it is."

"Well, John called and asked me to come out and look at the children."

"But he couldn't have! He's at his uncle's funeral in Indiana. I was wishing he'd be here so he could go to the neighbors to call for you, but he's not home yet. No, I'm sure. John didn't call you. He didn't even know the children were sick."

The doctor's eyes widened. "Well, I was sure. . . ." Suddenly, he started to laugh. "Hey, there's another John Miller south of town, isn't there?"

"Yes, I guess there is."

"I was sure it was your husband's voice."

"Well, anyway, I'm so glad you stopped by!" Mrs. Miller said, following the doctor to the door. "I was worried the children might be getting pneumonia or something. *Grohs dank.*"

As the doctor drove through the countryside, a young Amish couple walking alongside the road pulling several toddlers in a red wagon waved as he guided his car slowly around them. A row of boys in white shirts and black Sunday pants pedaled past from the opposite direction, and an elderly couple waved from a porch swing. South of town, the doctor slowed his car and read the name "John Miller" hand printed onto a mailbox.

Dr. Lehman climbed the steps of the farmhouse porch and knocked purposefully on the door. The girl who answered the door whispered over her shoulder, "*Maam! Die Doc is doah.*"

"*Ach*, Dr. Lehman!" a rosy-cheeked woman exclaimed, drying her sudsy hands on the corner of her apron. "*Kumm rei, kumm rei!*"

Purposefully, the doctor marched into the kitchen, his satchel at his side. Stuffing stray strands of hair under her *kapp*, Mrs. Miller called to her daughter, "Ella Mae, *schpring* to the barn and tell *Daett* that Doc is here. *Mach schnell!*"

"We just finished eating," Mrs. Miller explained, leading the way to the *sitzschtupp*. "Have a chair, once. John went to throw some feed down the *hoy loch* for the cows. He'll make fast and come in. You'll have a piece of *schnitzboi* while you're waiting, ain't?"

"*Schnitzboi!*" the doctor's eyes lit up as he sat down on the couch. Come to think of it, he was hungry. Lunch had been cut short due to the call. "*Schnitzboi* sounds too good to resist."

Where are the children? Perhaps they're all resting in a back bedroom, he thought, glancing at the bare walls, waxed hardwood floor, and plants on the windowsill beneath the sparkling glass. He couldn't see a fingerprint, much less a child.

The screen door slammed. He heard the water splashing at the wash bowl, and a moment later, the stocking-footed, muscular, bearded farmer strode into the parlor. "Howdy, Doc!" the big farmer boomed, extending a scarred hand toward the doctor. *"Vee gehts?"*

"Hello, John! How's the hand?"

"Ain't givin' me a speck of trouble. Healed up real nice after you sewed it up the day I got it in the *hoimacher*. Thanks to you or the kerosene!" The farmer lowered his large frame into a hickory rocker and crossed his legs comfortably. "I tell you, I can do most anything on the job. The boss sends me on a lot of errands. Why, the other day he sent me into an auto parts store for something, and the parts man took a look at my hat and beard and says, 'What's wrong? Did your buggy break down?' and I says, 'No, the rear end just went out on my horse!'"

Dr. Lehman and the farmer laughed together. "Now that was a good answer!" the doctor chuckled. "I'll bet that shut him up."

"Yeah, he had nothing more to say after that."

As Dr. Lehman finished the last spicy bites of pie, the farmer remarked, "I suppose you run into all kinds of situations yourself, Doc."

"I do," he agreed. "I sure do. Just the other night I thought I was being shot at."

"Ach yammah! Who'd want to shoot at a doctor?" John demanded.

"That's what I wondered when the pellets hit my leg. I ran for the house and called the sheriff. It turned out my path happened to intersect a neighborhood dispute just as the gun went off," he finished.

"Wow, Doc, you got a dangerous job. Hope it won't scare you off from doing house calls. Sure is awfully handy for us. Do you ever tell folks you won't do a house call?"

These friendly folks sure do like to visit, the doctor thought. "Yes, I've had to say no more than once. When I first came to town, I got called out to homes quite often. In fact, it seemed I got more calls at night than during the day! Finally, I caught wind that some folks hated to disturb their regular doctor in the middle of the night, so they thought it would be a good time to check out the new guy in town!"

"*Ach mei zeit!* That ain't too nice," John declared. "I wouldn't have gone."

"Well, John, I tell you, I was a shy one. I had to get up my courage and ask those night callers who their regular doctor was. If it wasn't me, I'd swallow hard and tell them they should call their own doctor."

"*Mei zeit*, Doc," John laughed. "I can't believe you'd have been as bashful as that! So, do you go every time you're called out nowadays?"

"No, I don't," Dr. Lehman replied. "But I do go out to homes for the elderly who can't come into the office, and to patients who are too sick to come in. I've had bedfast cancer patients, for instance, who have been able to stay in their homes because I go out and check on them. But, if the patient is able to come to the office, or would be better off going to the hospital, I don't go out to the house."

"You mean if someone was having a heart attack or something?"

"Exactly. Last week a woman called saying her husband was having chest pains. I got him on the phone and fired questions at him. When I heard what was happening, I told him if he really was having a heart attack, he could go into shock and die in my office. I said I wasn't equipped to handle a case like that here, and he'd better get to the hospital fast. And that was exactly what happened. He was rushed to the emergency room where he went into cardiac shock, but he pulled through because they were equipped to revive him. If I made him wait until I went out to his house to diagnose him, he would have died. I had a professor who advised students to sit down and drink a cup of coffee before responding to a house call from a suspected heart attack victim."

"Coffee! Whatever for? Was that supposed to make you figure out the problem better, or what?"

"No," Dr. Lehman laughed. "If a doctor goes out immediately and the patient dies from a heart attack, it looks bad for the doctor. However, if the doctor waits a little and gets there after the crisis has passed, the patient either will have died or will survive."

"So that's what you do?" John demanded.

"No, John, don't worry," the doctor smiled. "Actually, that's one part of med school I decided to disregard. For one thing, I don't drink coffee. For another, I've learned to pretty accurately diagnose heart attack symptoms over the phone."

"*Mei zeit,* Doc, you're not one of those quacks who asks folks to wrap a phone cord around their neck so you can diagnose them over the phone?"

"Oh no, John. No. Not like that. You see, I've learned to ask the right questions. And then I can pretty well tell if a person is suffering from a heart attack." Dr. Lehman glanced anxiously at the carved, wooden clock on the wall with the golden pendulum swinging inside the glass window. I do hope to hear Phyllis' solo!

"How are the children?" Dr. Lehman asked. He would get down to business if the Millers wouldn't.

"Healthy as ever!" John picked up a toddler and bounced her on his knee. "Healthy as ever."

"But, don't any of them have a rash? Or fever?"

"Not a trace, Doc, why?"

"But John, you called."

"Me? No, Doc, I didn't call. Must have been John A. Miller north of town, or John H. Miller west of town, John N. or John S. or John Z.," the farmer rattled on. "Or Jakey's Sam's John or One-eyed John."

"Yes! That's it!" The doctor jumped to his feet and picked up his satchel. "Now that you say it, that was John H. Miller's voice.

I declare, I sure wish these counties would assign street numbers," Dr. Lehman said walking to the door. "And it would help if everybody wouldn't have the last name of Miller!"

"Half the folks in Holmes County are Millers," John quipped, "and the other half wish they was!"

The doctor's hearty laughter rang through the house, and the door shut behind him as he set out in search of John H. Miller's residence.

Boy, I'm going to have to see if I can get these counties to assign street numbers, he thought as his Comet sped along the country roads. There could be three John H. Millers living along Route 2. According to the phone book, 40–some John Millers lived in the area, to say nothing of those who weren't listed because they had no phones! Nancy said that in Apple Creek alone, they had four patients named Levi J. Miller, and two of the wives had the same name. Something had to be done.

Though house calls certainly were more convenient for the patients than for the physician, Dr. Lehman valued the interaction with patients in their homes, as well as the variation from routine office calls. And variation they did provide. In fact, some of Dr. Lehman's house calls were more accurately barn calls or car calls.

On one home visit, the doctor asked about a son that had an enlarged spleen. "He's down in the barn, milking," the boy's mother told him. So, Dr. Lehman walked down to the barn and told the boy he wanted to check his spleen. "You don't need to bother going back to the house, if you don't mind laying down on this loading dock," Dr. Lehman suggested, gesturing to the platform on which the farmer set his milk cans for pickup. And on that unusual examining table, Dr. Lehman examined the youth's enlarged spleen.

One afternoon at a wedding, someone asked Dr. Lehman to check on a fellow lying in a van who had a terrible pain in his side. Was it an appendicitis? Dr. Lehman wondered as he walked to the parking lot. The condition was tricky to diagnose. Early in his practice, he diagnosed a case as an appendicitis, then discovered the child had pneumonia, instead. Pneumonia, he learned, mimics appendicitis symptoms in small children. Appendicitis, Dr. Lehman learned, is more prevalent in teenagers and people in their twenties. Though it was rare, the condition did show up occasionally in young children and elderly patients. But when it did, it was more difficult to diagnose.

Eventually, the doctor learned to accurately diagnose appendicitis, even over the phone, by simply asking the right questions or by observing the way a suspected appendicitis victim walked.

"You'd better get to a hospital," he warned the sick wedding guest in the van after examining him. "I suspect you've got an inflamed appendix."

When the diagnosis proved accurate and the appendix had been removed, Dr. Lehman quipped, "I couldn't turn water into wine at a wedding, but I could diagnose acute appendicitis!"

"You sure go out of your way to do house calls for your patients," folks told him.

"I never traveled as far for a house call as Dr. Eberly has," he always replied. "My colleague made headlines in the local paper when he traveled all the way to Haiti to care for a sick pastor friend!"

As he approached a farm, Dr. Lehman slowed down to study the name on the mailbox. For the third time that Sunday afternoon, he read "John Miller." And for the third time, he knocked at a door of a farmhouse.

"Why, Dr. Lehman! We've been waiting for you!" a tall, slender man greeted the doctor, holding the door open for him to enter. "Thought you got lost or something!"

"Well, I'm here!" the doctor smiled.

Flushed and spotted, the children reclined listlessly on the living room couches. Hacking coughs echoed through the room. "I saw you have a nice puppy outside," the doctor remarked to a young boy as he pulled out his stethoscope. "Does he have a name?"

Amiably, the doctor chatted with the children while he took their temperatures. He listened to their lungs, checking for pneumonia, and examined the small, raised spots.

"They've got measles, all right," Dr. Lehman informed the parents. "There's really not much I can give them. Since measles are a virus, antibiotics won't help, unless pneumonia or an ear infection should develop. About the only thing I can do is to offer them some cough syrup and Motrin to make them more comfortable. They probably won't feel like being too active for a couple of days. Five days after the rash started, they won't be contagious anymore. Until then, you'll want to keep them away from other children. Call me if they develop a deep chest cough and fever, or if you see signs of an ear infection."

Well, I finally got that call wrapped up, the doctor thought, packing his bag. Now, maybe if I hurry, I can drive straight to the church to hear Phyllis.

"Oh, by the way, Doc," Mr. Miller began, as he followed him to the door. "Joni Petersheims up the road think they got the measles, too. They were wondering if you could stop by and see their young'uns since you're out this way, anyhow. And my brother thinks his children have them."

"A measles epidemic," Dr. Lehman sighed as he headed up the lane of the Petersheim farm.

"Your children didn't have the MMR shots?" he asked the Petersheims. He was not surprised to hear they had not been vaccinated. Two-thirds of the general Amish population immunized their children, but nearly all of the Swartzentruber Amish opted not to. Since many of the Mount Eaton Amish belonged to the Swartzentruber group, Dr. Lehman and his colleagues saw whooping cough, measles, and mumps, diseases few city practitioners ever saw.

Soon after setting up his practice, however, Dr. Lehman was puzzled by the unusual number of requests for tetanus shots. "What makes tetanus shots the craze right now?" he asked one of his patients. "I thought you Swartzentruber Amish don't get vaccinated. Now all of a sudden everybody wants a shot!"

"Well, Doc, Monroe Miller chopped his toe with his hoe by mistake, and he got tetanus and nearly died," the patient explained. "We don't want to get tetanus, so we thought we better get ourselves a shot."

"I see. Tetanus, whooping cough, diphtheria, measles, and polio all have potentially serious side effects. That's why we recommend baby shots," Dr. Lehman replied.

Occasionally, he asked his patients if they have religious convictions against shots and discovered that, usually, the decision resulted from philosophical reasons rather than religious.

When polio broke out among Amish communities in Pennsylvania and Wisconsin, the Ohio State Health Commissioner worried that the large number of unvaccinated people in the Mount Eaton community posed an epidemic risk. "What can we do to get these folks vaccinated?" he asked Dr. Lehman.

At the doctor's suggestion, ads were placed in the *Sugarcreek Budget*. The advertisement brought many patients to Mount Eaton for vaccines, but still other families needed to be reached.

"I'll take the vaccines out to the Amish homes myself," Dr. Lehman offered. "I know where the folks live, and I'll explain the danger to them." And he did. Saturdays, evenings, and even on his days off, the doctor took the vaccines to his patients' homes, giving as many as twelve doses per home and a 100 doses a day. The hard work paid off, as Dr. Lehman never saw a case of polio in his office.

One Saturday afternoon before Labor Day, Dr. Lehman suspected he had a tetanus case on his hands. The young boy he examined appeared flushed and listless.

"It looks like a flu to me. Make sure he gets lots of rest and fluids," Dr. Lehman recommended. "And you can give him Tylenol to keep his fever down."

When the child's fever rose alarmingly high during the night, the parents were too polite to bother Dr. Lehman at that hour, and hired a driver to take them to the emergency room, instead.

Disgruntled at having his night disturbed, the pediatrician on call spoke sharply to the boy's father. "It's the flu, like Dr. Lehman said," he snapped. "Why did you bring a child in to the emergency room just for the flu? Take him home and put him to bed. He'll feel better tomorrow."

But he didn't.

When Dr. Lehman received an anxious call on Labor Day morning, he postponed the family outing and headed over to the sick child's home. After taking the boy's vitals, the doctor studied him thoughtfully. Fever, malaise, listlessness . . . but it's not the typical flu.

Dr. Lehman shut his eyes, trying to make a diagnosis. The boy's awfully sick—but what's the problem? he wondered, baffled and concerned. It wouldn't be polio, would it?

"I suggest you take him to Akron Children's Hospital," Dr. Lehman finally decided.

The tests at the hospital showed tetanus.

"Did your son have any scratches or injuries recently?" Dr. Lehman questioned the boy's parents.

"Well, let me think." The father studied the floor for a moment. "Yes, come to think of it, he did have a barnyard scratch about two weeks ago."

"Well, that makes sense. You can be thankful you brought him in for that tetanus vaccine some time back. It won't be as effective as if he had the full line of vaccines, but it's better than none."

When Dr. Lehman stopped by the child's home several days later, he was happy to see the child recovering from what could have been a fatal illness.

Once, several infected tourists introduced a measles epidemic into Holmes, Wayne, and Tuscarawas counties when they visited a local shop and infected two Amish boys. The youth caught the disease and unknowingly exposed their friends, relatives, and neighbors, who spread the germ to their acquaintances. Between office calls and house visits, Dr. Lehman had no spare time those days. On one afternoon alone, he saw 32 cases of measles.

After stopping at the Millers and Petersheims that Sunday afternoon, Dr. Lehman saw five more families with the measles. I suppose the choir's done singing by now, he thought, walking out to the car after the last house call. But maybe if I go straight to the church, I can at least show my face.

Suddenly, a large dog exploded out of the shadows, snapping and snarling at the doctor's legs. With a vicious growl, the hound lunged and snatched the leg of his trousers in his teeth.

"Let go!" the doctor shouted, waving his satchel at the dog. As the doctor shook his leg to free himself, he heard the sound of ripping fabric just as the farmer burst from the house.

"*Schick dich!*" the farmer shouted at his dog, who reluctantly released the shredded fabric and slunk behind the house. Quickly, the doctor pinched the fabric together where there once had been a seam and hobbled to the car.

"Well, that's the end of the house calls for today," he muttered as he drove out the lane. "No more house calls today or concerts, either, for that matter. At least not until I stop at home for another pair of trousers!"

8.

SLIT THROATS AND OFFICE DILEMMAS

As he lifted a corner of the bloody towel, Dr. Lehman could only stare at the jagged gash spanning the preschooler's throat from ear to ear. Rivulets of blood streamed down the side of the slender neck.

"Whatever happened?" Dr. Lehman asked, turning to the man in blood-splattered clothes.

"The dog got him, Doc," the father began. "You see, we were butchering the hogs and the children were running around having a grand time, when all of a sudden we heard the awfullest screaming. And here this big old German Shepherd had nailed our boy in the neck. The smell of blood must have driven the dog half mad," he theorized.

Only a fragile layer of tissue separates this child from death, Dr. Lehman thought, gently placing the flap of skin back over the throat.

It seems like every emergency in Mount Eaton ends up here at the clinic, he thought to himself, while realizing the folks in this community had few other options. Mount Eaton had no ambulance, and the hospital was 16 miles away. The Amish could more easily bring their injured to the clinic than locate a driver to transport them to the distant hospital emergency room. Besides, the community trusted Drs. Lehman and Eberly, and they charged only a fraction of the cost of an emergency room visit.

With the number of emergencies the Mount Eaton doctors saw, it was no surprise that one of Dr. Lehman's very first patients in his new office was a farm boy from Kidron who had mangled his foot in a farm accident. Not only did Sam Steiner's son have a compound fracture, but his foot had been cut up, as well.

"Sam, you and your brother Melvin, and the 17 or so boys you have between the two of you, are keeping us doctors busy. Didn't we treat another one of your boys not so long ago? And I suppose you soaked this wound in kerosene, too?"

"It works, Doc."

Dr. Lehman just smiled. With such large families of young farm boys running around, I suppose we'll be seeing more of the Steiners, he thought as he examined the injury. At least we're better equipped to handle emergencies now. I don't have to haul patients over to Dr. Eberly's office for X-rays anymore, now that we have our own X-ray equipment right here, including a portable electrocardiograph machine and a central hub with a laboratory and drug dispensary.

"Wow, this place is incredible!" Dr. Mayer exclaimed when he toured the new facilities. "All we ever had was a room or two in our house, and here you have four treatment rooms, a private office, receptionist cubicle, restroom, and even a storage room! You even have a loading dock to transfer patients into an ambulance," Dr. Mayer observed at the back of the clinic. "And if you ever need to consult with Dr. Eberly, he's only a step away. You sure have a good arrangement here."

"And good staff, too," Dr. Lehman agreed.

The energetic, willing nurse Dr. Lehman hired had become adept at giving shots, keeping records, ordering medicines, laying out the instruments she thought he might need, and assisting with baby deliveries. Rebecca fit well into the rural practice with her Amish background, speaking Pennsylvania German with patients who could better express themselves in their own dialect. Phyllis didn't fade out of the practice entirely; in fact, she continued to accompany her husband on night-time deliveries for a while.

As the practice grew, the doctor hired a young woman to handle secretarial duties. When Alice and her husband moved out of state, Dr. Lehman hired Nancy, a young ward clerk from Doctors Hospital to replace her. Later, Alice returned to the community, took nurses' training, and came back to work for Dr. Lehman as a nurse.

When Nancy came to Dr. Lehman's office, the only words she knew in the Pennsylvania German dialect were, *"Ich kahn net ferschtay."* Occasionally, she needed help to understand what an Amish patient was saying, like the time an elderly man called to request Dr. Lehman's services.

"My wife's done," the caller announced. "We need Doc."

"Okay, she's done, so what's she finished with?" Nancy questioned.

"She's just done."

"Is she done with her medicine?" Nancy asked, recalling that Dr. Lehman had issued the elderly woman a prescription.

"No, she's done. We need the doctor now!"

"But I have to know what she's done with." Nancy racked her brain, asking the caller about every imaginable thing the woman might have completed.

"Just tell Doc she's done and we need him. He'll know!"

"Doc," Nancy called softly, opening the door of the examining room after a quick knock. "A man is on the phone saying his wife is done and he needs you, but he can't seem to tell me what she is finished with."

Dr. Lehman set down the suture holder and looked up. "That's his way of saying she died. She's done living. He wants me to come pronounce her dead," the doctor explained patiently. "It's hard for some of the Amish who are so used to talking Pennsylvania Dutch to express themselves fluently in English."

"The doctor will be right out," the receptionist promised the elderly caller.

"Tell him to bring the embammer to."

"The embammer?" Nancy's eyes threw question marks at Rebecca. "What's an embammer?" she whispered.

"The embalmer," Rebecca whispered. "The undertaker."

"Okay," Nancy assured the caller, "we'll give the undertaker a call."

Rebecca warned the other staff that Mount Eaton Clinic was like a little emergency room. One never knew what would burst through the doors—like the child with the slit throat. Dr. Lehman tried to accommodate his patients when he could; however, if he felt he was not equipped to handle the case, he sent it on to the hospital. And he knew that the child lying on the table with the terrible throat injury was one of those cases he needed to send on.

"Give him a shot for pain," he told one of his nurses, "and I'll make arrangements for him to go to the hospital."

"*Mei zeit*, Doc, we was hoping you'd sew him up here. The hogs are half butchered and we're kind of in a hurry."

The doctor envisioned hogs scalding in huge kettles and slabs of meat waiting to be ground, seasoned, and stuffed into cleaned intestine casings. He understood the dilemma, but a child's life was at stake.

"I'd help you if I could," he spoke in his gentle but firm manner. "But I cannot treat this injury here."

"But Doc! Everything else you do here! Putting that tube down the throats of children who drink kerosene. And sewing up John Miller's hand when he got it in the *hoimacher*. It's as good as new."

"That was a hand and this is a throat. One mistake on my part, and your son will be dead. He needs a specialist."

"*Ach yammah*, we're awfully busy. But if that's what you say."

"There's no other option."

After he had seen the child off, Dr. Lehman called Doctors Hospital. "I'm sending you a child whose throat was slit by a German Shepherd. The voice box is exposed."

"Oh Doc!" the nurse groaned. "You always send us the most unusual cases!"

When Dr. Lehman made his rounds at the hospital the next day, he observed that the child seemed to be doing well and his neck was neatly stitched beneath the bandages.

"Did you ever get those hogs butchered?" he asked the child's father.

"Oh, yes. When we got home from the hospital, the meat was all canned. The neighbors and relatives finished it up when they heard about the accident."

"You Amish sure pitch in and help each other, don't you?" Dr. Lehman observed, turning to leave. "I'm glad it all worked out for you and that your son is doing so well. It looks like the surgeon did a good job."

"Yeah, not bad. But Doc, you could have done just as good!" the father remarked with a smile as the doctor walked out the door.

It seemed that no matter how bad the injury, the patients always felt sure Dr. Lehman could fix them up again—like the man who dropped a chainsaw on his head.

The moment Nancy heard the door handle rattle on a morning Dr. Lehman was out of town, she braced herself for the emergency she knew had arrived. When the mangled patient walked into the office, Nancy could only stare at the blood streaming from the deep, jagged laceration running across the top of the man's head and down the side of his bearded face. An eye dangled by little more than a thread of tissue, and blood trickled down into the man's beard and onto the floor. Nancy studied the bloody, mangled face and the dangling eyeball briefly. *What'll I do?* she wondered in desperation. *Doc's not even in town!* Finally, she managed to squeak: "What . . . happened?"

"Just dropped a chainsaw on my head," the man announced as matter-of-factly as if a twig had fallen on him. "I was trying to saw a limb over my head when the saw slipped from my hands."

"I'm sorry, but Doc's not in today. You'll have to go to the hospital," Nancy announced, reaching for the phone to call the ambulance.

"That's a shame. I thought surely Doc could fix me up." The Amishman's eye bobbed as he spoke. "Is he at home?"

"No, Doc's out of town. He and Rebecca are holding a clinic in Medina for the Amish who moved up that way. He won't be back until this afternoon."

"*Ach yammah.* That's a shame," he repeated. "They were all telling me that I'd have to go to the emergency room, but I says, 'Naw, you don't know Lehman. He'll fix me up.' Now he ain't in. If that ain't the berries."

Nancy forced herself to look at the bloody face. "The way that eye looks, if your driver jerked to a stop at a red light, I believe your eye would fly right out of your head. Come on back and I'll see if I can clean it up a bit and get a bandage on it before you head for the hospital," she suggested, trying to sound in control.

As the receptionist gave the patient a dose of Tylenol and helped him lie down on the examining table, she kept thinking, *I've got to bandage this eye, but how? Why couldn't this have happened yesterday when Doc was in? Or tomorrow?*

After a brisk knock, the door behind Nancy opened. She turned and a slender, white-jacketed man with closely clipped graying hair marched into the room.

"Dr. Eberly! Get in here quick!" In the stress of the moment, Nancy had forgotten about Dr. Lehman's colleague in the adjacent office. "Please! We got this gruesome chainsaw injury and Doc isn't in!"

Dr. Eberly studied the mutilated face with thoughtful concern. "Hmmm. A chainsaw wound. Let me tell you, you came awfully close to losing that eye."

The Amishman grinned crookedly at the doctor. "*Ach mei zeit*, am I ever glad you're in, Eberly. I was afraid I would have to go to the hospital. But now you can sew me up."

"Indeed not!" There was a no-nonsense tone to the doctor's voice. "One doesn't fool around with eyes. You don't realize how close you are to losing it."

"Oh, but Doc, I can still see. Just sew me up; I'll be fine!"

"No sir!" the doctor declared. "You might still be able to see out of your eye, but we want you to continue seeing out of it. Nancy, call the squad while I secure the eye with a patch."

"It's good you weren't here today," Nancy told Dr. Lehman when he returned that afternoon.

"And why is that?" he asked in surprise.

"Because a fellow came in this morning thinking you can fix anything, and he still believes it!"

The two doctors worked side by side, exchanging counsel and covering for each other. With Dr. Lehman's help, Dr. Eberly could take time off to pursue other dreams and goals he'd had for years. Once, when 20 tons of shelled corn and rice were shipped to Haiti during a famine, Dr. Eberly traveled there to help oversee its distribution.

"So how was your trip?" Dr. Lehman asked when his colleague returned.

"Doc, the amazing thing was, as hungry as the people were in the midst of that famine, they were even more desperate for medical help. They lined up every day for two weeks waiting to see me. My daughter Judy couldn't believe it when we used up every pill from those three large trunks we took down. One mother laid her dying baby on my lap and begged me to come back to their village. 'All our babies are dying,' she said. 'Can't you come and help us?' But Elton, there just wasn't time, and every last pill was gone."

I'd love to go and help care for those people who have no doctor, Dr. Lehman thought. Someday, I will. But for now, I'll cover for Dr. Eberly so he can go. After all, someone needs to care for ailments and emergencies that keep showing up at our door.

From one hour to the next, Dr. Lehman never knew what to expect. Most patients scheduled appointments, but some didn't have time to call. Often those unexpected callers brought critically serious injuries, like the slit throat and chainsaw victim. But others, like the hooked fisherman, ranged from embarrassing to humorous.

When Nancy looked up to see the fisherman signing his name on the clipboard, she was startled to see a fishhook caught in his nose and a line dangling from it. He looks like a bull with a ring in his nose! she couldn't help thinking, trying not to smile.

"Wow, that's quite a fancy decoration you've got there," she observed. "What kind of a new fad is that?"

The fisherman blushed slightly. "I did a dumb thing and caught a big sucker," he sighed peevishly.

"We've seen fish hooks in ears and eyebrows, too, so you aren't the first to do that sort of thing," Nancy consoled. "Have a seat. Doc will see you shortly."

The fisherman slumped into a chair. He lowered his head self-consciously, keeping a magazine in front of his hooked nose and looking as though he wanted to melt into the chair's vinyl upholstery.

"Better get that fisherman into one of the examining rooms before he dies of embarrassment," Nancy told the nurses.

When Dr. Lehman walked into the exam room some time later, it took him only a moment to gently push the pointed, barbed end of the hook the rest of the way through the tender nose cartilage. He snipped off the barb and pulled the hook back out.

"Ahhhh, that's better," the fisherman sighed, rubbing his sore nose. He sat back in his chair and flashed a smile that could have illuminated the whole room. "Boy, did I ever want to get that thing out before I met up with one of my buddies!"

"You're sure you don't want to save that hook?" the doctor asked. "You can tell all your friends that little hook caught a 200-pounder!"

"No way! Someone would be sure to ask what happened to the rest of the hook, and why the doctor had to snip it off!" the fisherman moaned and reached for the door. "No thanks. I don't ever want to see it again!"

As time went on, Dr. Lehman's patients learned to trust and respect his judgment. Not only did they bring their injured and ill to Mount Eaton Clinic, but occasionally they brought their non-medical problems as well, like the time a middle-aged man requested help for his mentally challenged son.

"Please give this to Doc," the father requested, handing a note to the receptionist.

Between patients, Dr. Lehman quickly scanned the note.

Dear Doc,
Please tell Elmer that his parents know best
as Lisa has gotten married and it would be useless
for him to think he could get her to go home with him
and help him on the farm. I think he will listen to you.

Though Dr. Lehman faced many medical crises at the clinic, occasionally he ran into dilemmas that had nothing to do with medicine. He generally sensed a deep respect from his patients, so he was perplexed when one man refused to come into the office.

"Doc," Rebecca whispered, holding her hand over the mouth-piece of the telephone one morning. "Danny Hershberger's neighbor is on the phone. He says Danny wants you to come out to their house immediately. One of the children is very sick."

Dr. Lehman sighed. "Why can't he come into the office? And why can't Danny talk to me himself? Let me have the phone."

"Hello, Dr. Lehman speaking. Is Danny right there? May I speak with him, please? Oh? He says he's not supposed to talk on the phone. Okay, tell him Dr. Lehman *asked* to talk to him, that way he won't be initiating the conversation. Thanks."

If it's a sin to talk on the phone, then I'll do the sinning for him, Dr. Lehman thought with the hint of a smile.

"Yes, Danny? You have a sick child? What's happening? I see. Get a driver and bring him in and I'll take a look at him. No, Danny, I can't come out to your house right now for those kinds of symptoms. Your child is not in critical condition and it won't threaten his life to come here to the clinic. Besides, my waiting room is filled with patients. I want you to hire a driver and bring your son in.

"Danny. Don't talk to me that way. No, I don't want to see your son die. That's why I want you to bring him in. You can't? Well, then I'll send my nurse out to pick up your son and his mother. Have them ready. Goodbye, Danny."

"I don't understand it," Dr. Lehman sputtered, hanging up the phone. "Why wouldn't Danny bring his son into the office? I've never seen anything like this before!"

When the nurse returned with a worried mother and a sick little boy, the doctor examined him, gave his mother a prescription, and sent the nurse to take them home again. Why was Danny so set against coming to the clinic? he wanted to ask.

The question plagued the doctor all week. Sure, the spacious brick clinic had electric lights, but electric lights had never been an issue before. He couldn't think of one reason a patient would refuse to come to his clinic.

Several weeks later, a man from Danny's church had an appointment in Dr. Lehman's office.

"Could I ask you a question?" Dr. Lehman asked the Swartzentruber Amishman. "Would you know why Danny Hershberger refused to bring his son to my office?"

"*Ei yi, sella kall.* So Danny wouldn't come in to your office, eh?" the Amishman asked, a lopsided grin tugging at his mouth. "I suppose it had something to do with the little talk the bishop had with him. Yep. The bishop heard Danny rode in a car to the horse races. He told Danny if he hears of him riding in a car again, well . . . ," the Amishman snapped his suspenders with his thumbs and his eyes twinkled with laughter. "I suppose after the bishop's little chitchat, Danny Hershberger don't ever want to ride in a car again, not even to the doctor's office!"

What next? Dr. Lehman wondered, shaking his head. In a country practice, one never knows what the next moments will bring.

9.

Quivering Sheets and Other Hospital Escapades

"Sometimes we almost drop the phone when Dr. Lehman calls," he heard one of the hospital nurses tell a new staff member. "I declare, he always sends us the most interesting cases. He doesn't call simply to chat and shoot the breeze. When we hear Dr. Lehman's voice on the other end of the line, we know an urgent case is heading our way. A man caught his hand in a piece of equipment, or a chainsaw fell on some guy's head, a boy fell in the watering trough, or a dog grabbed a child by the throat . . . ."

Another case for the nurses to fuss about, Dr. Lehman mused, taking one look at the preschooler with her leg twisted at an awkward angle between the knee and thigh.

"I was hitching the horse to the hay rake when he spooked and took off across the barnyard with the hay rake clangin' on behind," Pete explained. "Doc, I saw him head across the yard where my girl was playin', and I knew she was a goner. There wasn't a thing I could do. It was a terrible feeling. I saw the hay rake knock Esther off her feet and drag her across the yard. It's absolutely amazing she wasn't killed. I thought for sure she'd end up at the hospital, at least."

"It must have been a nightmare," the doctor sympathized, wondering to himself how he was ever going to tell Pete his daughter needed surgery, traction, *and* a hospital stay.

One of the greatest challenges in Dr. Lehman's practice involved bridging the gulf between his Amish patients and the technology a medical crisis demanded. Emergencies catapulted the Amish folk from the security of the tranquil farmstead and a close circle of friends and relatives into the unknown, sterile world of stainless steel, wires, and foreigners. And often, Dr. Lehman was the bridge spanning those two contrasting worlds.

Realizing the job he faced—informing the girl's family of what lay ahead—Dr. Lehman took a deep breath and began as gently as he could. "Pete, your daughter's leg is very badly injured. If it isn't treated properly, she'll never run again. In fact, without the right care, she'll scarcely be able to hobble around."

"But," Dr. Lehman continued, looking the young Amishman in the eye, "the good news is that the leg can be fixed. The bones are badly shattered, but if we screw the bones together, she'll be able to run again. We're going to have to take her to the hos—"

"*Mei zeit*, Doc!" the young father cried. "Does she have to go there? Why, she's only four! I've got the farm work to do and we've got a new baby, and who'll stay with Esther?"

Dr. Lehman read anguish in the young Amishman's eyes. "I'm sorry, Pete. I'd fix her leg here if I could, but she won't walk again if she doesn't have surgery."

"No!"

"And then," the doctor continued gently, "she'll need to have her leg in traction for several weeks."

Pete collapsed into a chair and buried his face in his straw hat. The hospital bill would be higher than the value of his rented farm, he knew. And his little girl would be separated from her family for several weeks. It was almost more than he could bear.

Dr. Lehman laid a hand on the man's shoulder. "Listen, Pete. Maybe we can work something out to put her in traction at home."

The disheveled head popped out of the straw hat. "You really mean that, Doc? You think they'd let us?"

"I'll tell you what," Dr. Lehman scratched his head thoughtfully. "I can't promise anything, but I know of a traction set-up that several mechanically-inclined men designed for a cousin of theirs. Dr. Smith allowed me to set up the patient in his home with this homemade device."

Pete stuffed his hat over his dark hair and shot to his feet, his eyes shining with hope.

"I can't guarantee what the surgeon will say, but I'll see what I can do," the doctor continued as Rebecca spooned pain medication into the child's mouth. "I'll put a splint on this leg to stabilize it. You came in your buggy, didn't you?"

Pete nodded. "Can't see as we can take her 15 or 20 miles in the buggy with the pain she's in and all," he sighed. "And I don't know how we'll get up to visit her."

"Well, I'll tell you what. I'll go ask my wife if she'd have time to drive you up to the hospital," Dr. Lehman offered, adjusting the splint. "And I have a friend at Doctors Hospital by the name of Dr. Finer who just got a bus route started to transport Amish patients, so there shouldn't be any problem with you finding a way to visit your daughter. And by the way, I have a pair of crutches here that she can use, so you won't need to buy any."

"*Vundahboah!*" Pete slapped his hand on his knee in delight. "Absolutely fantastic."

When Dr. Lehman called Doctors Hospital to notify them about the arrival of the injured child, the nurse answering the phone recognized his voice. "Oh no!" she groaned. "I don't have time for you and your emergencies today! It's a hectic day to begin with!"

"But you'll have to admit, Dr. Lehman does bring us the most interesting cases, and the nicest, most pleasant patients to care for," another nurse countered.

"I know," the first nurse agreed. "I suppose the reason it seems like he sends us the worst cases is because his Amish patients won't go to the doctor unless they've cut off their fingers or are half dead. Dr. Lehman does everything except major surgery right there at his Mount Eaton office, and he only sends the extremely urgent cases to us. So when Dr. Lehman calls, sometimes we almost drop that phone."

When Phyllis dropped off Pete and Esther at Doctors Hospital's emergency room, the grateful Amishman handed Phyllis some money. "I surely appreciate the ride and all Doc's doing for us. Tell Doc when we butcher, I'll bring him some steaks."

After surgery, Dr. Lehman stopped by Esther's room to check on the little patient and her family. "Well, Dr. Smith says he's going to let me put your daughter's leg in traction at your house if I stop by every day or so to check on her," Dr. Lehman announced with a smile. "So that means you can go home in a day or so, Esther!"

"And by the way, Pete," the doctor continued. "There's a house just up the road called the Amish House where you and your wife can stay for the night, if you'd like to. It's another service the hospital provides to try to accommodate your people, Pete."

"You mean this hospital has a special place just for the families of the Amish to stay?" Pete asked with amazement.

"That's right. I tell you, Pete, Doctors Hospital and I have an excellent working relationship. The staff here are very considerate of your people, and they'll do almost anything to accommodate your needs and wishes. And when you pay your bill, since you don't carry insurance, Dr. Finer arranged for a 15 percent reduction if you pay within 30 days."

"Well, ain't that something!" Pete told his wife as Dr. Lehman walked out the door. "Here we were all worried, and now Doc's got everything all worked out. I tell you, he's going to need more than steaks. Maybe you could make him a quilt."

"Or you could build him a hickory rocker," his wife suggested.

Leaving Esther's room, Dr. Lehman strode down the hall toward the maternity ward to check on an obstetrics patient. The creaking of the heavy doors, the odor of disinfectant, and the squeak of cart wheels called to mind a host of memories.

It was here, in the maternity ward of Doctors Hospital, that Brenda was born. He'd never forget his first glimpse of his daughter and the fierce desire that welled up inside him to protect the little, dark-haired cherub with his life. The nurses had better be sure they scrubbed their hands before handling this baby. He'd delivered scores of infants before, but the birth of his own child somehow was different. Now he understood the teary, starry-eyed dads at first seeing their child. Babies certainly were "bits of stardust blown straight from the hand of God."

January 1, 1967, two months after Brenda's birth, Dr. Lehman delivered the first baby of the year for Stark County. Phyllis still had the newspaper clipping of the event in her scrapbook. As the delivery room doors loomed ahead, the scene of that unusual delivery flashed through Dr. Lehman's mind.

When Laura Thompson called three days after Christmas saying that her contractions were six minutes apart and steady, Dr. Lehman told her to go directly to the hospital. Not only had Laura been on bedrest since Thanksgiving, threatening to deliver prematurely, but also her previous labors had been as short as two hours.

Dr. Lehman canceled his office appointments and raced to the hospital, fully expecting the Thompsons to be there and all set for the delivery. But they weren't. As minutes dragged into hours, he worried about his patient. Something's wrong. They only have a 15-minute drive, Dr. Lehman brooded, pacing the halls, peering out the window toward the parking lot, and tapping his fingers restlessly on the counter near the phone.

"She had her baby in the car, I know she did," he fretted, reaching for the telephone.

"No, they didn't have the baby yet," Laura's mother reported. "They called a while back and said the alternator went out on the car, so my son-in-law went to get them. I reckon they'll be drivin' in there any minute now."

The couple arrived but the baby did not. Dr. Lehman kept checking on the woman while making his rounds. When he stopped by three days later, the baby still had not come.

"Those walls are closing in on me. I'm tired of looking at them, and I'm sick of lying here," Laura complained in her West Virginia drawl on New Year's Eve.

Dr. Lehman shut his eyes a moment. The baby's full term. There's really no reason to make Laura climb the walls. Besides, there's a chance the infant could be a New Year's baby, which is always fun.

"We'll see what we can do," Dr. Lehman announced. "By the way, the area merchants have a gift package of clothes and baby supplies for the first baby born in 1967 in the area. And then there are always newspaper articles and pictures."

"Hey! Let's go for it!" Mr. Thompson cried.

"Yeah, right. You can talk!" his wife muttered from her bed. "The prizes and pictures might be nice, but I just want this over, and the sooner the better."

"Say, what's in that I-V, Doc?" Laura demanded a few minutes later.

"Oh, just some good old Mount Eaton water," Dr. Lehman winked.

"My friend's in labor over at Massillon Hospital," Laura told the nurses. "They'll call as soon as the baby comes."

"Well, they won't call before we call them," the nurse announced, "because Doctors Hospital is going to have the first baby of the year, not Massillon!"

As midnight approached, Mr. Thompson suddenly disappeared. A sure sign the action is about to begin, Dr. Lehman thought. He always knows just when to leave.

He glanced at the clock. "Well, Laura, what year do you want your baby born in?"

"Just let me have this baby, will ya!" Laura groaned.

Dr. Lehman smiled as he watched the minute hand inch upward. The feisty answer was another sign that the event was almost over.

The masked faces of the white-gowned group kept turning toward the clock on the wall as the room filled with the intensity of the final minutes of labor.

The hands on the clock reached their summit like a pair of mountain climbers who had conquered a challenging pinnacle. The stillness of the night erupted with the explosion of fire crackers, booming gunshots, and the cry of a newborn baby.

"12:01.5!" a nurse announced triumphantly as Dr. Lehman suctioned the wet, flailing infant.

"Wow! You did it!"

"Congratulations! You've had the first baby born in Doctors Hospital in 1967, and it's got to be the first baby—"

The jangling telephone cut the doctor short.

"Uh oh!" the nurse muttered, dashing out the door to answer the phone. "Maybe not."

A moment later, she came back with an entourage of nurses. "Well, Laura, your friend had the last baby of '66 and you had the first one in '67!" she beamed as the staff crowded around the isolette to admire the tiny celebrity.

"I *thought* you'd have the New Year baby," Dr. Lehman declared as he filled out the chart.

"Well, you did it after all, Doc," Laura smiled wearily. "You did it after all. And now when can I get out of here?"

"You can go home in the morning as soon as the photographers are finished with you."

"Dr. Lehman!" the nurses protested. "That's not even 12 hours! Mothers should always stay at least 48."

"She's fine and her baby's doing great," Dr. Lehman announced decidedly. "Besides, this is the fourth day she's been in here, and she has a family at home."

The nurses just shook their heads. That was Dr. Lehman. He didn't keep his patients in the hospital an hour longer than necessary. Dr. Kenneweg and other surgeons released their Amish surgery and Caesarean patients after a 24-hour stay instead of the week-to-ten-days other patients were kept. The staff knew that Dr. Lehman's Amish patients would be well cared for in their homes under his watchful eye. And Dr. Lehman knew Laura and realized she'd be ready to go in several hours if all went well.

"Okay, Laura, off to your room you go," Dr. Lehman announced with a wave of his hand. "I suppose your husband is waiting for you there. And you better get some sleep; those photographers will be here before you're ready for them," he called as the orderly wheeled the mother out the door.

The staff at Doctors Hospital all remembered the excitement of New Year babies, but it was the Amish emergencies Dr. Lehman sent that really made them talk.

"I've got a woman on the way who's all set to go," Dr. Lehman warned the obstetrics staff on one occasion.

Hearing the whine of the gurney wheels and the groan of the heavy doors, a couple of nurses rushed into the hall to the side of the cart pushed by a teenage girl. A nurse accompanying the stretcher to the delivery room froze as the sheets began to shiver and twitch mysteriously in the center of the cart.

"Ma'am, you didn't by any chance have your baby yet, did you?"

"I think maybe I did," the patient acknowledged with a shy smile.

"Oh no!" the aid gasped, gripping the side of the gurney to keep from fainting. "Oh please."

The ward door swung open and Dr. Lehman strode through, his footsteps echoing through the tiled hall.

"Hey, Doc!" a nurse called. "You missed the action, she's already had her baby."

"She's had her *baby?*" he asked matter-of-factly, wriggling his hands into a pair of rubber gloves. "Well, then I guess the excitement is only half over. She's having twins."

"Aaaarrrgh!" the aid shrieked, trying to get out from behind the gurney. "Let me out of here!"

"There isn't time!" a nurse snapped. "We can't move this cart; the baby is coming!"

The young aid collapsed against the wall, hiding her face in her hands. As Dr. Lehman calmly delivered the baby, the aid nudged the cart aside and ran to the restroom.

"A typical Lehman case," a veteran nurse remarked to a new nurse. "Trust Lehman to send us some excitement and then to get here in the nick of time to calmly deliver the baby!

"There's one story you've got to hear," she went on. "Lehman had an expectant Amish patient who was recovering from an appendectomy when a nurse noted a strange quivering under the sheet. The nurse asked her if she had her baby, and the woman said sweetly, 'I think I might have.' And sure enough, when the nurse pulled back the sheet, there was the baby. The patient was still kind of numb from the surgery, so when she felt some abdominal discomfort, she associated it with her appendectomy and couldn't detect the labor pains. The baby came before any of us knew what was happening. I tell you, those Lehman cases . . . ."

On a different occasion, Dr. Lehman delivered a set of twins in two different counties. When a patient went into labor on the way home from a doctor visit, the woman stopped at Barb's house, in Wayne County, where she delivered a baby. Discovering the second infant, and noting that it was breech, Dr. Lehman drove the parents to Doctors Hospital. There, he rotated and delivered the baby, recording Stark County as the location of birth for that twin and Wayne County for the other.

Another infant was born right on the county line when Dr. Lehman was taxiing an Amish couple to the hospital. As he eased off the road to deliver the baby, he pulled alongside a sign announcing, "Entering Stark County, leaving Wayne County." Now I have to decide which county that baby was born in! he mused as he prepared to fill out the birth certificate.

Dr. Lehman discovered that not only could twins arrive in different counties on occasion, but they also could arrive in different months. In one case, the first twin was born just before midnight on October 31, and the second one arrived a few minutes later on November 1.

Yes, Dr. Lehman and the hospital staff shared exciting moments, but there were tragedies as well. If only the ambulance with the breech baby could have arrived 10 minutes earlier. If only there wouldn't have been a detour. If only the driver would not have gotten lost. If only . . . .

But there *had* been a detour. In his search for an alternate route, the driver *had* gotten lost, and by the time the ambulance arrived at the hospital, there was no fetal heartbeat. Dr. Lehman rushed to the stretcher as the orderlies carried the mother into the emergency room. Lifting the infant's body up at a 90 degree angle, Dr. Lehman instantly dislodged the head and delivered the child, but it was too late. The nurses and paramedics stared at each other in shock. And then, as no amount of effort revived the lifeless body, they sadly turned away from the blue, lifeless form.

Why couldn't someone else have delivered that child the way Dr. Lehman did and saved the child's life? everyone wanted to ask.

"We tried every trick we knew," a medic murmured, "but the baby just wouldn't come. We didn't have the right touch, I guess."

"God must have allowed it to happen for a reason," the parents responded in quiet resignation. "His hand is over all."

That breech tragedy is one of those cases a person would like to delete from memory, the doctor thought as he walked down the corridor of the maternity floor after checking on little Esther's broken leg. But there was no delete button to push.

"Dr. Lehman!" a nurse called, rushing into the hall as he passed a labor room. "Get in here! You're just the one we need! Quick!" she cried, grabbing his arm and dragging him into a labor room. A hasty exam revealed the woman was fully dilated and the baby was definitely breech.

Dr. Lehman turned toward the door. "Just a minute, Paula. Let me go talk to her doctor."

"No!" the nurse gripped his arm in desperation. "Please, don't leave! Her doctor is in the midst of delivering another baby, and when I told him this baby was breech, he said to set her up for a C-section, but I know you can deliver breech babies, Dr. Lehman! Please?" she pleaded, tossing him a pair of gloves.

A moment later, Dr. Lehman handed the nurse a squalling infant. Quickly, he checked the baby's respiration, heart tones, reflexes, muscle tone, and color, allowing a high of two points for each of the five factors. "An Apgar score of nine after one minute," he reported.

"By the way," he said, turning to the new mother. "I'm Dr. Lehman."

"Boy, Dr. Lehman, am I ever glad to meet you!" she replied with a wide smile.

Paula leaned weakly against the counter as she filled out the chart. "Have you ever heard of a breech baby with an Apgar of nine out of 10?" she asked her colleague. "Maybe after five minutes, but an Apgar score of nine on a breech baby at one minute after birth? It's absolutely amazing! And what's even more amazing is that Dr. Lehman walked up the hall at just the right moment. I tell you, I've never seen a doctor who can deliver breech babies as slick as Lehman does. He sure was a God-send today. What would we do without Dr. Lehman and his horrendous cases, his pleasant patients, and even his knack for delivering breech babies?"

10.

THE CASE OF THE RARE BLOOD FACTOR

The memories of the past days gripped Dr. Lehman's thoughts, strangling his heart like an invisible python inside his chest as he guided his car through the slumbering countryside. He didn't notice the sprawling farms peacefully blanketed by the pale light of the moon. All he could see was Pastor Albert's wife and their infant lying lifeless and pale in the cold casket.

Rebecca, too, was quiet and pensive as she sat in the passenger's seat that night. After a bit she remarked, "I just can't get my mind off Mary and the baby. I just feel so sorry for Albert and the children. Here they were looking forward to this new baby, then she's overdue and her uterus ruptures."

The doctor sighed deeply. "So, you were thinking about Mary and the baby, too. It must be awfully hard on her doctor. One death in a family is hard enough, but two must be devastating."

"Four," Rebecca corrected. "Albert's father died of a heart attack in November, then Albert's brother was killed in February when he ran into a pile-up of cars in the fog and his semi caught fire. And now Mary and the baby."

I hope I don't ever have to experience losing a mother in my practice, he thought, never guessing he'd stand at the brink of just such a crisis within the week.

A glowing kerosene lantern in the window illuminated the yard as the doctor picked his way carefully through the darkness. He held a hand ahead of him to catch any clothesline waiting to snare him.

"Ah, good. It's Doc," the young Amishman sighed, opening the screen door for the doctor and his nurse. "Glad you're here."

When the doctor walked into the lamp-lit bedroom, the lines of anxiety on the youthful face melted into a smile. It was her first delivery and she didn't know quite what to expect, but now that Dr. Lehman had arrived, everything would be fine.

As the night wore on, labor seemed to progress slowly, so Dr. Lehman napped in an adjacent bedroom until his nurse notified him that Elizabeth was ready to deliver.

With the stoic control that characterized many Amish patients, the woman endured the long night and delivered a beautiful six-pound daughter. There was nothing about the delivery to indicate problems down the road.

"You have a maid coming to help with the work, don't you?" Dr. Lehman questioned as he packed his bag. "Remember to take it easy. No stair steps this week or heavy lifting. That's what your hired girl is for. And let me know if there is any unusual hemorrhaging."

"We'll take good care of her," Mose assured him from his wife's bedside. The golden glow of the lamplight spilled over the blanketed bundle in the young mother's arms. The new parents gazed down at the cherubic face, counting each tiny finger and toe, their faces glowing as they marveled over the miracle of life. Dropping by the Yoder house 24 hours later on a routine checkup, the doctor observed that both mother and newborn seemed to be doing fine.

A week later, Elizabeth casually mentioned to her sister that she had hemorrhaged profusely that day and had nearly fainted when she tried to get up. But that must be normal, she figured.

"It certainly isn't normal," her sister told her, urging her to send her husband to call Dr. Lehman immediately.

Dr. Lehman knocked at the door a few minutes after he received the call, knowing his Amish patients didn't call unless it was urgent.

"I'm going to send you to the hospital for a blood transfusion, Elizabeth," he explained after examining her. "You've lost a lot of blood."

"Oh, Doctor," the young mother was nearly in tears, "but the baby!" she cried, looking from the tiny bundle in the crib to her husband. "*Ach*, Mose, I just can't leave her!"

"*Du muscht*, Elizabeth. You want to be here to raise her," Mose countered kindly but firmly. "The *maut* will take good care of her."

The doctor caught the young husband's eye. "Mr. Yoder, it's serious. It could be a matter of life and death."

At the hospital, Mose hovered protectively at his wife's side, observing the nurses and technicians scurrying in and out of the room, checking Elizabeth's blood pressure, taking her temperature, drawing blood, and starting an intravenous drip.

"Your patient has a temp of 103," the nurse reported to Dr. Lehman.

"Then start her with penicillin along with the blood expanders and fluids in the I-V," he ordered.

A lab technician rushed the blood sample to the lab. Something's strange, Judy Kauffman observed, examining the flocking cells under the microscope. I've never seen blood cells like this.

"Take a look at this, will you?" the technician asked a colleague. "Have you ever seen anything like it? What blood type does the woman have, anyway?"

The colleague squinted into the microscope, adjusting the slide. "Boy, that's strange, Judy. Why don't you ask the new pathologist who's moving in from New Jersey. He stopped by the hospital today when he came to town for the weekend. He just finished a course on blood banking. Why don't you ask his opinion?"

"Dr. Michael Durishin's around? Great! He'll know." The technician looked up to see the young doctor walk into the lab. "Just the man we need! Have you ever seen anything like this, Dr. Durishin?"

The young doctor studied the sample silently for a few moments, adjusting the knob of the microscope and moving the slide around beneath the lens. Finally, he straightened with a sigh. "Very unusual, indeed. Let me talk to her doctor."

"Dr. Lehman," Dr. Durishin began, holding the phone in one hand and the glass slide with the drops of blood in the other. "We have a bit of a problem here. There's something atypical about Mrs. Yoder's blood. It's different than any type I've ever seen. Actually, there's no blood in the hospital to match the type she has."

Dr. Lehman was silent for a moment, then he asked, "What's her hemoglobin level?"

"Let's see," Dr. Durishin scanned the chart in front of him. "Hemoglobin level's 4.6."

"Four point six! Less than a third of what it should be. What about the hemocrit? Where's it at?"

"Fifteen percent."

"Oh boy. Well under normal range," he thought out loud. "That doesn't sound good, especially when we don't even know what blood type she has! Why do emergencies always happen on weekends when only a skeleton staff is on duty? Do you have any idea what blood group this might be?"

"Well, come to think of it, at the course on blood banking at Ortho Diagnostics, we learned about a rare blood group called Tj(a-). I'll tell you what. Judy and I will study the blood again, and then we'll overnight a sample out to Ortho Diagnostics in New Jersey."

"Great. Keep me posted."

The pathologist and lab technician continued to examine and test the blood, adding reagents to samples of Mrs. Yoder's blood to test compatibility with her type. However, the antibodies in the red blood cells of Mrs. Yoder's blood reacted, clustered, and clotted no matter what blood type Dr. Durishin and Judy added. Not one drop of blood in the hospital was compatible with her unusual blood type, and giving a patient incompatible blood could be fatal.

In the race against the clock to find an answer for the young mother, Dr. Lehman paced the floor, prayed, and researched the problem, reaching for the phone the instant it rang.

Please, Lord! Surely someone else has the same blood type Elizabeth has. But what type does she have?

Dr. Durishin worked feverishly in the lab, researching, talking to the research laboratory in New Jersey, and overnighting a blood sample to Ortho Diagnostics for testing.

Hours seemed like weeks as Dr. Lehman waited for the results. He hated to see any patient die, but a dying mother was a heart-wrenching scenario. When Dr. Lehman answered the phone, he knew Dr. Durishin had news.

"Ortho Diagnostics called," Dr. Durishin exclaimed breathlessly.

Dr. Lehman gripped the phone, hardly daring to breathe.

"We were right. It is the rare Tj(a-) phenotype! Their lab confirmed that it's definitely Tj(a-)."

"The Tj(a-) phenotype!" Dr. Lehman whistled. "You mean my Amish patient actually has this rare blood? And all this time we've been sending out blood work to a lab in Columbus, and they never detected it. Will it be difficult to locate blood?"

"That's the question now—whether any blood can be found. I just don't know. I'm warning you, Dr. Lehman, it's very rare."

"Try every avenue you can," Dr. Lehman urged. "Time is running out."

Leafing through a hematology book, Dr. Lehman found little information on the Tj(a-) phenotype. With a blood this rare, it would be extremely difficult to find a donor who could give blood for the dying woman.

In her hospital room, the mother lay listlessly, her eyes sunken in her pale face. Now and then they rolled upward as she wondered when the angels would come for her. It seemed as though Elizabeth could almost feel the wind of their wings over her face.

Dr. Lehman paced the floor of his office until he could stand it no longer. Grabbing the phone, he dialed Doctors Hospital lab. "You still haven't located any blood?" he questioned. "How about testing Mrs. Yoder's relatives? There's a good chance one of them will have the same blood factor."

"Tell them it's a matter of life or death for Elizabeth," Dr. Lehman instructed his nurse as she prepared to drive out to the homes of Mrs. Yoder's siblings. "And assure them it won't harm them in the least."

When two of Elizabeth's sisters tested positive for Tj(a-), Dr. Lehman was ecstatic until he learned that both were pregnant and ineligible to donate blood. None of the other relatives' blood matched.

"Give Mrs. Yoder more blood expanders," Dr. Lehman told the nurses, knowing what she really needed was blood. The vise that seemed to grip his heart tightened with every passing hour. *Dear God, we need help.*

Meanwhile, Dr. Durishin called blood banks across the nation, inquiring about the availability of units of Tj(a-) blood.

"Never heard of it," was the inevitable response.

Finally, Dr. Durishin heard of a man in one of the western states who supposedly had the rare blood factor. However, when the pathologist called the potential donor, he learned the fellow suffered from a bleeding ulcer, and, therefore, was not permitted to donate blood.

When the phone rang, Dr. Lehman answered in his characteristic authoritative voice.

"It's on the way!" the caller shouted.

"What's—?"

"We've got a unit of Tj(a–) blood on the way!" Dr. Lehman recognized the new pathologist's voice. "It's coming, Doc!"

"Where? How?"

"We found one donor—a healthy male in Bellefontaine, Ohio. A state highway patrolman is on the way with a unit," Dr. Durishin spoke so fast the words practically tumbled over one another. "And listen to this! There are two more units of frozen blood cells on the way from Massachusetts General Hospital, so I believe we're all set!"

"Wonderful!" The doctor sank wearily into a chair as the stress of the last hours drained away, leaving him feeling as though he hadn't slept for days. *Thank you, Lord!*

When he drove to the hospital to check on his patient, he explained to Elizabeth and her husband what had been taking place.

"*Ach* my, you mean someone actually gave some of their own blood to save my life?" Elizabeth wiped tears from her eyes. "I just can't believe someone would do that for me." Her voice softened to a whisper. "I thought I was done, Doc. I could almost feel the angels."

A smile brightened the young face and a tint of pink hinted at her thin cheeks as she asked, "Now when can I go home to my *buppeli?*"

"As soon as you can get up without hemorrhaging or feeling faint, we'll release you," Dr. Lehman promised. "But then you'll need to stay off your feet for a while, and you must call if you have any more problems."

"Do you think this will happen the next time I have a baby?"

"Not necessarily, but you and your sisters who have the Tj(a–) phenotype will probably need to have your babies here at the hospital from here on out, just as a safety precaution. Then if we run into an emergency, we could get blood for you more quickly."

"Don't you have those sisters down there with that rare blood type?" the Red Cross agent asked Dr. Lehman when she called his office some time later. "We really should check their relatives and collect some blood to freeze for an emergency."

"An excellent idea," Dr. Lehman agreed. He instructed Rebecca to send out letters to Mrs. Yoder's extended family, explaining the urgency of testing their blood since it could save their own life or the life of another person in the future. Out of 25 relatives tested, around 10 were found to have the Tj(a-) phenotype.

"We'll store the blood in Cleveland," the Red Cross agent offered when a number of healthy males donated blood.

"That's very kind of you," Dr. Lehman responded, "but I'm concerned about the time factor. Cleveland's a good hour's drive away, and in an emergency, every minute counts. Timken Mercy Hospital is in Canton, just a 15-minute drive away. They have blood storing and thawing capabilities, too."

So, a decision was made to store two units at Timken Mercy Hospital at all times. However, if a donor was available to give fresh blood in a serious crisis, this would be the favorable option.

In the back room of the office, Rebecca hung a genealogy chart on which one of the Red Cross workers had begun to record the family trees and histories of those with the Tj(a-) phenotype. Because of her Amish background, the nurse knew many of the patients, their parents, and who was related to whom. Those Rebecca didn't know, her mother did. The nurse's Amish connections enabled her to fill many of the blanks on the chart that stretched the entire length of the wall.

An interesting pattern began to emerge. Every single person with the rare blood factor was a descendent of Bishop Sam Swartzentruber, after which the Swartzentruber Amish Church had been named.

At the Red Cross' suggestion, Dr. Lehman asked Rebecca to take blood samples from the umbilical cords of newborns they delivered to test them for the rare blood type. Over the years, the Red Cross came to the community regularly to draw the rare blood from donors. Eventually, around 65 people in the area tested positive for the Tj(a-) phenotype. Through continual testing, Dr. Lehman discovered that, over time, the blood type of patients with the Tj(a-) phenotype actually mutated to a more common blood type.

Rebecca kept careful records on each person that had the Tj(a-) blood factor, noting the addresses and whether or not they were able to donate blood. Sooner or later, there would be another emergency and Dr. Lehman wanted to be prepared. It could mean the difference between life and death.

It was midnight when the call came from the hospital. "We have a patient of Dr. Eberly's here with the Tj(a-) blood factor. The surgeon feels it would be beneficial to use fresh blood in this case rather than the stored units. Can you locate a donor immediately?"

"We'll find one," Dr. Lehman promised. "I'll call my nurse. She knows where the potential donors live."

In the darkness of night, Rebecca drove her car to an Amish home. The dog growled and snapped at her heels as she walked through the dark yard and knocked loudly at the front door.

A moment later the door opened and a blinking Amishman stood with a lantern in one hand. *"Yah? Veah ist es?"*

"It's Rebecca from Dr. Lehman's office," she answered in Pennsylvania Dutch. "I'm sorry to bother you, but Esther Stutzman desperately needs your type of blood up at the hospital. Can you get ready and come with me?"

When the Amishman pulled on his shoes and told his wife what was happening, he followed the nurse to the car and the two of them went on their way to the hospital.

A second emergency arose some time later, and a messenger went to the home of a healthy male with the necessary blood type. "He's not at home," a brother informed the messenger. "He's taking some chickens to the Kidron Livestock Auction."

"He's got a rare blood type, and we have a critically ill patient who desperately needs some of his blood."

"If you'll drive over toward the auction, you could catch up with him," the brother suggested. "If you want me to, I could go with you since I'd recognize his wagon."

On Kidron Road near Gerber Poultry, they spotted the Amishman in the wagon with the crates of squawking, flapping chickens in the back. Pulling alongside, they flagged down the buggy.

"What's the problem?" the Amishman looked warily from under his hat brim.

"We have an emergency and need your type of blood immediately," he was told. "Can you come with us right away?"

"But the chickens?"

"I'll take care of them," his brother assured him. "You go. They need your blood." The donor may have smelled like chickens, but his blood was priceless.

When a family with the Tj(a-) blood phenotype moved from Ohio to Michigan, the local Red Cross office called the Michigan branch and informed them of the family's rare blood. There was silence on the other end of the line, and then the Michigan agent whispered, "How can we get them to move back to Ohio again?"

Word spread about the country doctor's patients with the rare blood type. News reached a prestigious research institute, who contacted Dr. Lehman's office.

Nancy interrupted a patient examination to inform the doctor that he had a long distance phone call. "It's from a Dr. Kevin Brown from the National Heart, Lung, and Blood Institute from Bethesda, Maryland. Can you come to the phone?"

"Dr. Lehman," Dr. Brown said after identifying himself. "We understand that you have patients in your practice with a rare blood phenotype called Tj(a-). We are researching a theory and need samples of this rare blood type. We'd also be interested in samples of other blood types taken from the community, as well, to use as a control group."

Dr. Lehman gave a low whistle as he hung up the phone and wiped the palm of his hand across his forehead. "Wow. The National Heart, Lung, and Blood Institute is asking for blood from my Swartzentruber Amish patients! Isn't that amazing! I'm sure we can round up a few donors."

Dr. Lehman sent the requested samples to Dr. Brown, and some time later, the results of the studies were published in the April 28, 1994 issue of the *New England Journal of Medicine.* Though Dr. Lehman didn't write the article, his name was listed with the authors because he had collected the blood for the study.

Quickly, Dr. Lehman scanned the table of contents for the article. "Resistance to Paravirus B19 Infection Due to Lack of Virus Receptor (Erythrocyte P Antigen)," the title read. Beneath the title were seven names, including Elton D. Lehman, D.O.

"Hey, Phyllis, look at this!" He handed his wife the article full of technical analysis. "In essence, that study found a new way to treat certain viruses," he explained. "But the interesting part is that my Swartzentruber Amish patients' blood made the study possible!"

"So, whatever happened to that Yoder woman first identified with the rare blood? Do you hear from her anymore?" Phyllis wondered.

"Yes, I do, which reminds me, Dr. Durishin told me they've renamed Tj(a-) blood. Now they call it Yoder blood! How do you like that? Anyway, I delivered 12 more children for Elizabeth and Mose without any problems. The last one weighed over 11 pounds. Imagine that! She was a little apprehensive every time, of course, but things always went well."

Dr. Lehman traced his finger around the edge of the *New England Journal.* "I tell you, Elizabeth's one grateful woman. She was so touched that someone donated blood to save her life that, as soon as she was able, she became a donor herself. They tell me that every time the blood mobile comes to Mount Eaton, they can count on Elizabeth being there. She says, 'Someone saved my life by giving blood, and now I want to help someone else in return.'

"You know, Phyllis," he continued. "It's so awesome to see God at work in these kinds of experiences. Technically speaking, Dr. Durishin shouldn't have been at the hospital that day. He wasn't even working at Doctors Hospital yet, since he still had another month to go before completing his residency in New Jersey.

"His family had moved to the area so the children could start school. And since he hadn't seen them for a month, he traveled from New Jersey to visit them for the weekend. He decided to stop by Doctors Hospital while he was here to tie up a few details, and he just happened to be in the blood bank when the rare blood case came in! Just happened," he mused. "Does anything ever just happen in life?"

11.

THE QUANDARY OF THE AMISH BISHOP AND THE TELEPHONE

D r. Lehman mopped his forehead with a handkerchief and glanced at his watch. The battery–operated fan made feeble ef– forts to stir up the steamy air in one of Barb Hostetler's birthing rooms while the labor patient rested quietly on the bed.

She's not making much headway, he realized in dismay. The husband sat nearby, his bearded face buried in *The Farm and Dairy*.

Dr. Lehman fretted about his patients waiting back at the of– fice and paced the length of the narrow room. God, what shall I do? It's so hard to just sit here. It was the dilemma the doctor faced with increasing frequency as he found himself torn by nu– merous patients needing him at the same time.

"I don't know if I should go or stay," he told Barb, who was on her hands and knees scrubbing the kitchen floor. "I've got patients back at the office, and there's not much sign of action here. But I don't want to leave if she's going to need me."

"*Ach yammah*, it's hard to know what to do," Barb sympathized. "Sometimes a labor will piddle around most of the day, and then others come so fast the driver can't get there, like the baby who was born in the patient's front yard while she waited for the driver to come."

"I've never been too concerned about the babies that come so fast that I can't get there to deliver them," Dr. Lehman replied, tapping his fingers on the table as he studied the clock on the wall. "The ones that come that fast are generally not complicated deliveries. Well, I suppose I ought to head back to the office for a bit. But I'd just feel so much better leaving if you had a phone and I knew you could reach me quickly if you needed to."

And I could communicate with the office and see if they have any emergencies there, he thought.

As he drove back to the office past the peaceful farms and grazing animals, he thought about how comfortable he had become delivering babies in homes. Sure, delivering infants outside of a hospital setting is a little lonely without the backup of staff and technology available at the hospital. But home deliveries are actually more fun than the ones in the hospital, he thought. And they don't have the stack of paperwork that goes along with hospital births. However, when I'm needed in several places at the same time, the fun fizzles out. If only Barb had a phone!

Back at the clinic, Dr. Lehman extracted a bean from a child's nose, bandaged a laceration, and cared for the most urgent cases as swiftly as he could, and then he headed back down the country road to Barb's place. He could not shake the uneasy feeling gnawing at his heart as he pressed the accelerator as hard as he dared.

Entering the Hostetler house, an empty silence greeted him. The uneasiness pounced heavily on his heart and he dashed through the rooms, threw down his satchel, and caught the baby just as Barb stepped aside for him. "And now, what's the little fellow's name?" he asked, snipping the cord.

"Elton."

"Yes? I asked what you'd like to name the boy."

"Elton."

The doctor stared at the father. "You mean you want to name your son Elton?"

"Yep, that's the name we decided on."

Dr. Lehman's cheeks reddened. "You must have run out of names after 14 children," he finally stammered.

As Dr. Lehman examined the baby, the father pulled out his wallet. "Don't know that I can do much today, but I'd like to pay a little on the bill."

"That's not necessary," Dr. Lehman smiled with a wave of his hand. "I never charge for delivering a baby named Elton."

As he drove back to the office, he thought of other namesakes he had in the community. The new baby was neither the first nor the last Elton he delivered, including Elton Hostetler, Barb's own grandson.

Meanwhile, back at the clinic, the phone was ringing.

"Aden N. Yoder here," the caller identified himself. "My wife's needin' Doc."

"What's wrong?" Nancy wondered. "Is she sick?"

"She got stomach pains."

"Does she have the flu?"

"No, it ain't the flu. It's her stomach."

Whatever.

"I warned Doc she goes early."

"Oh, she's having a baby. I'm so sorry, but the doctor is out at another delivery."

"Can you call Eberly?"

"I'm afraid Dr. Eberly is out on a call, too." Nancy's toes curled to think of a woman delivering her baby alone. "How close are her contractions?"

"I don't know about them contraptions, but I could see the baby's eyebrows."

Nancy nearly dropped the phone. "One of the doctors should be in soon. I'll send them right out. If anything—"

Then the line went dead.

As Dr. Lehman trudged wearily up the back steps of the clinic, Nancy met him at the door. "Hurry! Mrs. Aden N. Yoder back at Maysville's been waiting for you! I suppose the baby's come already. It sounded awfully urgent."

"But I just came through Maysville! If only I had known. I tell you, I've got to install a phone out at Barb's."

Nancy began to laugh. "Did you forget Barb's husband is a bishop? There won't be any phones on that property, I can assure you!"

Several months later, a worried young woman sat on the edge of an examining table. Her eyes shimmered with tears as she nervously twisted the ties of her *kapp*. "Oh, Dr. Lehman, do I have to go to the hospital? Isn't there any other way? Couldn't I just take it easy at home?"

Dr. Lehman studied the patient's chart. "Kathryn, I just don't know quite what to say. Placenta previa can be a life threatening condition for you and your baby. You really ought to be hospitalized." The doctor closed his eyes and thought a moment. *What do I do? She'd probably be fine out at Barb's place. I just wish she'd have a phone.*

"Technically, you really don't need a lot of care," he told the distressed patient. "What you do need is to stay off your feet and have someone monitor you. I really think you'd be fine at Barb's, if she'd let you come. There'd be no meals to worry about, and her girls would take care of you."

"Oh yes, Dr. Lehman! And then Andy could drive over in his buggy and visit me every day." Kathryn's eyes shone. "Yes! I'd much rather stay at Barb's house than go to any hospital!"

"Well, I guess it would be okay with me, if it's all right with Barb. If you'd start to hemorrhage again, the Fredericksburg squad could get you to Doctors Hospital in about the same amount of time it takes to get a team together for a C-section. You might have to be out at Barb's for a month, though."

The Quandary of the Amish Bishop and the Telephone

When Dr. Lehman stopped by Barb's house the next week to check on his patient, he found Kathryn propped up comfortably on the couch surrounded with pillows and knitting a baby afghan. Her rosy cheeks glowed as she chatted in Pennsylvania German with her husband sitting comfortably beside her on one of Barb's padded hickory rockers, his stocking feet resting on a hand-braided rug. The pressure lamp hissed in the background, lighting the orderly room. A fire crackled in the potbelly stove, and the savory scent of roast beef filtered in from the kitchen.

There had been no further signs of trouble, Dr. Lehman was relieved to hear. In addition, he noted the mother's blood pressure was satisfactory and the baby was active with a strong heartbeat.

"It's not too much for you to have her here, Barb?" Dr. Lehman wondered, walking into the kitchen where Barb was mashing potatoes.

"*Ach*, no. She's no bother at all," Barb waved aside the concern. "Why don't you stay for supper, Doc?"

"Thanks, that's very kind of you, but some of my colleagues from Doctors Hospital are coming to our house tonight for dinner."

"You mean your wife cooks?" Barb's helper asked with wonder. "Don't you go out to eat at a restaurant every night?"

"Yes, she cooks. And no, we don't go out to a restaurant every night," Dr. Lehman smiled. "Actually, I'd rather eat Phyllis' meals than any restaurant's. But really, Barb, Kathryn seems happy here, doesn't she? It's much nicer for her to be here than in the hospital. And cheaper, too. I just would feel more comfortable if you had a phone." He looked up to see Barb's husband walking into the room. "Hey, there's Bill!"

A broad smile lit the doctor's face. He extended his hand toward the tall, thin, bearded man with the gaunt face, walking slightly humped as if the bishop carried the burdens of his entire flock on his thin shoulders.

"How are you, Bill? Are things going well at the job?"

"Just great, Doc. Cold weather's moving in, ain't?"

The gray-bearded Amish bishop and the doctor chatted like old friends. Bill always had an interesting scrap of news or a humorous incident to relay.

"Did you ever hear about the English woman who stopped by the Amish farm to complain about the calves? You didn't? Well then sit down, you gotta hear this one." Bill gestured to a hickory rocker. "Barb, have you got any cinnamon buns for Doc? He's got to have a roll and a cup of tea if he can't stay for supper. By the way, is it warm enough in here, Doc?"

Dr. Lehman set his satchel beside the rocker and sank into the quilted cushion. "It's very comfortable, Bill. You keep that wood stove well stocked."

I have a couple of minutes before I need to run, Dr. Lehman thought, glancing at his watch. And Dale Carnegie says to create a relationship with folks, listen to them, and give them reason to want to do what you are requesting.

"Tell me about the English woman and the calves." The doctor cut into the soft, warm roll and sipped the steaming mint tea.

"Well, they tell me this actually happened, Doc. An English woman was pretty up in the air about all these baby calves tied to the hutches around the barn—taken away from their mothers and all. She told the farmer she had a mind to report such inhumane treatment, and the farmer should be ashamed of himself for doing that. Well, the farmer didn't say much, and was real calm-like till she got done fussin'. Then he says, 'Lady, it's like this. Them cows is career women, and we're just runnin' a day care center for their young'uns.' And Doc, she didn't have another word to say."

The doctor and the bishop laughed together.

"That was some quick thinking, wasn't it?" Dr. Lehman drained the last drops of tea from the china cup and then shared his dilemma. "Well, Bill, I was just asking Barb if there is anything I can do to get a phone on the property for you. The time you'd save not having to run up to Lytles to call could save a life someday. Like with Kathryn here, if she'd start hemorrhaging again, every minute counts. I missed several deliveries because there wasn't a phone here. I know your people don't want phones in your houses, but couldn't they make an exception in this situation?"

"Yeah, I know what you're saying." Bill raked his fingers through his long, gray beard. "I just don't want to make problems for anyone in my church." He continued to stroke his beard and added, "But maybe I could say something to the other ministers and see what they think."

After a delivery at the Hostetlers several weeks later, Barb set a generous slice of pecan pie on the table where the doctor was filling out his paper work. "Bill asked the ministers about the phone."

"Oh?" Dr. Lehman looked up expectantly.

"It's not going to work, Doc," she sighed. "They say they can't start making exceptions, even for the bishop's house, because then others will want to have phones in their barns, too, and then it will interrupt family life with people wanting to talk on the phone when they should be spending time with their families, instead. I'm afraid the answer is no."

The doctor thought for a minute as he forked a syrupy bite of pecan pie. *We've just got to have that phone!*

"What if I paid for the phone and had it installed in the shop? Then it would be my phone and not yours. Do you think that would be allowed?"

Barb shrugged. "I'll ask Bill. By the way, I suppose things went okay for Kathryn at the hospital?"

"Very well, Barb. We didn't have a lot of extra time, and I wouldn't want to try delivering a placenta previa case anywhere but at a hospital—at least if we knew ahead of time. But see what you can do about that phone, Barb."

Weeks passed. The Amish ministers met and discussed the appeal once again. "Your farm would be connected to the world, even if you didn't own the phone," the other ministers protested.

The doctor attacked the problem from every angle and prayed about it every time he drove the 20-mile round trip to Barb's house and back. There has to be an answer! There must be. Lord, what can I do?

"Barb, I've got an idea," Dr. Lehman suggested to the midwife during one visit. "Let's make one more appeal. What if I buy a camping trailer, pull it onto your property, and put a phone in it? The phone and the trailer would belong to me." The doctor's eyes showed his excitement. "You often use the neighbor's phone anyway. Would it be that much worse to use *my* phone in *my* trailer?"

Bill had been supportive of his wife providing this service to their church women from the very beginning. He handcrafted small cribs for the babies and patiently endured all the interruptions to their family life, asking only that Barb be awake when he left for work as foreman of Curry Lumber Company. The bishop was very sympathetic and saw the need for the phone, so he agreed to intercede once again.

"Dr. Lehman really cares about us plain folk," the bishop told the ministers. "He's tryin' to help us and wants a phone for the good of our womenfolk. He wants to pay for it from his own pocket. Is there any reason he couldn't buy a camping trailer with his *own* money and put his *own* phone in to try to save the lives of *our* women?"

Bill met the doctor at the door the next time he came. "Why don't we go out and find a good spot to put that trailer," he suggested. "I was thinking about a place under the trees, say 50 feet or so from the house, and I have a bell here we'll hook up inside the house so we can hear when the phone rings."

A compromise had been reached. Dr. Lehman would have his phone in his trailer on the Amish bishop's property for the benefit of the Amish folk.

12.

I'm Not God

"I just wish there was something I could do," Elton mumbled to himself while paging through the newspaper. " I just *wish.*"

"What happened now?" Phyllis questioned, shutting the living room shades.

"What a day," Elton sighed as he dropped the newspaper onto the floor beside the recliner and clasped his hands behind his head. For a moment he stared at the design of the plastered ceiling, his eyebrows knit in troubled concentration.

"We sent a baby to the hospital from Barb's today. I just wish there was something I could do."

"What was wrong?" Phyllis wondered, straightening the couch pillows and gathering up the childrens' books scattered on the coffee table. "What happened?"

"Well, the mother had gone into labor six weeks ago and then stopped. Today, when the baby was born at Barb's, we couldn't get him to breathe. Barb said I worked harder at resuscitating him than the mother did delivering him," he remarked, a lopsided grin sliding across his face and then vanishing again.

"We got the boy breathing and gave him oxygen. But he won't make it, Phyllis. Little Davy, as they call him, doesn't have a chance. I noticed when I cut the cord that it was barely attached and that the placenta was black. He couldn't have been getting much nourishment the last number of weeks from the appearance of the placenta and the condition of the cord. He never did gain consciousness.

"Now Davy's started having seizures, he's hypoglycemic, and there are signs of cranial hemorrhage. There's absolutely no way the boy will pull through. If only there was something I could do," he finished wearily.

"But, Elton, you're not God."

"I know. I know. The nurses at the office tell me that all the time. But there are some cases I want so badly to cure—to prescribe pills, give a shot, or do something to restore health to a life that is slipping away. I tell you, nothing is more heart-rending for a physician who is trained to prescribe remedies and bandage wounds than to stand at the side of one he so desperately longs to help and to know there is not a thing in the world he can do! Phyllis, it's agonizing," the doctor exclaimed in exasperation.

"Like Lisa's case," Phyllis agreed softly.

"Exactly," Elton groaned. He could still see the small, angelic face in the little casket. Until his last breath, Dr. Lehman would never be able to erase from his mind the agonizing torture of standing beside the lifeless body of his four-year-old niece, Lisa Lehman. The bitterest form of anguish ripped his heart as he realized there was not a medical procedure in the world he could perform to restore her to life after a car had struck and killed her.

It was Merlin, his own brother, who had given from his personal savings to help pay medical school bills, offering encouragement and support after Dad died. It was Merlin who had helped him locate his first office. And then there was not a thing he—Dr. Lehman, who was trained to stitch lacerations and set broken bones—could do for his brother's crushed little daughter and his broken dreams. He was not God.

"But, Elton," Phyllis went on, "we all deal with situations beyond our control. Even the mechanic cannot fix a car that is totaled."

"But I'm dealing with irreplaceable lives, and that's the difference! Phyllis, the Troyers have two little girls about Brenda's age who were praying a long time for a baby brother. Now Little Davy, whom they've prayed for for so long, is going to die before they'll ever have a chance to hold him. I just think there's got to be something I can do. But there isn't."

"Elton, you're a physician, not God."

"But sometimes there are situations I want so desperately to change."

"But if God allows everything that happens for our good, like your patients always say, then are you saying you would work differently than God does?"

"No, I wouldn't want to say that. I'd just like to spare my patients all the grief I can."

Later, Dr. Lehman attended a Medicaid meeting updating doctors on the latest forms physicians needed to fill out for Medicaid patients. Sitting in a boring lecture was absolutely the last way he cared to spend his evening, especially since he had been up most of the night before. From the front row, he listened halfheartedly to the droning Medicare representative. In his first inactive moments in 18 hours, intense weariness overcame the doctor. His eyes drooped and his head began to nod. Now and then a soft snore escaped from the tired doctor in the front row, rising to a crescendo until the snores and snorts competed with the voice of the distracted speaker.

"He must have had a hard day," the lecturer winked at the audience.

"Yes, and he was up most of the night delivering several babies," Dr. Lehman's nurse wanted to say, but she smiled, instead.

The speaker continued emphatically. "A diagnosis *must* be listed on every form in order for us to process your payment."

The audience groaned.

"Medicaid cannot . . . ."

A resonant snore distracted the speaker momentarily and then he continued shrilly, "Let me repeat. Medicaid will not pay for any case that does not list a diagnosis. Is that clear?"

With a loud snort, Dr. Lehman's eyes blinked open and he sat straight up in his chair. "I want you to know that we are physicians and not God!" he announced emphatically. "And there's no way we can have a diagnosis for every situation. Sir, I am not God!"

A rumbling of assent filled the room, accompanied by nods of approval. Dr. Lehman's colleagues smiled at each other. That was Dr. Lehman for you, standing up for what he thought was right.

Well, Doc, his nurse chuckled to herself, I'm glad it's finally sinking in. We've been trying to tell you that for a long time. You're not God.

"Phyllis, you won't believe it," Elton remarked to his wife one evening. "Do you remember Little Davy that we sent to the hospital from Barb's a couple of weeks ago? Well, he went home today."

"You mean he died?"

"No, his parents took him home."

"How did that happen?"

"He came out of his coma and rallied, and now he's doing fine!"

"Wonderful! What did you do?"

"Nothing unusual, really. I can't explain it. Those nurses all call him the little miracle baby, and Barb says his mother was praying like only a mother can."

Three years later, Barb called Dr. Lehman to her house to deliver another child for Mark and Jeanie Troyer—a boy, the brother Davy had been hoping for.

"Two girls and now two boys," Dr. Lehman observed. "What a nice family."

Several hours after the baby was born, Mark brought Davy in to see the new baby. The little blond-haired boy sat on the edge of his mother's bed, beaming down at his new brother and stroking the tiny fingers.

"Now I have two farmer boys!" Mark announced proudly. "Little Davy, here, is my little shadow, going wherever I go, doing whatever I do. He's even got his own little shovel, don't you, Davy?" the father squeezed the toddler's knee. "Our little miracle boy, aren't you?"

The following day was one of those balmy autumn days that energized farmers to finish harvesting their crops. When the frantic call came into the office, Nancy managed to decipher a few hysterical, jumbled words—something about a man on the way to the office with a child who was accidentally driven over by a tractor.

Almost before Nancy could hang up the receiver, the distraught father dashed through the door with his limp little boy in his arms. A horrified hush froze the waiting room as the patients stared at the eyes bulging from the crushed little head.

How on earth did he get here so fast? Nancy wondered while her shaking fingers dialed the nearest squad. "We have an emergency!" she called to the nurse, who flew to open the office door and ran to locate the doctor, who was tending to another patient.

Icy fingers gripped Dr. Lehman's heart as he stared at the limp, bruised form in the farmer's arms.

"Davy!" he murmured. "Oh, Lord, not Davy!"

Lord, help us, the doctor groaned inwardly, laying the toddler gently on the exam table as the nurse prepared to start an I-V. At least he's breathing, Dr. Lehman thought, trying to assess the extent of the injuries. It looks as though the tractor tire almost missed his head. Almost.

The paramedics rushed into the room, gently lifted the child onto the stretcher, and carried him out to the ambulance. Grabbing his bag, the doctor climbed into the ambulance behind the pale, young father. "I'm going along," he announced. Never mind that the office was full of patients. This doctor went where he was needed most.

"Which hospital?" the driver called above the shriek of sirens as the squad headed out the lane.

"Timken," Dr. Lehman shot back. "They've got a neurosurgeon."

As the ambulance flew over the hills and sped around the curves, the doctor labored over the child fighting for his life. He gave him oxygen, checked his vitals, made him comfortable, and monitored the I-V.

"Let's see, how old is he?" Dr. Lehman asked the father, who held his son's little hand and gazed down at the boy with moist, anguished eyes.

"Three."

Three—almost Lisa's age.

"Can you tell me what happened, Mark?" Dr. Lehman asked gently above the wailing siren.

"Davy wanted to go with me on the tractor." His voice broke, and for a moment the father wept quietly.

Dr. Lehman placed a hand on Mark's shaking shoulders as the farmer continued brokenly.

"He could have stayed in the house with his sisters, but he heard I was planning to chop some haylage quick before we went to see the baby, and he thought he had to go along. Davy always was my little farmer boy, shoveling silage with his own little shovel. My shadow, I guess you'd say, and I liked havin' him with me, so I didn't make him stay in the house."

Mark blew his nose before continuing. "We was riding along, and then I stood up and reached back to pull the rope to start the chopper. Davy slipped off the seat. He must have fallen asleep, is all I can figure out. I saw him fall. I jumped after him, not even taking time to shut off the tractor. My foot was caught, and the tractor almost got me, too, but I pulled free. And there he lay," Mark's sad voice died away.

"I could see by the tread that the wheel almost missed his head. Almost. But it had driven over just the side of it. I ran to the house with him in my arms, and by the time I got to the vehicle, his eyes were bulging already."

Dr. Lehman's heart wept with the father, knowing how small the chances were for the child to survive the crushing weight of the monstrous tractor tire. As he left the operating room several hours later, Dr. Lehman walked slowly to the anxious father huddled forlornly in a corner of the waiting room.

"We lost him," Dr. Lehman said gently, placing his arm on the father's shoulder. "Mark, let me assure you, we did everything we could to save your son, but Davy's injuries were just too extensive. But even if your boy had lived, he would not have been normal." The doctor closed his eyes, searching for the right words, and then he continued, "Some things are hard to understand, Mark. You can't blame yourself. It was just one of those things."

Dr. Lehman wept silently with the young father for a few moments. And then he said, "Mark, I called Barb and told her to give your wife some medication to help her relax, but I told her not to tell Jeanie, because I figured you'd want to do that. I'll drive over to Barb's with you if you want me to."

"Please do," Mark nodded, mopping the tears from his face with his red handkerchief. "I'd like that."

Together the two of them set out on one of the most difficult tasks they'd ever undertake.

"You didn't sleep too well last night," Barb casually explained to Mrs. Troyer, handing the mother several pills and a small glass of water.

"No, I didn't," Jeanie smiled, reaching for the capsules. "I never sleep good away from home."

"Here, let me rub your back. Maybe that will help you relax." As Barb expertly kneaded and massaged her shoulders and spine, Jeanie sighed deeply and her eyes drifted shut. What mother didn't look forward to Barb's nightly massages? Only one more night here and she'd be taking the new baby home to Davy and the girls.

Jeanie's breathing deepened into the even breaths of slumber. Barb straightened slowly, shook her head sorrowfully, and tiptoed from the room. Get some sleep while you can, she thought.

An hour later, Jeanie awoke to hear muffled voices at the foot of her bed. Blinking, she saw the curtains part and her husband walking slowly toward her. In the doorway stood Dr. Lehman.

In the pale glow of a lamplight, she noticed that the hands of the clock pointed to 10. What were the men doing here at this hour? The tortured look in Mark's red eyes and the pain she read on Dr. Lehman's face sent Jeanie's heart racing in panic.

"Davy . . . died," Mark sobbed, collapsing into her arms. The two clung to each other, crying together in unspeakable anguish.

"How?" was all she could say. And then he told her.

A hundred memories seemed to surge over Jeanie. Memories of prayers for an unconscious newborn. Memories of the miraculous recovery. Memories of his sunny presence around the farm, memories of the fair-haired boy sitting on the edge of this very bed, his shining face gazing adoringly at his new little brother.

God had heard their prayers three years ago and healed their Davy, giving him to them for three short years. And now after he gave them a second son, God had called Davy home.

"God must have a reason," Jeanie whispered.

"You don't blame me, Jeanie, do you?" Mark pleaded with a tortured look in his eyes that melted her heart.

Looking into her husband's miserable face, Jeanie couldn't bear to intensify his suffering. "No, Mark," she whispered. "God must have allowed it for a purpose." The tension in her body eased as she decided not to struggle against what had taken place, but to quietly accept it.

"I'm going to let you go home," Dr. Lehman said gently after the sobbing had subsided and he had explained the details of the injury. "Mark says you'll have help, and it will do you more good to be at home with the rest of your family than to stay here."

As the doctor drove home in the darkness, a deep pain

throbbed in his heart. He felt as though he had lost his son, and in a way he had, for his patients were like family to him.

It took the doctor a while to unwind that night as he relived the day, telling Phyllis about the tragedy. He couldn't help but think of the sleepless night the Troyers would spend. Bringing a new baby home should be one of the happiest moments a family could experience.

"So what did you tell them?" Phyllis wondered, wiping her eyes.

"I didn't say much. I just tried to be there for them, and that, I think, is more important than lots of words they won't remember or can't comprehend in the intense pain of the moment.

"A lot of the plain folk just accept that God orders the events of life, and whatever happens he allows for a purpose. And, Phyllis, I find people who are able to trust God like that are able to cope with grief much better."

Several years passed before Dr. Lehman heard much from the Troyers again. Then one Sunday afternoon, Jeanie Troyer called the Lehman residence. "Mark was riding his horse. The horse fell on Mark's leg and it's bent straight out the side. He's in awful pain."

"I'll meet you at my office right away," the doctor replied.

"But Dr. Lehman, I know it's Sunday and—"

"That's fine. Bring him to the back door, then he won't have as far to go to the X-ray machine."

"Why, it's Sunday! Most doctor's would send their patients to the emergency room," Mark exclaimed when Jeanie told him what the doctor had said.

"That's Dr. Lehman for you. He never sends his patients away just because it's not office hours."

"Your horse fell on you?" Dr. Lehman questioned, as he helped the groaning patient onto the X-ray table.

"Yeah," Mark moaned, his face contorting in pain. "I was out for a Sunday afternoon ride. A mutt jumped out at the horse. He shied, lost his footing, and fell on my leg. My foot was still in the stirrup and bent sideways."

The man nearly fainted in pain while Dr. Lehman took an X-ray. Holding the film up to the window, he could see a severely fractured bone. He's probably got several torn ligaments, the doctor thought, studying the X-ray image.

"With a break like you've got, you'll need surgery," Dr. Lehman informed Mark as he studied the X-ray. After the operation, Mark wore a cast on his leg for nine weeks while his wife helped milk the cows. Two months after the cast came off, the Troyers called Dr. Lehman again. He delivered another healthy son for the couple at Barb's house.

Jeanie's thoughts went to Davy, the music at his funeral, and the rainbow. "The neatest thing happened the afternoon of Davy's viewing," Jeanie shared with Barb. "It was a gorgeous autumn day, and there was hardly a cloud in the sky. It definitely wasn't raining. Mark was looking up into the sky, wondering about his little farmer boy and then he saw it—a lovely rainbow. He looked again, and sure enough, he hadn't imagined it. There was a rainbow in the sky without a cloud or a drop of rain!" The woman paused for a moment, her face radiant with the precious memory.

"Yes, and I always said it was like God's special message to Mark that everything was okay. You know," she continued, "it's amazing how a death can change one's perspective. Heaven seems so much closer now, and things that used to be so important now seem so . . . so trivial. I guess there's something about heartbreak that makes a person grow."

"She's right," Dr. Lehman agreed when Barb shared the story with him. "Suffering can refine a person's character. Like they say, 'Suffering makes men and prosperity makes monsters.'"

"I guess it's good I'm just a doctor and not God, or I might want to spare all my patients the heartaches that make them better people," he acknowledged. "Yes, I'm very glad I'm not God."

13.

AMISH CHURCH AT BARB'S

Barb's white double-knit curtains were pulled back to one side of the window, revealing dozens of buggies and bicycles lining the white fence posts of the bordering pasture. Dr. Lehman stood at the window, watching the Amishmen in their white long-sleeved Sunday shirts, black pants, vests, and black shoes solemnly file into the backless benches inside Bill Hostetler's barn. Rows of mothers with babies on their laps, stooped grandmothers, and young girls, all in dark dresses and white *kapps*, sat silently on the adjacent benches.

Dressed as miniatures of the older generation, the children sat quietly next to their parents, their eyes sparkling at the treat of having a church service in a barn. Many Amish families emptied their homes of furniture or swept out their buggy sheds when their turn came to host *gmay*, but Bill and Barb swept out the upper floor of the barn, chased away the cobwebs, and set up benches under the lofty beams. The Hostetler house needed to be kept available for expectant mothers every day, even Sundays. And the conspicuous presence of Dr. Lehman's car announced the arrival of someone's baby.

Walking into Barb's kitchen that morning, Dr. Lehman had noticed the plump, golden loaves of homemade bread, and colorful jars of home-canned pickles, red beets, and jellies spread across the kitchen counters. Platters of luncheon meat and sliced cheese, Amish peanut butter,[4] and plates of cookies along with coffee and tea would complete the noon meal the entire church would share. The plates of cookies and crackers on the table would be served to the small children during the long services.

During the winter months, the women served huge kettles of *bohnesupp* after *gmay*. Yes, Dr. Lehman knew all about the *bohnesupp* that the Amish women prepared. He had learned about the tradition of serving bean soup for the church lunch when an ingredient other than the 12 gallons of milk, four pounds of navy beans, four pounds of butter, and 18 loaves of homemade bread had found its way into the soup.

Straight pins weren't listed as one of the ingredients for bean soup. But somehow, one of the pins that the Amish women used to close their dresses, fasten their aprons, and secure the *kapps* onto their hair had dropped into the kettle of *bohnesupp* that particular Sunday noon. The stray pin made itself known when it washed down a man's throat with his last gulp of broth and lodged there, pricking him with every swallow.

Though the patient could feel the pin, and an X-ray in Dr. Lehman's office verified that a pointed object was lodged in the man's esophagus, Dr. Lehman couldn't see it, nor could he reach it with any of the instruments in his office. So, he sent the patient on to the emergency room where the surgeon on call also attempted unsuccessfully to reach the offending object. While the surgeon rushed to the other side of the hospital to locate an instrument he thought might extricate the pin, the Amishman coughed, shooting the pin right out of his mouth.

Barb's menu did not include *bohnesupp* on this warm summer day. Cold sandwiches were served instead during summer months, so no pins would be swallowed accidentally today.

Sitting on a hickory rocker next to a window, the *Family Life* magazine in his lap, Dr. Lehman listened to the musical strains wafting from the Amish church service while he waited for a baby to arrive. He thought of his family worshiping at Longe-necker Mennonite Church, where Phyllis was involved with the music and Pastor Albert was preparing to deliver one of his in-spirational sermons. I wonder how the Sunday school class is going for my substitute teacher, he thought. I hope Phyllis re-members to bring home the offering for me to count and de-posit.

Church was a central part of Dr. Lehman's life and he hated to miss a service, even to deliver a baby. When he shared his feelings with his pastor, the minister placed his hand on Elton's shoulder and said, "Doc, when you are serving others, the church is there with you."

God's presence certainly isn't limited to steepled buildings, he thought, listening to the slow, sustained notes of the *Lobleid* song floating through the open window.

"We sing the *Lobe* song so slowly," a patient once told him, "that if I'd arrive just as the song started, I could unharness my horse, tie it up, walk to the service, and the congregation would still be on the first note." That was stretched a little, Dr. Lehman thought as he listened to the first note dying away.

After an opening devotional and a kneeling prayer, the con-gregation rose respectfully to its feet as the minister prepared for the Scripture reading. And then the singsong cadence of the German preaching filtered into the room. Dr. Lehman listened with fascination to the preacher's voice rising to a passionate crescendo and then dying away, rising again with emphasis and intensity, and then fading into a mournful wail.

"*Ein Psalm Davids, Lobe den Herrn* . . . . "[5]

Either Bill or his son-in-law must be preaching, Dr. Lehman realized, though he couldn't tell which. Perhaps even a grand-son. If the preacher was of the younger generation, he had mas-tered the singsong style well as he read: "Bless the Lord, O my soul: and all that is within me, bless his holy name. Bless the

Lord, O my soul, and forget not all his benefits: Who forgiveth all thine iniquities; who healeth all thy diseases . . . . "[6]

As Bill's congregation worshiped in his barn, the German preaching wakened dusty memories from Dr. Lehman's mind, and he found himself recalling the German preaching he heard as a child at Sonnenberg Mennonite Church decades before.

In his boyhood home, church had been as much a part of the doctor's life as breathing. Every time the doors of Sonnenberg Mennonite Church opened, all 14 members of the Lehman family were there. Father was the church chorister from as early as the doctor could recall. Yes, the Lehman family was deeply religious, but Dr. Lehman often said that being born into a Christian home doesn't make one a Christian any more than being born in a garage makes one a car.

Although he had attended a Christian school and made a formal commitment to the church through baptism, Dr. Lehman first experienced the joy of his faith at 16, when George and Lawrence Brunk brought their tent meetings to Wayne County. He could still see the slogan, "The whole Gospel for the whole world," emblazoned on the side of the evangelists' trailer.

In his mind's eye, Dr. Lehman remembered the tall brothers with the commanding presence and thunderous voices. That first week of tent meetings was pure misery, he recalled, sitting under the fiery preaching that seemed to bring heaven down on the tent canopy. How hearts were stirred as the evangelist's deep, rich voice rolled across the tent, leading the old Gospel hymns with conviction that drew many to the altar seeking God's touch on their lives. Hundreds turned to God and lives were changed in Holmes, Wayne, and Tuscarawas counties.

Dr. Lehman's heart, too, had been stirred to renew his commitment to God. As he milked the cows every afternoon during the first week of meetings, he was worried that if a cow would kick him, he'd have to miss the evening service. When the service began, he could hardly keep his seat through the soul-piercing sermon. However, as the service closed with an altar call, Elton couldn't pry himself out of the folding chair to walk forward. For almost a week, the boy struggled before walking to the front of the tent where he recommitted his life to God.

That night, Dr. Lehman released the load of guilt he felt, as a deep peace filled his heart. It had been a defining moment in his life. From there on, he based his decisions on what he thought God wanted him to do and not just on what he wanted to do.

Through the years, Dr. Lehman sensed God's presence in his life, not just on Sunday mornings but every day of the week, at home, at the office, at Barb's, on the road, or wherever he happened to be. At times he sensed God's spirit gently guiding and nudging his heart. And more than once, he was grateful he had listened to the gentle, inner promptings.

In one situation, a distraught patient called Dr. Lehman one weekend. His pet had been hit by a car and he wanted Dr. Lehman to give him something to put his injured animal to sleep. Dr. Lehman always liked to accommodate his patients whenever possible, yet he didn't feel good about giving this patient the requested drugs. After thinking for a moment, he told the caller, "You know, I'd like to help you out, but I'm not a veterinarian. Perhaps you could check with the local vet about caring for your injured dog."

Some time later, the patient called Dr. Lehman again. "You know," he said, "I want to thank you for not giving me something to put my dog to sleep. You see, I didn't have an injured animal at all," the caller confessed. "I was planning to use the drugs to take care of an annoying relative. Thanks so much for not giving the drugs I asked for that day."

Being sensitive to those inner promptings not only saved the life of a person that day; they also may have saved his own life during the flood of '69.

On July 4, 1969, Dr. Lehman worked night rotation at the emergency room of Orrville Community Osteopathic Hospital.

As the last bursts and flashes of fireworks faded away, the heavens seemed to split open, dumping lakes of water upon the countryside.

After a long night of treating firecracker burns and accident victims in the emergency room, Dr. Lehman headed out of town, ready for a good nap before heading to Longenecker Mennonite Church. At least I don't have to prepare for a Sunday school class this morning, he thought, as he swung by Doctors Hospital to check on a few patients.

Dr. Lehman could hardly keep his eyelids open as he headed for Mount Eaton after making his rounds at Doctors Hospital. Beyond the water droplets batted back and forth between the windshield wipers, he could see rivers streaming down the sides of the road. Lakes of water flooded fields and yards, while streams rushed across the roadway ahead. Water sprayed as high as his car roof as he plunged through the flooded streets.

Driving through the village of Brewster, Dr. Lehman slowed as he approached a bridge where the stream had swelled until it surged over the roadway.

A voice urged him to turn back as he approached the swiftly flowing water. He braked and looked around. I've driven through other streams just as deep as this one, he thought, easing off the brake pedal.

"Stop! Turn around!" an inner voice warned.

He braked again and watched the rushing water ahead of him for a moment. The stream is flowing pretty fast, but it'll take so long to go another way, and I'm exhausted. Slowly he released the brake. Surely the water can't be that deep.

"Go back!" the inner voice urged with an authority that could not be disregarded.

With a weary sigh, the doctor shifted his car into reverse, turned around, and headed back the way he had come. After a lengthy detour, he approached Mount Eaton where water streamed down the hills along the sides of the road. Realizing the road to their church in the hollow would be impassable, the Lehmans attended church in Mount Eaton that morning, instead. Sunday afternoon, a member of Longenecker Church called to say that the songbooks were floating down the aisles of the building. What did Phyllis want done with them?

"Don't bother cleaning them up," she had replied. "We were just ready to order the new edition anyway."

When Dr. Lehman drove to Doctors Hospital several days later, he was startled to see a sign near Brewster blocking the road. It was the same spot where he felt the urge to turn around, he realized suddenly. Drawing to a stop, he read the sign barricading the road: "Road Closed Ahead. Bridge Out."

Goosebumps stood on his arms as he stared at the gaping hole in the roadway ahead and the rushing water beneath. *If it wouldn't have been for that voice, I could have driven over the edge of the road and into the river.* He shuddered as he turned his car around once more, not daring to think of what could have happened and feeling grateful to God for his safety.

Beyond the window at Barb's house, Dr. Lehman saw shafts of sunlight falling on the worshiping congregation.

The notes of the parting German hymn, *"Lebt Friedsam,"* floated across the meadows, and Dr. Lehman observed Barb placing her arm around the weary, laboring woman on the bed of Barb's delivery room. She encouraged, "I know just what you are going through." And then, they ushered a new life into the world.

Suddenly, Dr. Lehman understood what Pastor Albert had been trying to convey. Praise and adoration were only one aspect of worship. Another dimension involved channeling God's love to those in need. And that was what life was all about.

14.

MY SON!

Has it been a year since that accident? Dr. Lehman asked himself, drawing his eyes away from the gruesome journal entry to the open window. It was a warm sunny day when the call came in, just like this one. He glanced back at the words he had recorded into his journal exactly one year ago: *September 1970: Shotgun injury.* Yes well, there was no use brooding over the accident. It was history.

"So long, everyone," he called on his way to the door. He noted with amused fascination his small son kneeling beside a doll, a stethoscope dangling from his ears, his face masked with concentration. The toddler slowly moved the disk across the doll's chest.

"Dr. Brent, can't you get any heart tones?" Brenda asked, hovering over her small brother with convincingly genuine concern.

"Dr. Brent," Dr. Lehman murmured softly, savoring the sound of the words. "Dr. Brent."

Setting down the satchel, he knelt beside his son, pulled out his own stethoscope, and placed it on his chest. "Here is a good location to get heart tones, Son," he said, pointing to the left side of the doll's chest. "Now you should be able to pick them up," he advised, tapping furtively on the underside of the doll to create a rhythmic tick in the stethoscope. "You can tell your patient that her baby will be fine, Dr. Brent."

"Daddy play?" his young son invited hopefully.

"No, Daddy doesn't have time," Brenda announced wisely as her father stowed away his stethoscope and picked up his bag. "He's got sick folks to take care of. Daddy can't play today."

Dr. Lehman met his wife's eyes. He knew what she was thinking. He always had time for his patients, but he was a father, too! Phyllis didn't verbalize her thoughts. Instead, she asked, "You'll have your two-way radio turned on in case I need to reach you while you are on the road?"

"Yes, today you should be able to get in touch with me," he replied, almost hoping a call would come in so he could try out the new pager and two-way radio. If he had known that after today, every beep from the new pager would send a stab of anxiety through his heart, he wouldn't have been so eager. But he couldn't have known.

"Dr. Brent," the doctor mused as he walked down the steps to his car. Deep within him stirred a longing familiar to every father—that secret desire for his son to follow his footsteps, to shoulder his vision, and to reach those goals he was personally unable to attain.

What tools will those hands hold 25 years from now? Dr. Lehman wondered as he headed north on Route 241. A pen? A hammer? A violin? Or . . . a stethoscope? What kind of a person will my boy become?

Across town, Dr. Eberly, too, was heading out. He had duties to tend at the office and a house call to make that Saturday morning. Life seemed to be dashing past faster than he cared to see it go. It was one of those seasons in life that one longed to freeze right where it was to enjoy it a little longer. The days of all six children gathered around the dinner table every evening were already past. Judy had married Andy Miller and they moved to northern Canada.

It was special to have his son Morris home again after doing church work in northern Canada, Haiti, and southern Texas. But it wouldn't be long until Morris would leave the nest, too, he realized. The boy's heart and thoughts seemed to be in Canada with the nurse he had met. When Dr. Eberly left the house that morning, he noticed that his son was making a pair of lamps for his girlfriend. No, Morris wouldn't be home much longer either. Where had time gone?

The four youngest of the six Eberly children seemed to be hurtling into adulthood, as well. His daughter Kathy now worked at the clinic, and Elaine, Loretta, and James would begin the fall term at Hartville Christian High School next week. Time was rushing on.

As Dr. Eberly headed out on a house call that Saturday morning, he thought he heard a dump truck barreling through town. Not until he saw the flashing lights of the ambulance on the way back to the clinic did he realize that the sound he had heard had not been a dump truck at all, but the terrible crunching and ripping of metal.

Someone's severely injured or worse, he realized, noting a crumpled pickup and a mangled car crushed like a discarded tin can under a careless heel. Maybe I can help, Dr. Eberly thought, pulling to the side of the road and grabbing his house call bag.

Driving up Route 241 that sunny September morning, Dr. Lehman couldn't help but recall his son's invitation to join his play, and Brenda's response that Daddy had more important things to do. Life just slips away with the urgent crowding out the important unless we schedule time for what really counts in life, he realized. How will I impact my son's life if I never have time to build a relationship with him? Somehow, I've got to find more time for the children. Maybe this afternoon we can toss a ball together. But no, that would never work. Whenever his patients drove by the house and spotted him outside, they always remembered an urgent question they needed to ask about their latest ailment or injury. If we could only find a little private corner somewhere, he thought.

As he drove up Route 241 toward Massillon, Dr. Lehman noticed the profusion of blossoms oblivious to the frosty fingers of autumn lurking around the corner. Corn shocks, mums, and pumpkins clustered at roadside stands, forecasting summer's coming demise.

Watching a pair of squirrel hunters disappear into the woods, Dr. Lehman thought, I hope they are careful with their guns today. He could still feel the cold horror when he heard the words: "We've got a young squirrel hunter that accidentally shot himself in the abdomen." If only he could erase the memory of those bloody organs and loops of intestines spilling from the boy's abdomen as he lay on the back seat of a car behind the clinic a year ago today.

"Call the squad!" Dr. Lehman had ordered as he groped amid the mangled mess to find a severed artery.

Thank God, Mount Eaton finally has an ambulance of its own, he thought, listening gratefully to the approaching siren. Only days before, the vehicle had been purchased from a neighboring township for one dollar.

As the medics sprang from the vehicle and yanked the stretcher from the ambulance, Dr. Lehman struggled to staunch the blood that gushed past his fingers like water through a sieve. Gently, the medics eased the boy from the car onto a stretcher and into the back of the panel truck.

"I'm going along," Dr. Lehman announced, following the stretcher into the ambulance. He's lost a lot of blood, the doctor thought, compressing the spouting artery as the ambulance doors slammed behind him.

"Hemostat," he ordered, his voice steady and calm in spite of the tension he felt. He took the clamp from the medic and clinched the gushing artery.

"I-V needle." His fingers traced the youth's arm as his eyes searched for a raised vein. *Boy, all his veins are collapsed. Maybe this one.* In a quick motion, he jabbed the needle beneath the pale skin.

As the doctor worked, the boy lay quietly looking around but never uttering a groan. *Incredible,* the doctor observed. *His abdomen's blown apart and he lies there as quietly as if he were relaxing on the living room couch. Is it shock, or what?*

Dr. Lehman bent over his young patient, his face lined with compassionate concern as he adjusted the oxygen flow, took vitals, and monitored the intravenous solution—every move precise, confident, and deliberate.

As the ambulance wailed through the countryside, the doctor gazed sadly at the boyish face. *Son, are you ready to die?* he couldn't help wondering.

Fifteen minutes later, the ambulance lights flashed against the walls of Doctors Hospital's emergency room. Orderlies dashed through the hospital doors as paramedics eased the stretcher out of the vehicle. Dr. Lehman spoke briefly with the emergency room physician and followed the gurney down the maze of halls to the operating room. Quickly, he scrubbed, pulled on a gown, mask, cap, and rubber gloves, thinking about the wounded hunter and his family. *If only Doctors Hospital had a trauma team!*

Furrows of concentration lined Dr. Lehman's face as he assisted the surgeon in tying off the gushing arteries. Instruments flashed. Words were short and clipped. Muscles tensed as every effort was made to save the slipping life. But the teenager's pulse faded. His shallow breathing slowed to an occasional gasp.

Breathe. . . breathe. . . . Please, breathe!

Silent tension gripped the nurses and doctors waiting for the teenager to breathe again. But the only sound was the blip–blip of the I-V and the hissing of the oxygen.

There at the side of the operating table, Dr. Lehman felt as though he stood on the bank of an unseen river where a soul slipped its moorings and vanished beyond the horizon into eternity. The surgeon's shoulders sagged and his weary eyes met Dr. Lehman's. "I'm sorry. I wanted so much for your patient to pull through. He was so young."

"You did all you could," Dr. Lehman replied quietly. "You couldn't have done anything more. Unless . . . unless we had a trauma team here."

"I know, Dr. Lehman," the surgeon agreed. "We've got to have a trauma team."

They never had time to say goodbye, Dr. Lehman realized, as he approached the young hunter's family.

"We can't question God," the young man's father whispered when Dr. Lehman broke the news that the wounded hunter had not survived surgery. "He has a reason for letting this happen. God always brings good from every situation he allows."

How does one survive the death of a son? Dr. Lehman wondered as he parked his car next to Doctors Hospital that Saturday in September, one year later. How does a father cope with the death of those dreams, hopes, and ambitions when his son's life is snatched away?

He felt a tinge of pain as he recalled the crestfallen expression on his young son's face as he left that morning. Somehow we must savor the moments we have, he thought, turning off his new two-way radio and clipping his pager onto his belt.

"Howdy, Doc!" a colleague called, meeting Dr. Lehman in the hall as he made his rounds. "We were just talking about your young squirrel-hunting patient that was in here some time ago."

"A year ago today."

"Has it been that long? It's kind of amazing how that young boy's death was the impetus for our hospital putting together a trauma team. Those patients of yours are always quoting some Bible verse about everything working out for our good. Well, it seems they were right this time."

They usually are, Dr. Lehman thought, spreading out his paperwork on a table in the hospital library. They usually are.

When the pager began to beep a moment later, a gratified smile flashed across Dr. Lehman's face. Well, what do you know. They said the pager wouldn't function inside a major steel structure like this, but it works better than I hoped, he thought, scooping up his charts. Somebody must be in labor, he assumed, strolling to the nearest phone to call his wife.

"Elton, we just got word that Morris Eberly was killed instantly in a car accident," Phyllis informed him. "Dr. Eberly came upon the scene and the car was so badly mangled, he didn't recognize his son."

In his mind's eye, Dr. Lehman saw his colleague's son—once tall, trim, dark-haired, and vibrant—now a crushed, lifeless shell lying under a sheet in an icy morgue. *No! Not Morris Eberly!*

From what the family could piece together, Morris had needed a few electrical parts for the lamps he had been making for his girlfriend. A little before 8:30, he hopped into his red Volkswagen Beetle and headed west on Route 250 toward a hardware store.

Approximately half a mile west of Mount Eaton, the right-front wheel of the VW slipped off the berm and into a gully washed out from the flood of '69. Morris whipped his steering wheel in a desperate effort to bring the car back onto the road, and the Volkswagen spun directly into the path of an oncoming pickup truck cresting the hill.

Arriving at the scene on his way home from the house call, Dr. Eberly didn't recognize the mangled car. "We got a fellow here we need you to check out," a medic called from the ambulance.

As he climbed into the vehicle, he glanced at the young man lying on the stretcher. He's about the age of my son, Dr. Eberly realized, noticing the dark hair falling away from the youthful face that had shifted from the blow he had received on the side of his head. Quickly, he pulled out his stethoscope, but he couldn't find any heart tones. He knew the boy was dead. Dr. Eberly searched the victim's pockets for his billfold to locate an identification card, but his pockets were empty. He asked the ambulance driver if he could see the wallet, but the driver ignored the question.

There was something familiar about the face from the eyes on up. Surely it's not my son, he thought, scanning the corpse for a clue. But how can I be certain? Then he remembered Morris once caught a finger in a V-belt, and he had personally taken care of that wound. Lifting the limp hand, he saw the stump of a finger.

"Give me the wallet!" the doctor demanded. As he reached for the billfold, he instantly recognized the leather wallet he helped his son make. As he climbed out of the squad truck, Dr. Eberly asked the medic, "Do you know who you've got here? You have—*my son.*"

Dr. Eberly drove back to the office. "Cancel all my appointments," he told his nurse. "If anyone calls, tell them my oldest son was killed." Then he took his daughter Kathy home, broke the news to his wife and his younger son, and located his teenage daughters. Then he called his daughter Judy in Canada and asked her to break the news to Morris' fiancée. Instead of an engagement announcement the following week, there would be a funeral. The next several days, Dr. Lehman covered for his colleague while caring for his own patients' emergencies, as well.

The following Tuesday, 600 people crowded into the small country church to pay their respects to Morris Eberly that unseasonably hot September day. Hundreds of youth, from as far south as Haiti and as far north as northern Canada, met to mourn their mentor and friend. Mourners tried to fan away the oppressive heat. Others studied the picture on the memory card of a clean-cut youth with dark hair and thoughtful eyes.

"We've grieved and wept over Morris' accident," Dr. Eberly told Dr. Lehman later. "But, Elton, we're not getting hysterical. God is in control, and we can't try to wrest that authority away at a time like this, demanding answers and rebelling against what has taken place."

The next months, Dr. Lehman often found himself looking at his young son in a new way. Children are gifts that come without guarantees of how long we may keep them, he realized. I must find time to cherish my children and interact with them while I can. But how do I find time for my family when I need to be available for my patients 24 hours a day? he wondered. Even on Sundays, which he always set aside for church and family time, the doorbell and telephone rang.

Finally! A few moments to relax and to catch up on some sleep, he thought, propping up his feet one Sunday afternoon. Just as he shut his eyes, Brent popped into the room, toting his new kite. "Hey Dad! It's a great afternoon for flying kites!"

"Oh, I don't know. Maybe later," he began to say, stifling a yawn. Then on second thought, he added, "I think that's a pretty grand idea," he said, reaching for his shoes. "It's a beautiful afternoon to fly a kite. Let's go!"

15.

TWILIGHT RENDEZVOUS

It's time, Dr. Lehman realized, gazing across the brilliantly cloaked trees beyond the valley. This is the season of the year that young Amish couples will soon be slipping in the back door of the clinic. One of these next evenings, I suspect there'll be a twilight rendezvous for a couple or two.

He glanced at the clock. It was soon time to head back to the clinic for evening hours. What would it be like to end every day at five? he wondered a little wearily. What would it be like to have an uninterrupted night, and to know every weekend is free? Certainly such a peaceful, predictable life would be less exciting, he reminded himself.

But once in a while, especially on holidays, a quiet, predictable day would be welcome to the country doctors in the heart of Ohio. "If I could just have Christmas to myself, I wouldn't mind so much giving up every other day," Dr. Mayer had told Barb on the way home from a delivery one Christmas Day. Barb knew the feeling. She had been called away that noon just as she was serving the holiday meal to a house full of guests.

Dr. Lehman, too, knew all about holiday calls. Of course, his patients needed him the day Phyllis' family had come to celebrate Christmas at the Lehman house. "You'll be passing my house on your way to Barb's," he told the prospective parents. "So why

155

don't you stop by and I'll check how things are progressing. That way I'll have a better idea how soon I'll have to leave my guests."

When the couple arrived, Dr. Lehman soon realized that there was no time to waste. "Move your cars!" he urged his guests. "I got to get these people down to Barb's *fast!* Would several of you please give me a hand and we'll carry her out to my car?"

The guests scattered to move their cars. Phyllis' niece's husband, a football player, supported the woman around the middle while other guests held her shoulders and legs as they carried her out to the car.

Later that afternoon, Dr. Lehman rejoined the party. "Well, we got to Barb's in the nick of time, and I was sure glad we made it," he reported. "That couple got a special present this Christmas— twins!"

"Between emergencies and baby deliveries, I never know when I'll be needed next," Dr. Lehman sometimes said. Just because the office doors are locked at 9:30 on the two evenings he held office hours, that didn't mean patients would stop calling and coming.

"I read about a kindergarten teacher who told her class to draw pictures of what their fathers did on their job," Dr. Lehman told Phyllis once. "'What's happening here?' she asked the girl who drew circles all over her paper. The child looked up at her teacher and said, 'Why that's my dad doing his rounds!'" he finished with a laugh. "But seriously, she might have been more accurate than she realized. Some days, the life of a doctor goes around and around with no break in sight!"

As the last buggy pulled away from the hitching post one evening, the phone rang. My day's not over yet, he realized, glancing at his watch. Nine-thirty. The children would soon be asleep. Somehow I've got to find more time for Brent and Brenda. But how can I when my patients need me 24 hours a day, seven days a week, every day on the calendar page?

"Eli Schrock says they are heading for Barb's," Nancy announced. "Do you have a word for him?"

Dr. Lehman thought for a moment. "Let's see. They'll be coming right by my office on the way out to Barb's. Why don't you ask them to stop by and I'll check to see how things are progressing? Then, I'll know if I have time to go home and say good night to my family before heading over."

"Do you want me to stay?" Nancy asked after she hung up the phone.

"That's not necessary. You might as well go home."

Nancy finished straightening the rooms, placing instruments on their chargers, and covering the examining tables with fresh paper. Dr. Lehman called Phyllis to tell her what had developed. As the receptionist pulled on her coat, she noticed the glow of buggy lights in the parking lot.

"The Schrocks are here!"

"Then you may as well stay," the doctor advised.

Nancy draped her coat over her chair, ushered the couple into a treatment room, and helped the woman onto the examining table.

"Get your coat, Nancy," he said a moment later, his voice calm but businesslike. "Take the obstetrics kit out to the car. We're heading for Barb's now!"

Dr. Lehman pulled on his overcoat, grabbed his bag, and suddenly he could tell the baby wasn't going to wait to get to Barb's. "Nancy, get back here!" he called.

As Nancy dashed into the room, Dr. Lehman calmly shoved back his coat sleeves and caught the baby.

"Suction syringe," he ordered in a steady voice. "Cord clamps. Scissors."

"A little girl," Nancy cooed, snatching a large pad from a drawer and wrapping the baby in it.

"This is the youngest patient I've had in this office for a long time!" Dr. Lehman remarked.

"*Ei γi γi!*" the young father laughed shakily. "So you've delivered 'em in your office before, eh?"

"Ah yes, we've had other babies born here," the doctor acknowledged. "But not too many. Actually, Dr. Eberly unexpectedly delivered twins in his office. Before he knew it, those babies were there."

After Dr. Lehman had carefully examined the infant, Nancy weighed and measured the newborn. She washed her and dressed her in the clothes the father brought in from the suitcase in the buggy, and wrapped her tightly in a hand-made flannel blanket. Then she washed the instruments and placed them in the autoclave to sterilize them for the next delivery.

"Well, I don't suppose you'll want to go out to Barb's anymore tonight," he asked. Eli searched his wife's face inquiringly.

"Let's just go home," she said with a weary smile. "Won't the children and *Mommi* be surprised!"

"I'll take you home in my car," the doctor offered as he jotted a few final notations on the chart. "I don't like sending mothers out on a buggy ride so soon after a delivery."

"There's probably never a time when you can say your work day is over," Mr. Schrock observed, looking at the clock.

"No, but that keeps life full of suspense and excitement!" he replied, switching off the light. "And besides, I enjoy my practice so much that sometimes I say I've never worked a day yet! But really," he continued on a more serious note, "I wish I could find more time for my family."

"That's very important," Eli agreed, stroking his beard. "Not too many things are more important than spending time with your children. You know, on the farm we have our busy times, too, and it's not like we have lots of evenings just to go out and play ball or go fishing with the boys, but we take them with us wherever we go. If I go to the auction, I take a couple of the youngsters. If I milk the cows, feed the chickens, or hoe the garden, the children are there, too, following me around and helping as they can. And while we are working or riding in the buggy, we talk about things that are on our hearts. I don't suppose you could take your children with you?"

"That's a great idea," Dr. Lehman agreed, "catching moments together whenever you can. With my patients needing me around the clock, I'll have to do that more."

Taking his children with him proved to be an ideal solution to finding more time with Brent and Brenda. As he began taking them on house calls and to the hospital, nursing homes, and the office on occasion, he could tell it made his children feel important and involved in their father's practice. In addition, he found that taking the children along made evenings and Saturdays more enjoyable for him, his family, and his patients, as well.

Brenda was still a preschooler when she first accompanied her father to Doctors Hospital, coloring quietly next to the friendly receptionist while he made his rounds. Sensing the girl was good with numbers, the receptionist showed her how to connect incoming phone calls to the correct room by placing the cables into the proper receptacles. She also taught her alert pupil how to answer in-house phone calls.

"I'm going out on a house call. Want to ride along?" Dr. Lehman asked Brenda one afternoon. "Nothing contagious," he assured his wife. "Just checking in on an elderly bedfast patient."

"Now when we go out to the houses after dark, there often aren't any outside lights," he explained to his daughter as they walked across the yard toward the house. "So we hold our hands out in front of our faces to feel for clothes lines so we don't hang ourselves on them."

As she entered the farmhouse, Brenda noticed the kind expressions on the faces tinged with concern for their loved one. The strong scent of kerosene tickled her nostrils as she glanced around at the sparse but comfortable furnishings in the clean, orderly room. Across the room, a small girl with a dark dress, matching apron, and bare feet watched Brenda shyly from the doorway. Brenda smiled back and quietly followed her father into the grandmother's bedroom. Since the little girl's grandmother was not feeling well, this wasn't the time to play, Brenda knew.

While Dr. Lehman took the vitals of the wrinkled lady on the bed, Brenda stood quietly by the window.

When he had examined the patient and packed his stethoscope into his bag, he asked the elderly grandmother, "Would you like my daughter to sing a song for you?"

"Why, sure!" the woman answered feebly, her eyes brightening as she slowly turned her head to study Brenda. "Yes, I'd like that very much."

So Brenda walked to the bedside and began to sing confidently, "Jesus loves me this I know, for the Bible tells me so."

Father always said her singing did more for his patients than any medicine he had, so she sang with all her heart, hoping the little girl's grandmother would soon feel better again.

"He does love us, doesn't he," the grandmother whispered, closing her eyes and sinking back into her pillow with a contented sigh.

Brenda tiptoed out of the room behind her father, listening to the grateful expressions from the patient's relatives and feeling very thankful to have a dad who knew how to make people feel better.

And again, the following week, he would say, "Brenda, I need someone to sing for my patients tonight. You know, that does them more good than anything I have in my bag."

"Well, it's time to head for the office," Dr. Lehman remarked one evening after supper.

"Do you suppose a boy will come in tonight who shot his foot with his BB gun?" Brent wondered.

"We had a case like that the other week, didn't we? Never can tell what emergencies we'll see throughout an evening," Dr. Lehman replied, noting the higher-than-usual percentage of emergencies showing up during evening hours. "But I can tell you, I think some Amish couples might be slipping in the back door tonight."

"Did you say slipping in the back door?" Brenda asked. "Why don't they come in the front door like everyone else?"

"Because these young couples don't want anyone to see them and spoil their secret."

"Why don't they want to be seen? What's the big secret?"

"Well, Brenda, the couples I expect to see coming in the back door the next few weeks are engaged to be married. But no one is supposed to know about it until their bishop announces it at their church two weeks before the wedding. It's kind of like a game. The Amish couples and their families secretly prepare for a wedding. They make furniture for their house, can garden produce, make quilts, and do lots of other things without letting anyone find out about it. It's a really great accomplishment for any young couple to do all this without anyone guessing that they are getting ready for a wedding."

"That would be hard to do! But what do they want at your office?"

"There's a law that every couple who wants to get married has to take a blood test first. The Amish bishop doesn't announce the wedding until he sees the results of the blood test. If these couples are seen coming into my office, everyone knows they are planning to get married, and that's supposed to be top secret. So, I play the game along with these couples and allow them to sneak in the clinic's back door after dark."

"Sounds like fun!" Brenda laughed.

There was always something exciting happening at their dad's office. He always had stories to tell when he got home. One night he told them about a boy who got a four-inch splinter in his seat when he slid down the side of a hay wagon. Dr. Lehman had to call a nurse back into the office to help him get it out. "I'm sure his ride home was a little more comfortable than his ride into my office!" Dr. Lehman quipped. Another night, he told of a patient who needed Dr. Lehman to dig a metal sliver out of his arm. Frequently, there were lacerations to stitch or broken bones to X-ray—like the child who broke his leg on the trampoline.

That night, as darkness extinguished the last glow of twilight, Dr. Lehman listened for the creak of buggy wheels and the clopping of horses' hooves as he paged through the syllabus for the course he was taking on the latest medical procedures and techniques.

In front of the clinic, Alice and Nancy also listened for the creaking of buggy wheels as they straightened the examining rooms, put the instruments in sterilizers and on chargers, and pulled the charts for the following day. Nancy paused as she heard the faint sound of clopping hooves. Sure enough, the buggy stopped behind the clinic.

A moment later, the back door opened softly, shutting with a gentle click. At the same instant, the receptionist heard the clip-clopping of another horse's hooves on the parking lot, and the creaking of a second set of buggy wheels. She rushed down the corridor to the Amish couple running towards her.

"Quick!" she called, leading the way down the hall toward an examining room. "This way!"

White *kapp* strings flying, the bride-to-be ran down the corridor with the muscular farm boy at her elbow, urging, *"Dabbah schpring!"*

"In here!" Nancy whispered, and the two dove through the open doorway. As she closed the door behind them, she noticed the couple peering out a corner of the curtained window, trying to detect the identity of the other prospective groom tying his horse to the hitching post.

Please, don't recognize the other couple! Nancy breathed. I should have put them in a front room so they couldn't have looked out the window toward the hitching post! she chided herself. The back door clicked shut again, and the cautious padding of stealthy footsteps filtered up the hall.

Only after the second couple was safely stashed into a room across the corridor did Nancy remember that in her haste, she had forgotten to ask the names of the couples. Let's see, one couple was Ben and Anna. Yes, that was the first couple, I'm sure of it, she thought.

Opening the door of the first room, she whispered: "Here you go, Ben, fill out this form, and Anna, here's—"

The woman's eyes widened and shot her smiling partner a triumphant look. Aha! "We're not Ben and Anna," the young man smiled impishly.

"Oh no!" Nancy groaned. "Then you're Joe and Mandy! Please, you won't let the cat out of the bag, will you?"

The couple smiled smugly, not promising a thing.

Now I've done it! What couple will want to come to an office that gives away their secrets?

It took only a minute for Alice to draw the blood. "I'd turn right at the end of the lane and take another way home, if I were you," Nancy advised Joe. "The other couple might recognize your horse under the street light if you go through Mount Eaton."

"You mean Ben and Anna might recognize my horse?" he teased.

"If I find out you told anyone, I'll inform folks of your news," she threatened as the couple escaped into the darkness.

In the second room at Nancy's whispered suggestion, Alice took her time drawing the blood, listening to the hoof beats dying away in the distance. I'm going to keep them here until I'm sure Joe's got his buggy out of town, she decided. I'm not taking any chances.

"So who else was here tonight?" Ben asked mischievously as he paid the $7.50 fee.

"Would you like me to give away your secret?" Nancy retorted.

"You wouldn't do that, would you?"

"Not intentionally, and I won't purposely spoil anyone else's secret, either."

After the couple left, Nancy straightened the examining rooms and headed home. As Dr. Lehman locked the door, he heard the clopping of hooves on the gravel outside the clinic. Someone must be in trouble, he realized. A laceration? A broken bone? Or a baby case?

"Oh good, I was hoping you'd still be in," a farmer called, ushering a worried-looking mother with a toddler into the waiting room. "Johnny got into the kerosene. *Mei zeit,* I don't know how he got that lid opened. Most of a cup was missing, I'd say, but some was splashed on his clothes, too."

"You're a thirsty little adventurer, aren't you?" Alice laughed, playing peek-a-boo with the toddler back in the examining room, popping out from behind her clipboard as she jotted down his weight.

While she waited for Dr. Lehman to come, a large painting above the examining table caught the worried mother's attention. The scene depicted the inside of an adobe frontier home where a young girl lay across several blanket-covered chairs. Her wavy auburn hair flowed across the pillow and the eyes in her pale face were shut as if she were asleep or unconscious. A woman with her hair pulled back into a bun and who appeared to be the sick child's mother, sat at the table with her head buried in her arms while a tall man, presumably the child's father, stood with a hand on the woman's shoulder, looking anxiously toward the doctor. Spoons and empty cups lay on a table at the patient's side. The bearded doctor stood next to the patient, his chin resting in cupped hands. His eyes held a thoughtful gaze tinged with compassion.

A lot like Dr. Lehman's expression, the mother holding the toddler thought as she studied the painting. Except when Dr. Lehman thinks, he thinks with his eyes shut! she mused as the doctor swept into the room.

With a word from the doctor, Alice smiled winningly at the toddler and wrapped him securely in a blanket with his arms tight against his sides, and laid him on the table.

Speaking soothingly to the wide-eyed child, Dr. Lehman fed a tube down the child's nose and into his stomach. Like most Amish children, the toddler had been trained to obey and to cry quietly, so he didn't struggle, but looked at the doctor with large moist eyes that leaked a tear now and then. Slowly, Dr. Lehman pulled back on the plunger of a large syringe at the end of the tube.

"There it comes!" Alice cheered. "A little more. And a little more."

"That's great!" the doctor encouraged. "I believe that's about it."

"Oh, thank you, Doc," the worried mother exclaimed, as Dr. Lehman gently pulled the tube out of the child's nose. "Do you think he'll be okay?"

"He'll be fine," Dr. Lehman patted the child's head. "Just keep the kerosene out of his reach, and he'll be all right," he smiled as he ushered the couple out the door and flipped off the light.

He hadn't been home long when the phone rang. Another baby was arriving down at Barb's. It was late when he crawled wearily into bed that night, scarcely sleeping at all when the phone began to ring again.

"You awake, Doc?" the caller asked.

"Uh, yes," he mumbled, lifting one eyelid a crack.

"I knew you'd be," the caller rattled on. "Those baby cases are always keeping you up in the night. I couldn't sleep no how, so I said to myself, 'Now why don't you give Doc a call and chat with him? He's sure to be awake.'"

At least I don't have to go out! Dr. Lehman thought, sinking back into his pillow as he listened to the elderly patient share what was on his heart.

"I'm telling you, Doc," the caller continued. "Days just drag since the children don't want me to drive anymore. And nights are even longer."

The doctor listened patiently as the man went on and on about the frustrations he experienced. Finally, he finished his call, saying, "Well, Doc, one can't count on a lot of folks these days, but I know I can always count on you. You're always there when I need you. Just like tonight. Thanks for listening. Now you'd better get some sleep while you can, Doc. Never know when that next call will come."

16.

BLIZZARD BABIES DON'T WAIT

Like wild wolves stalking the same slumbering prey, the wind slashed through the night as the winter storm fronts collided and clashed over northern Ohio. Barometers plunged to record-shattering depths as blinding blizzards buffeted the state in what reporters would call "The Storm of the Century." Victims strained in the ferocious grip of the storm hour after hour, as their vehicles struggled along snow-smothered roadways. And then, like a helpless hare beneath the paw of a massive arctic wolf, the countryside lay still—strangled in crises spun into legends for decades to come.

On a hill above Mount Eaton, a house hunkered beneath the drifts, its lights flickering valiantly through the storm. Beyond the snow-spattered windows, pajama-clad youngsters nestled against their mother as she read Laura Ingalls Wilder's story about the blizzard adventures in *The Long Winter*.

"I hope our daddy doesn't have to go out in the storm tonight like Laura's Pa," Brenda whispered at the end of the chapter.

Across the room, the doctor listened as the storm clawed at the windows with icy shards of snow and howled down the chimney. He snapped closed the biography that no longer held his attention. Then he tossed another log on the fire and walked to the window for the umpteenth time. Still snowing.

"Wind chill factors as low as 60 degrees below zero," the weather forecaster announced. "Record snowfalls . . . more than 34 inches of snow have fallen the month of January . . . 60-mile-an-hour winds . . . visibility near zero . . . semi trucks, cars, and farm buildings buried under 20-foot drifts . . . ."

He stared out into the whirling whiteness beyond the windowpane, listening as the broadcast continued to describe the devastation of "The Great Blizzard of '78." "Hundreds of stranded motorists . . . food shortages . . . disrupted electrical services . . . unheated homes . . . a rising death toll . . . President Carter declares Ohio a federal disaster area . . . ."

It's even worse than the blizzard of '68, Dr. Lehman thought, recalling the storm that had paralyzed central Ohio a decade before. He could still remember the apprehension he felt as the phone began to ring. He could still feel that sinking feeling as he recognized the caller's voice during the blizzard 10 years before. Not tonight, please not tonight, he remembered thinking. But Mrs. Beachy's twins were arriving, storm or no storm.

"We'd never get through to the hospital," Dr. Lehman and Mr. Beachy agreed. "It would be foolish to take the risk."

"If we could just get you to Barb's," Dr. Lehman thought out loud.

"Barb and Bill aren't that far away," Mr. Beachy agreed. "But you'd never get through with your car."

Glen Shoup! Dr. Lehman thought with sudden inspiration. Glen's dad has a four-wheel-drive dump truck! A short time later, Mr. Shoup's truck was plowing through the storm toward Barb's place with Mrs. Beachy in the cab and Dr. Lehman and Mr. Beachy huddled in the exposed bed of the coal truck. Icy pellets of snow scoured the men's reddened faces and swept inside their upturned coat collars.

Will we make it? Dr. Lehman wondered as the truck labored through drifted country roads. But then he saw the welcome lights of the Hostetler home winking through the storm. Once in Barb's house, he shed his snowy coat and boots and headed straight for the potbellied stove. Before long, the twins lay wrapped in warm quilts in the hand-made cribs near the radiant warmth of Bill's glowing wood stove.

Many snowy nights, Dr. Lehman and Glen headed for Barb's in the four-wheel-drive truck. They'd stop for Rebecca and often pick up the prospective parents along the way. After helping the woman into the cab, Dr. Lehman and the patient's husband would climb into the back of the truck. As Dr. Lehman warmed his hands at Bill's fire those nights, he'd always ask, "Well, Barb, how many women have you got here tonight?"

"Seven, Doc," she replied one snowy evening. "They're everywhere, I tell you—on every bed and couch. We've made beds for the babies on tables."

"Seven! Barb, it's time to send some home!"

"*Ach*, they're desperate enough to get in when the baby is coming," Barb fussed. "But they're never quite as desperate to leave through the storm. It's awful hard for them to find drivers with vehicles that can get through these roads, and besides, they don't want to get stranded in a ditch with a newborn."

"Get the mothers and babies who have been here the longest ready to go, and I'll ask Glen to take them home," Dr. Lehman instructed.

Barb couldn't help but smile as she bundled the babies. She knew that's what he'd say. If anyone could make things happen, Dr. Lehman could!

"We got three-foot drifts in our lane. Ain't no way your car could make it through," another caller informed Dr. Lehman during the Blizzard of '68. "No way a'tall. I'll fetch you at the end of the lane in the buggy."

He's right, Dr. Lehman thought, studying the drifted lane, as he climbed into the buggy and pulled a heavy blanket over his knees. I'd never get through in my car. The buggy bounced across the field as the farmer guided the horse toward the lights of the farmhouse, where Dr. Lehman safely delivered another blizzard baby.

I really ought to get a four-wheel-drive Jeep, he thought, riding in the buggy across the field after the delivery. But they're just too expensive. Why, they cost half as much as I paid for my house—all of $5,000 dollars! It sure would be nice to go anywhere I wanted to whenever I needed to.

I'm afraid it would take more than a Jeep to get me through this storm, Dr. Lehman thought as he finally climbed into bed early that Sunday morning. Even Glen's truck won't get me through those drifts if this storm keeps up, he worried, tossing sleeplessly and wondering when the next call would come.

He was not the only person awake that stormy night during the Blizzard of '68. Five miles away, Samuel Steiner stood at the window of his Kidron farmhouse, gazing through the blur of white to the drifts barricading his farm. Already, Sunday services were canceled for most of the area's 85 churches, including the congregation the Mennonite pastor served. And the snow was still coming down as thickly as ever. I've got to keep the drive open, Steiner thought. This could be the night.

While neighbors slumbered under layers of quilts and comforters, the storm muffled the tractor's hum, cloaked the glare of its headlights, and erased every path Samuel carved through the drifted lane. All night long, he drove the tractor in and out of the lane as the snow blower blew the accumulating snow over the banks. This lane could be the lifeline for his wife and unborn child, he realized.

As dawn began to push up the dark shades of night, Samuel Steiner saw that although he had managed to keep his lane open, Wenger Road had drifted shut. What'll I do, Lord? he wondered, picking up the phone to call his family doctor. I'll never get my wife to the hospital through those drifts.

"There's no way we can get to the hospital," he told Mrs. Eberly. "The snow must be waist high out on our road some places!"

"Well, we've got a problem," Mrs. Eberly replied. "You can't get to the hospital, and Dr. Eberly's stranded in a snowdrift on his way to another delivery. Maybe Dr. Lehman can help."

When Mrs. Eberly called Dr. Lehman, he assured her he'd try to find a way to get to the Steiners.

"But how are you going to get through?" Mrs. Eberly questioned. "No one is going anywhere around here, and anyone who tries gets hopelessly stuck."

"I'll find a way," Dr. Lehman promised determinedly.

As the rising sun unveiled a wonderland of glittering whiteness frosting every tree, barn, and meadow, a rumbling engine brought the Kidron town folk to their windows. *What kind of vehicle can plow through these roads?*

At the Steiner home, the little boys had been hustled outside to play in the snow. They watched incredulously as a fire engine rumbled up the lane. *The barn must be on fire, but where was the smoke?*

The crimson engine pulled up on the bank in front of the barn and stopped. The passenger door opened and a warmly dressed man climbed out into the snow, holding a black satchel in his gloved hands. Turning, he helped a woman down from the truck and strode toward the house.

"Why, it's Dr. Lehman!"

"Praise the Lord! You got here!" Samuel welcomed Dr. Lehman and Rebecca. "I was praying you'd find a way."

"Whatever it takes, we'll get here for you!" Dr. Lehman laughed, shedding his snowy coat and boots. "The fire truck was the biggest piece of equipment available, and we had to get through!"

"What a special baby!" the Steiner girls exclaimed a short time later when the nurse handed them a pink bundle. "We haven't had a baby girl in our family for over 12 years! She was born in a blizzard, delivered by a doctor who arrived on a fire engine, and they say her story'll be in the newspapers, too. What a *very* special baby!"

But Samuel Steiner thought Dr. Lehman was the special one, exerting such efforts to reach folks who weren't even his patients.

"How are the boys I stitched up some time ago?" Dr. Lehman asked as he pulled on his coat.

"Both of their cuts healed up as nice as can be," Samuel replied with a smile, referring to the tractor accidents two of his eight boys had in the last number of years. "Thanks to you and—"

"The kerosene!" Dr. Lehman finished as he headed for the door. "Boy, I've seen that stuff work so well I can almost recommend it. Almost. Someday I'd like to do a study on kerosene and find out how it works."

As the fire engine labored past the cheese factory a few moments later, Dr. Lehman felt a twinge of nostalgia. He fondly recalled the days he had driven his pony cart down this same road, hauling milk cans from their farm to the cheese factory and dreaming of becoming a fireman or a police officer.

"If only I could have seen this sight when I was a youngster!" he laughed. "I would have given my pocket knife to see myself riding down this road in a fire engine!"

"What are you going to be riding in next, Elton?" his wife asked him that afternoon.

"Well, I haven't ridden in a manure spreader yet," he replied.

"Elton Lehman! A manure spreader!"

"Yep, that's right," he said with a hint of a smile. "Doc Mayer told me that he couldn't get through a patient's lane, so the farmer came out with a horse–drawn manure spreader. The farmer must have been too busy to hitch up the horse to the buggy, so he just put a chair in the manure spreader he had been using. Mayer says he put his foot on a wheel, climbed inside, sat on the chair, and set his bag on his lap. 'At least he didn't spread me over the fields,' Mayer always says when he tells the story."

"You'd better buy yourself a Jeep," Phyllis urged, "or you'll find yourself on the back of a manure spreader one of these days!"

In the spring of 1971, Dr. Lehman headed for the Jeep dealership. "I should have gotten it sooner!" he said of his '71 Jeep Wagoneer the next winter. "I can sleep so much better just knowing I can get to my patients when they need me. It's the best tool I ever bought for my practice."

When the Great Blizzard of '78 blew in, he told Phyllis, "I don't know if I'd sleep all night if I didn't have a Jeep parked in the garage."

It was a mild, rainy afternoon when the Weather Service first began to issue winter storm warnings on Wednesday, January 25, 1978. By 9 p.m., forecasters were issuing blizzard warnings. By midnight, winds picked up and meteorologists knew a storm of unprecedented magnitude was in the making. But not even they foresaw the collision of two storm centers over Ohio in a dangerous and rare occurrence.

At 3 a.m., the storm fronts collided. Winds as high as 100 miles-per-hour slammed through Ohio, toppling billboards and mobile homes, crashing windows, and downing electrical lines as well as thousands of trees. All air, rail, and highway transportation came to a halt. For the first time in its history, the Ohio Turnpike closed down, stranding hundreds of motorists.

More than 12 million pounds of milk were dumped, since milk trucks could not reach the dairy farms and farmers had no surplus storage. Farm buildings collapsed, livestock perished, and people, too, lost their way and froze in the storm.

But the worst blizzard in Ohio's history didn't deter the arrival of infants. Babies have a timetable all their own. They arrive when they are ready, not waiting for weather to clear. Somehow, Thursday morning, Dr. Lehman's Jeep made it to the hospital through the blizzard in time to deliver a baby. That afternoon, Barb called. "I really hate to call you, Doc, but . . . ."

"That's all right. I can at least try to make it," he replied calmly. "I'll bring Nolan Byler, the med student who's been helping out at the clinic. Nolan told me if I go out on calls, he'd like to go along."

"It'll be good to have an extra pair of hands in case you get stuck, Doc."

"Oh, Barb, I've got the Jeep!" he laughed.

"I know," she replied, "but I've never seen a storm like this. And those Jeeps might be good, but they can't go everywhere a horse can."

"Like into a barn stall, for example?" he quipped.

So, Dr. Lehman put his Jeep into four-wheel drive and headed into the storm to pick up the med student and then on to Barb's. The drifted snow seemed to blot the roads from the countryside. At times it was almost impossible to see where the gravel road ended and the ditch began. The blizzard winds buffeted the Jeep, and the snow swirled around the car like a thick white scarf. Dr. Lehman struggled to see beyond the hood of his Jeep.

"Kind of a switch from the weather in Haiti, isn't it?" Dr. Lehman asked the fourth-year med student, who had just returned from a trip with Dr. Eberly.

"It's a switch, all right," Nolan agreed, wiping his fogged glasses with a handkerchief and pulling a cap over his curly hair. "But it just looks like home to me. Snow's our natural habitat in Minnesota."

"So, I hear you're thinking about coming to Mount Eaton to practice?" Dr. Lehman asked congenially, straining to see the road through the swirling veil of snow.

"I've been considering it," Nolan replied. "Dr. Eberly offered that we could both work out of his office for a while. Eventually he'd move to the basement office."

"I see. Well, we could sure use another doctor in Mount Eaton," Dr. Lehman acknowledged, "one who understands our

Amish patients. It's been hectic the last while. And I'd love to have more time with my family."

The two talked intermittently about the rigors of med school and the challenges of the profession. "Stay focused on where you come from and on where you're going," Dr Lehman encouraged.

"I have a question for you," Nolan said as the Jeep crept slowly through a countryside smothered in vast whiteness. "There's a lot of stress in a country doctor's life—just like today, trying to get to a patient through almost impossible circumstances. How do you manage the pressures that go with this occupation?"

Dr. Lehman drove silently, concentrating on the snow-covered road ahead. All he could see was an immense whiteness. A deep drift loomed ahead, and the doctor stepped on the gas pedal, sending the Jeep shooting through the snow and blasting icy pellets into the night.

Suddenly, a pair of headlights exploded through the curtain of snow and a snowplow flashed past so close it practically polished the Jeep's paint. Dr. Lehman whistled softly. "Are there angels out in blizzards, or what? We almost hit head on."

But there was no time to worry about the close call, for there were new problems to solve. The glow of the headlights revealed mountainous drifts blocking Harrison Road.

"No use trying that way. Maybe we can try Kidron Road."

The Jeep plunged through the drifts clogging Route 250 and then groaned to a stop. Dr. Lehman stared into the darkness. Not a track marred the mounds of white that buried the road ahead and obscured any trace of its existence. The men looked at each other. Dr. Lehman shook his head. "That's what you call closed. Not even a horse could tackle that road. I wonder about Kidron Road." He glanced left and then right. "Can't turn left, that's for sure, but maybe I can go right and then loop around."

The wind whipped the snow across the drifted roadway, making it impossible to see just how deep the drifts actually were. Backing up, he made a right turn onto Kidron Road and jammed the gas pedal to the floor as the engine roared and the tires spewed snow. The four-wheel-drive vehicle lunged into the drifts, grumbled, griped, slowed, and stopped.

Ahead, the snow lay even deeper, totally barricading the street. Jamming the Jeep into reverse, he spun the vehicle around and headed back the way they had come. Suddenly the Jeep pitched to the right and slowed to a stop, deep in a drifted ditch. He threw the transmission into reverse and then back into drive again, but the vehicle only grumbled and refused to budge. The wheels whirred and shrieked on the snowy slope, but the Jeep wouldn't even rock. It was hopelessly hung up in a deep snow bank.

"If I only had a shovel!" Dr. Lehman sighed, assessing the situation. "I've never needed one since I bought the Jeep. Maybe I should wake a farmer and see if he can pull me out with his horses," he muttered, climbing back inside the Jeep.

"I remember seeing the lights of a house back just a little ways," Nolan said, turning up his coat collar. "I'll run back and see if I can borrow a shovel."

The student pulled his hat over his ears and thrust his hands into his gloves, then headed into the storm. As Dr. Lehman watched him disappear, he realized his future colleague already demonstrated a servant's heart—a needed quality for a successful country practice in a world of house calls and around-the-clock emergencies.

Hunched against the wind, the dark figure emerged from the snowy curtain a moment later with a shovel over his shoulder. The two men shoveled and pushed until the Jeep finally climbed onto the road once again.

The Jeep had not gone far when the right wheel suddenly sank into the snow, pulling the Jeep deep into the ditch again. The icy wind pelted his face with icy bits of frozen snow as Dr. Lehman surveyed the buried Jeep. Not even a shovel could help this time, he realized.

"Well, I guess we'll have to wake another farmer," he decided. "I'm guessing we'll need a couple teams of horses to get us out of this fix."

The nearest Amish farmer gladly hitched up his horses and chained them to the Jeep, but the vehicle wouldn't move. No matter how hard the horses worked, the vehicle barely budged.

Dr. Lehman thanked the farmer and offered to pay him for his efforts. The farmer waved the money aside. "I'm not takin' your money, Doc. You're out here in the storm trying to get to someone in need. I'm not takin' a cent from you. Just wish I could-a pulled you out."

"I suppose a snowplow will come along toward morning," Dr. Lehman remarked, settling back in his seat for a nap.

As the two doctors sat in the stranded vehicle wondering how to survive until morning, they noticed a faint glow in the distance. Soon, a pair of headlights and a flashing yellow light pierced through the snow.

"Talk about a welcome sight!" Dr. Lehman laughed as a salt truck pulled alongside the Jeep. The driver hopped out of the truck, fastened a chain to the Jeep, and slowly eased the vehicle back onto the snow-covered road once again.

Soon, Dr. Lehman found a road he could get through and pulled into Barb's lane. "What's wrong, Doc, do you need a horse?" Barb asked when he told her what had taken so long. "Mr. Troyer here got in with his horse and buggy a long while ago, and even his baby beat you here."

"The baby came?"

"Yep. Blizzard babies don't wait, do they?"

Later that evening, Dr. Lehman headed the Jeep back toward Mount Eaton. "I don't think I ever answered your question, Nolan, about handling stress in our profession. A number of my patients have a motto on their walls with the simple prayer you've probably often heard, 'God grant me the serenity to accept the things I cannot change, the courage to change the things I can, and the wisdom to know the difference.'

"Nolan, if I can do something to help a situation, I give every ounce of energy I've got. For instance, one of my greatest challenges has been reaching my patients in any kind of weather, as you can see. I've done everything in my power to be there for them. I've arranged for snowplows and loaders to open the road for me, and for a fire engine to take me through another storm. I rode in the back of four-wheel-drive dump trucks, in bobsleds, and buggies, and now I've bought a Jeep.

"We tried our best to reach my patient in time tonight, but we were battling elements beyond our control. And so, when we came up against a circumstance we couldn't change, like the storm here, we calmly accepted it and went on. They say it is not one's circumstances that cause stress, so much as one's reaction to those circumstances.

"During my tenure as assistant deputy coroner," he continued, "I've seen how the inability to accept crises often drives some folks to suicide. And then, on the other hand, I've seen some of my patients quietly resign themselves to the most heartbreaking tragedies a person can experience."

The next day, the blizzard winds whipped the drifts higher than ever, and Dr. Lehman had a patient that needed to get to the hospital. Even my Jeep won't get through, he realized. Perhaps I could call the township. So Dr. Lehman did, and arranged for a snowplow to open the way to the hospital, all 15 miles from Mount Eaton to Massillon.

Saturday came and went, and the storm surged on, piling more snow over the paralyzed region. Mullet Coal Company's large loaders tried to carve paths through the mountainous drifts, but the winds blew the roads shut again. No one is going anywhere tonight, Dr. Lehman thought as he stood looking out the window that Saturday night and as Phyllis finished another chapter of *The Long Winter*.

Suddenly, he felt little hands tug at his pant legs. "I want to kiss you good night, Daddy!"

He picked up his daughter and kissed her cheek. "Good night, honey."

"It's so stormy out," Brenda observed at his side. "I hope you don't have to go out tonight, Daddy, like Laura's Pa did."

"At least we don't have to carry in wood like Pa," Brent remarked. "And Daddy has no beard to get all frosty white!"

If the power goes out, we'll wish for my patients' wood stoves and oil lamps, Elton thought as the children headed for bed. The power is already out in some parts of the state.

After tucking the children into bed and listening to their prayers, he sat at the fireside for a long while, watching the flames that seemed to leap tauntingly toward the wind, howling and shrieking down the chimney. As he sat listening to the cry of the storm, he seemed to be waiting for the call he knew would come.

The wind howled around the houses of Mount Eaton, smothering the countryside in the heaviest snow the villagers had ever seen. His patients curled up under afghans at their firesides hoping no emergency would send anyone out in such a storm. But at the Lehman house, the phone was ringing.

It was Barb. "Doc, we got a woman all set to go."

"What? Who on earth could get to your house through all this snow, Barb? Nothing's been moving up this way for hours!"

"Mike Miller brought his wife in. *Ach* my, they had such a time of it in that buggy, I tell you. Why, it's been days since the storm started anyhow, and he thought for sure the road would be open past our house. But just before he got here, the horse got stuck in snow up to its belly."

"You've got drifts as high as a horse's stomach on your road?"

"That's what they say. Three feet deep, I'd say. Well, anyhow, Mike's poor horse couldn't move back or forth, so Mike got out of the buggy and shoveled a path to the field since it wasn't as deep there. Then when he got the buggy to our lane, the snow-plow had piled up a huge mountain of snow, and so he was shoveling again. Poor man. You can imagine he was half frozen when he stumbled into the house. Why, it's way below freezing out there! Well, anyways, Doc, we need you here now. That baby's coming."

"But Barb! There are 36 inches of snow on your road! If a horse couldn't get through on its own, I'll never make it. Right now it's snowing and blowing so hard I can hardly see the trees right outside my window."

"It's a bad storm, Doc," the midwife agreed. "Almost worse than the winter of '68."

"Barb, I don't see how I can get through, but I'm going to try."

As Dr. Lehman warmed his hands next to Bill's wood stove later, Barb walked into the room with a surprised smile on her face. "Well, Doc, I'm impressed. Your Jeep got you through those drifts, and you didn't even have to get out and shovel, and the man with the horse did! I'm impressed.

"But Doc," she went on. "Your work's not over. I've heard several men brought their wives into the area on snowmobiles so they could be close. *Ach* yes, desperate fathers and determined doctors always find a way, don't they, Doc?"

"They have no choice, Barb, because blizzard babies don't wait!"

17.

Coroner Duty

"What do you expect to find tonight, Doc?" Glen Shoup questioned as Dr. Lehman guided his Jeep through the dark countryside.

Dr. Lehman shivered involuntarily, adjusting the heat on the dashboard. "Suicides are the most difficult for any coroner, but the gunshot cases make it worse. It won't be a pleasant experience, I'm warning you. I don't even like to go out to suicide scenes by myself. That's why I wake my good buddy, Glen, at 1:00 in the morning to ride along with me."

"I often wondered why you ever took the position of assistant deputy coroner, Doc, as busy as you are and as unpleasant a task as it is," Dr. Lehman's friend revealed.

"Believe me, it's not because I enjoy the job or because I need something to keep me busy, but I've done it as a service to the Amish community."

"We're not heading to an Amish place tonight, are we?"

"Nope. I don't know if Hank was a churchgoer of any kind or not," he replied, eyeing the farm just ahead eerily illuminated by red and blue flashes of light.

As Dr. Lehman stepped into the barn, the scent of hay tickled his nostrils. He could hear the cows lowing and stamping restlessly in their stanchions below. A naked light bulb suspended from a dusty beam illuminated a tractor, hay wagons, and a combine. The sheriffs in their black hats weaved through the barn toward Dr. Lehman and his companion, their footsteps echoing hollowly across the worn, wooden floor. The last fragments of conversation faded into dusty cobwebs as a tense, sober silence gripped the barn.

As a cluster of men stepped aside, Dr. Lehman saw the soles of the farmer's muddy work boots, the overall-clad body, and the rifle sprawled across the wood floor of the barn. The body lay where it had fallen when the bullet ripped through the neck. No one had moved it since. No one was permitted to move a body without the coroner's permission.

Gently, Dr. Lehman nudged the body, rolling it onto its back. A piece of tablet paper protruded from the chest pocket of the blood-splattered overalls. Slowly, he reached down and pulled out the folded note. There was silence except for a faint rustle as he unfolded the paper.

"Kenny gets the tractors. Burt can have the cows. Jenny gets the car," he read silently. "Always did like the pastor at the little white church, have him say a prayer for me if he knows a good one."

And that was it. Dr. Lehman handed the letter to the sheriff. The scene swam before him and his stomach churned as the doctor filled out the forms and then asked Glen to accompany him to the most difficult part of the entire task—talking to the farmer's family.

"Things have been going bad, and it looks as though we'll lose the farm," Burt shared brokenly in the farmhouse kitchen. "We knew Dad was down about losing the family farm, but we never figured he'd actually . . . ." his voice died away. "If only . . . ."

As Dr. Lehman and his companion drove away into the night, their thoughts were too tangled in the scene behind to talk. The heavy darkness seemed to wrap its shroud around the Jeep as the men drove through the black countryside.

Then, finally, Glen spoke. "Doc," he asked, "what drives someone to do a thing like that? I mean, lots of folks have tough times."

"Good question, Glen," Dr. Lehman sighed. "I don't really know, but a guy would have to be feeling like there's not much left to live for. You know, we all have our down days and I suppose the thought of suicide flashes through most minds at some point, but a person can't dwell on those thoughts, because thoughts lead to actions."

As the men drove on in silence, Dr. Lehman thought of other coroner cases he had officiated. He'd seen other patients pull through times that were more devastating than the loss of a farm. What makes the difference? he wondered.

Dr. Lehman found it difficult to sleep some nights after returning from death scenes and morgues. And if *he* could barely sleep after he tended the child who was accidentally mowed over by a garden tractor, how did the family and the driver of the mower ever survive? And what about the Showalters, who lost half their family in a tragic accident? How could they continue to go about the daily tasks in a house that was so filled with memories, yet so empty and still?

Perhaps the Showalter tragedy etched such a deep impression onto his heart because it was his first coroner case. Or perhaps it was because the crash occurred right outside his bedroom window. Either way, he would never forget February 4, 1973.

It was late that particular Saturday evening when Dr. Lehman and Phyllis returned home from a birthday celebration for Elton's brother Dave. As Alice pulled on her coat, she reported that the Lehman children were sound asleep. Earlier, they had taken their customary walk up the sidewalk to Hilltop Market for an ice cream bar and then had a great time playing games and reading stories. A patient had called, and she had been able to answer the question satisfactorily. Before long, the lights were out in the Lehman home in the town square.

In Wilmot, just East of Mount Eaton, a light glowed on the porch of the Showalter home where the mother waited for her boys to come home.

"It might be late, Mom," Elwood and Eugene had advised. "After the evangelist is done preaching, he's gonna talk to the young folks at a youth rally, so don't worry if it gets late."

At home, Joan Showalter listened to the clock striking midnight.

Just across town, six Swartzentruber Amish youth guzzled another round of drinks at the Golden Buzz Saloon. By the time the gang stumbled out to the car that an employer had helped them buy, the driver had pledged to cruise through Mount Eaton at 90 miles an hour, no matter what.

In the second floor of the Lehman home, lights shone from the window of the room where Glen Shoup and his friend Eli Showalter were on their knees praying for Elwood and Eugene. All evening, Eli could not shake the burden on his heart for his younger siblings.

Meanwhile, his brothers had responded to the evangelist's invitation to rededicate their lives to Christ at the youth rally and were on their way home. On their way, Elwood and Eugene planned to drop off two friends, who had caught a ride home with them. Stopping in Sugarcreek, they left Pastor Albert's son Myron at his home. With Eugene at the wheel of the white Maverick, Elwood in the center, and a 15-year-old friend Adrian Schlabach on the passenger's side of the front seat, the three boys headed north toward Mount Eaton around 12:30 a.m.

As they approached the intersection of 241 and 250 alongside the Lehman home, the traffic light in the square of Mount Eaton turned yellow and the Maverick coasted to a stop.

A right turn would have taken the Showalter boys home to Wilmot, but they were dropping off Adrian first. When the light turned green, the little Maverick turned left onto Route 250. At that instant, the carload of Amish youth flew into Mount Eaton at nearly 90 miles an hour, sailing beneath the red light and exploding into the rear of the white Maverick. The car's gas tank erupted, turning the Maverick into a flaming bomb as it flew down the road, crashed into a tree and telephone pole, and wrapped around them.

As the ripping and crunching of metal splintered the silence of the night, Glen Shoup dashed to the second floor window of his apartment. The whole road was aflame with the gas spilled from the smashed, blazing car. "Let's go, Eli!" he shouted and bolted down the steps.

Downstairs, Dr. Lehman leaped from his bed and flung back the curtain of the window facing the village square. Scanning the scene, he observed the crushed, torched vehicle. Just beyond, he spotted the glowing taillights from a second vehicle that had struck the side of a neighbor's house. Instantly, adrenaline surged through his body.

"Call an ambulance!" he yelled, throwing on a shirt and grabbing his satchel.

As Glen ran down the road, he noticed three forms writhing in the orange glow inside the car. *God, help us!* he thought. *Someone's got to get them now.*

Taking a deep breath, he yanked open the driver's door of the Maverick. Smoke belched from the car, stinging Glen's eyes as he reached into the flames and wrestled the driver from the burning car. The flames roared in his ears and Glen knew he had only seconds to free the two passengers. Not stopping to think what would happen if the gas tank exploded, Glen dove back into the car and yanked out the center occupant, ignoring the excruciating pain of his scorched palms.

I *can't* go back in again! Glen cried, laying the boy on the road and watching flames spew sparks into the night. Gingerly, he touched his blistered palms. But I can't let the poor boy roast. *God, help me.*

Yanking the cuffs of his shirt sleeves down over his blistered hands, Glen plunged into the flames again and groped through the smoke for the last passenger. The boy slapped frantically at the flames burning his hair and devouring his shirt as Glen grabbed him and yanked. But the boy wouldn't budge. His leg's pinched between the seat and the door that was smashed against the tree, Glen realized in horror. Agonizing shrieks pierced the air as Glen backed out of the scorching furnace of suffocating smoke and flames. "Don't let me burn to death!" the trapped passenger screamed.

Dr. Lehman ran down the road dodging pools of burning gasoline and scanned the scene. He spotted the two bodies sprawled on the grassy strip next to the burning vehicle. If that gas tank explodes, they're gone, he realized, sniffing the air laden with gas fumes and smoke. Gently, he eased the boys back from the searing blaze.

Flames from the burning vehicle leaped into the night sky, casting eerie shadows across the motionless bodies. Dr. Lehman knelt next to the victims and searched for a pulse. If the flames were that intense, their lungs will be damaged by the smoke and the heat, he thought.

Treat the most severely injured first, Dr. Lehman reminded himself, scanning the scene. He noticed several figures walking around near the car that had hit the house. They're probably not as critically injured as these two, he thought. Holding a finger over an artery on the boy's neck, he thought he could detect the faintest throb.

A burly truck driver ran up to scene just as Glen emerged once again from the burning car shouting, "I can't get him! He's stuck, I can't get him out!"

"Let's try one more time," the trucker yelled. "We can't let him burn. Just one more time."

Running to the passenger's side where the car was molded around the telephone pole and tree, the two men tried to lift the boy through the window, but his foot was thoroughly wedged between the seat and the door.

"Just pull," the trucker shouted. "If we leave him, he'll die anyway!"

"God help us!" Glen cried. Smoke billowed around their faces as the two men each grabbed the boy under an arm and strained to pull him free. A crunching, ripping sound filled the air, and the body slowly began to ease out of the window. As they carried the boy away from the car, Glen noticed the zippered leather boot had been ripped off of the boy's foot.

The angry roar of shooting flames, wailing sirens, and the smell of burning rubber filled the night. The flashing lights of police cars, fire trucks, and ambulances illuminated the mangled skeleton of the car in a red, pulsating glow. Firefighters trained streams of water on the blackened, twisted Maverick, and clouds of steam and smoke bellowed from the hissing car.

"Does anyone know who these boys are?" Dr. Lehman asked the growing crowd, not recognizing that the charred victims were his patients and members of his church.

A bystander ventured, "Some lady from Wilmot drives through here every day in a little white car."

Hearing the words "white car," Eli Showalter shoved through the crowd. "My mom owns a white car," he whispered hoarsely, bending down to examine the charred faces of the bodies lying on the road. Recognizing a scrap of shirt, Eli cried, "Oh my God! These are my brothers!" and his knees buckled as he crumbled to the ground.

Glen leaped forward and caught his friend. He and a bystander led Eli to the steps of Spector's Store, where they helped him lie down.

While the medics eased the victims onto stretchers and loaded them into the waiting ambulances, Dr. Lehman gave the paramedics a quick rundown of the patients' conditions.

As the last ambulance drove off into the night, neighbors stood in a silent cluster staring at the blackened, twisted metal.

"Three of the boys from church were in the accident," Dr. Lehman told his wife. "Eli Showalter will tell his folks, but someone really ought to call the Schlabachs and tell them about Adrian."

"I can call them," Phyllis offered. "Was anyone else hurt?"

"They took five boys to the hospital from the other car. I suspect at least one had head injuries, but mostly there were cuts and likely some broken bones. All six should have gone, but one refused." Dr. Lehman rolled up his sleeves and scrubbed his bloody, soot-blackened arms while he spoke. "I feel like I ought to run up to the hospital, now that I'm the assistant deputy coroner."

As he walked out to his car, he eyed the five-foot strip of grass and sidewalk separating the children's bedrooms from the road. "It's time to move," he muttered. "This is no place to raise a family."

Nothing could be done to help the Showalter boys, Dr. Lehman discovered to his sorrow. The next morning, Joan and Ken Showalter were informed that both of their sons were dead.

When Dr. Lehman examined Adrian Schlabach, the 15-year-old boy from church, he discovered the hair had burned off the back of his head. The youngster's shoulders were scorched and his hands were blistered from trying to extinguish the flames on his head. In addition, there were symptoms of head injuries.

"It appears at the time of the accident, your son was asleep with his head slouched against the back of his seat," Dr. Lehman told the Schlabachs when they arrived. "And that's what saved him. With an impact like that from the rear, if Adrian had been awake and sitting up, the blow would have snapped and broken his neck."

"Do you think he'll pull through?" the parents worried.

"He needs attention tonight," Dr. Lehman declared, examining the injured youngster. "Tomorrow might be too late. With his head injuries, he really should have the specialized care of a neurosurgeon." Dr Lehman closed his eyes and scratched his head in concentration. *Lord, what do I do?*

Suddenly, his eyes popped open. "I'll tell you what. I know a neurosurgeon over in Canton I can call. I might be able to arrange to have Adrian transferred to Timken Mercy Hospital."

"Oh, could you please!"

"I'll do what I can. Two tragedies in one youth group is devastating enough. We can't have a third."

"Sure, send him up," the neurosurgeon replied without hesitation when Dr. Lehman explained the situation. "I'll take care of the boy."

The ambulance pulled away from the hospital and Dr. Lehman walked slowly down the hall. He had been to the morgue before, but never on coroner duty. Shivering in the chilly air, Dr. Lehman needed every ounce of resolve he could muster to open the door to the morgue. How he longed to dash back up the hall to find his patients, where he could bandage their wounds and prescribe treatments for their burns. But his patients were here.

The door creaked open and he stood in the entrance for a moment, studying the pair of carts draped in white sheets. A hundred thoughts seemed to surge through his mind.

I can't do this. These boys are my patients. They're from my church. He thought of the Showalters who had driven away from the hospital as Adrian's stretcher was lifted into the ambulance. How are they going to survive this terrible tragedy? Two sons in one night!

And then he thought of Pastor Albert. He'd be able to steer his parishioners through this horrible nightmare. After all, Albert had lost a wife, child, brother, and father all in nine months' time. But how will the Showalters ever be able to forgive the drunken driver? he wondered, studying the sheet-covered stretchers.

He jumped as footsteps echoed through the hallway behind him. "Ah, there you are, Elton," Dr. Questel murmured. "I was looking for you. Not a nice initiation, is it? We may as well get it over with. The hearse will soon be here."

Dr. Lehman glanced over the report the senior coroner handed him. "Eugene Wade Showalter, 16, junior at Fairless High School. Elwood Dean Showalter, 15, a sophomore at Fairless High School."

"We'll do Elwood, the younger one, first." Dr. Questel drew back the sheet to reveal a head of singed, softly waving hair above a boyish face. He pointed to the shriveled nubbins of ears on either side of the head. "You'll find under intense heat the cartilage of the ear shrinks to a small knob–like ball. And there, see how the skin is peeling off his face?"

Elwood, Doc sighed, looking down at the charred face. Your life was ahead of you. Why did those boys have to drink tonight?

"Just what I suspected," Dr. Questel remarked, manipulating the head. "See how the head flops from side to side? Clear evidence of a broken neck. It's the kind of injury you'd expect when a person is hit from behind at a high rate of speed. The head jerks back on impact and the neck snaps. Now, you try it. I want you to learn the feel of it."

Taking a deep breath, Dr. Lehman took the youth's head in his hands.

"Put a hand on either side of the head, like so. There. Now swivel and tilt the head. It feels real loose and wobbly, doesn't it?"

It did, Dr. Lehman agreed, resting the head back onto the sheet.

"Now, on the form under cause of death, jot in 'broken neck,'" Dr. Questel explained after examining the rest of the corpse for other injuries and draping the sheet back over it.

Walking over to the second cart, Dr. Questel lifted the corner of the sheet exposing the scorched body. "This was the driver. His hair was burned off his head."

"I don't suppose they'll be able to view him," Dr. Lehman shuddered.

But Mr. Desvoignes, the elderly Mount Eaton funeral director, had other plans. "We're going to view these boys the way they are," he insisted. "I want youngsters to see first-hand the horrible consequences of driving under the influence of alcohol." As predicted, the brothers' funeral deeply touched the community.

While paging through the newspaper some time later, Dr. Lehman read that the driver of the speeding car was found guilty of involuntary manslaughter and drunken driving. "Thirty days in jail and three years probation! What a slap on the wrist for snuffing out two lives!"

"But think of all the suffering he's going through, all the pain of regret and rejection," Phyllis reminded him. "It'll haunt the fellow for rest of his life."

The Showalters would not sue the driver, he knew, nor would Adrian, despite the trauma and pain the accident caused. The Schlabachs and Showalters believed in restoration instead of revenge. And their forgiveness, Dr. Lehman knew, was a key to their own healing. But what a task it would be.

"I just thank God my boys were ready to go," Joan shared with those expressing sympathy. "Dwelling on the positive side of the tragedy helps me to survive. They were ready to go, and I know where they're at."

"I've seen it again and again," Dr. Lehman shared with Glen Shoup. "At death scenes and in the morgue, I've observed first-hand how folks who don't have hope are tempted to end it all when difficult moments come. And yet, I've seen others face the most heart-rending circumstances by drawing on the grace God provides in those hours."

18.

A Dog in Doc's Bed

How did I ever find this little corner of Eden? Dr. Lehman wondered as his Jeep threaded up a blacktopped driveway just a stone's throw from the clinic. Every time I head up this lane, I marvel how we ever got this property in the first place, he thought, cresting a grassy knoll and parking in the circle drive in front of the stone, L-shaped home.

Walking through his house, he glanced at the view framed by the plate glass windows. Prettier than a painting, he thought, looking across the wooded hills, plowed fields, and farmsteads in the valley below. Sliding open the glass door, he stepped out onto the deck.

Dr. Lehman marveled at this piece of paradise tucked away just a short walk from his office. He and Phyllis could sit on the deck at the end of the day and take in the sunset without another soul in sight while the children played to their hearts' content. Thank God we didn't build a house on the corner of Harrison Road and Route 241, he thought, looking out over the valley. God knew I needed this quiet, hidden retreat at the end of a long day.

The day he had changed his mind about building a house on Harrison Road had been an invigorating spring day much like this one, when the sun gently woke the tulip bulbs from their long winter slumber.

"Let's fly your kite over at the field where we are going to build our new house," Dr. Lehman suggested that spring afternoon. Though the small yard offered no place to fly a kite, there was plenty of space on the acreage he had just purchased. Besides, he and his son would have a few moments alone, uninterrupted by the patients who always dropped by when they spotted their doctor outside the white Victorian house.

"I can't wait until we build the new house. Then you can go outside with me every day without people stopping to talk to you about their problems," Brent announced as Elton parked his car at the edge of the field.

"I can't wait either, Son," his father remarked, thinking of the safe haven he and Phyllis would create for their family away from the loaded semi trucks that roared passed Brent's tricycle on the sidewalk. They'd build a quiet retreat where they could sit together on the deck and watch the sunset away from the gaze and intrusion of every passerby. Yes, the new lot was a start toward more family time together, he hoped as he watched the kite lift into the air.

"Higher, Daddy, higher!" Brent shouted as the kite dipped and soared in the sky as they ran together across the field. The tension of the doctor's heart unwound and disappeared into the breeze as the kite string slipped through his fingers.

I've got to spend more afternoons like this with my son, he realized. Maybe after the house is built I can go out and play with Brent without every sick person around Mount Eaton stopping by for a free diagnosis.

Running through the field with his son at his side, the father's spirits soared with the kite that strained to reach the clouds.

"Look at all those carriages, Daddy!" Brent called, gesturing to a caravan of buggies winding down the road in their direction.

"Did you ever see so many in all your life? Where'd they all come from, Dad?"

"Must have had church up there somewhere," Dr. Lehman replied as the clopping of horses' hooves grew louder. "They're probably coming home from their church service."

As the buggies approached, the occupants recognized the doctor's car parked at the edge of the field. The whole line of horses and carriages drew to a stop.

"Howdy, Doc! *Vee gehts?*" an elderly man called, waving his black hat.

"Nice day out, ain't?" another man called.

"Your boy there's a-growin', Doc. Next time we see him, he'll have one of them stethoscopes hangin' 'round his neck!" a bearded man laughed.

"Hey, Doc, by the way, them pills you gave for my throat, my stomach won't take 'em . . . ."

"My wife fell the other day," another patient inserted, "and her knee flamed up . . . ."

As the last buggy drove away, the doctor looked down at the forlorn little boy sprawled beside the wilted kite in the grass. In that instant, he made his decision. Tomorrow, I'll go search for another building site—one secluded enough to protect my children and those few moments we have together.

When he first spotted the quiet, isolated hill beyond his clinic, he wondered why he had never noticed it before. As he climbed to the top of the knoll, he gazed out over one of the loveliest panoramic views he had ever seen. For hours, he sat on that grassy hill behind the clinic, studying the pastoral valleys, streams, patches of fields, and belts of woodland that lay to the north of Mount Eaton, with only a distant road in sight.

I can't believe no one else has built here, he thought, watching the shadows shift with the setting sun. This is where I want to build our house, he decided. With a view like this, we must have lots of picture windows and a deck or two. We'll finish a walk-out basement apartment for Mother, and, of course, we'll plant flowers and ground cherries and pumpkins, he planned.

When he inquired about purchasing the land, he soon discovered why it still lay vacant. "I'm sorry to tell you that there are mine shafts under the property," the owner told Dr. Lehman. "It's not fit to build on."

"Would you mind if I'd have someone check where the shafts are located?" the doctor asked, not ready to give up his dream.

"At your expense," the owner replied.

The contractor discovered tunnels 12 feet below the surface at the ideal depth for building. "That will never work," he warned.

"Try drilling test holes to the west," Dr. Lehman suggested.

"No tunnels there!" the contractor announced several days later. "You will have your house."

On that secluded hill, near the clinic yet out of sight, the Lehmans savored a little piece of Eden those few short minutes Dr. Lehman was at home.

I haven't had much time to spend with Bev since we got back from Hawaii, Dr. Lehman thought, as he stood on the deck of his home overlooking the picturesque valley that spring afternoon. I think I'll take her along to the nursing home with me today. She might be young, but the residents love her little songs.

"Where's my little sunshine?" Dr. Lehman asked as Phyllis joined him on the deck. "I thought I'd take her with me to the nursing home."

"The last I saw Bev, she was playing with the new lamb," Phyllis replied. "I tell you, Elton, that girl's a little Mexican jumping bean. I don't know what I'd do if we still lived out there by the road. I know I wouldn't have a moment's rest! She's always up to something—which reminds me, your mother said when she answered her phone the other day, she heard a childish voice saying, 'Hello, Mrs. Lehman. This is Doctors Hospital. Your son says the reason you can't smell is because of your nerves. Good bye.'"

"That's my girl," the doctor laughed as he watched his youngest daughter skipping across the yard shouting, "Daddy! Daddy! You're home!"

He caught his little girl in a big hug. "I haven't seen much of my little sunshine. Where've you been hiding?"

"Oh, Daddy, I wasn't hiding. I was just down comforting the baby lamb we got from Nancy 'cause she's lonely without her Momma."

"How would my girl like to go away with Daddy this afternoon?" he asked. "I'm going to visit some nice folks at the nursing home, and you can ride along if you want to."

"Oh yes, Daddy! Yes! I wanna go!" Bev was impressed and felt very important. Usually Brent or Brenda were given the privilege of accompanying Dad on calls. Brenda often told her sister how she would sit at Doctors Hospital's information desk and color while Dad made his rounds. The kind operator at the hospital desk let Brenda put through the incoming phone calls, even allowing her to answer in-house calls once in a while. And it was always Brenda that Dad took to the nursing homes to sing for the folks. Beverly could sing, too, the folks would find out. Why, she could even make up her own songs! Wouldn't Dad be impressed!

A few minutes later, the doctor and his little daughter rode down the drive in the Jeep.

"Oh, Daddy, we had the grandest time when you were in Hawaii. Nancy's dog slept in your bed with us," Bev confided as the two of them headed down Harrison Road toward the retirement home.

"What! The dog slept in my bed when I was gone?" The right tires of the Jeep crunched briefly over the gravel on the side of the road, and then swerved onto the macadam again. "I thought I told Nancy I didn't want her dog sleeping in my bed! Why, I really didn't want that creature in the house at all!"

"It's okay, Daddy. Missy is the cleanest little dog you ever did see, and brave, too." Bev bounced up and down on the passenger's seat, her little face peering up over the door through the passenger window as she spoke. "Why, she kills groundhogs that are much bigger than her and drags them up to the house. And when we ate dinner, Missy sat by my chair and I dropped food right from my spoon into her mouth and . . . ."

Dr. Lehman's face turned a shade of green, and he dug his fingernails into the steering wheel.

"And Daddy, Brent ran around the house barefoot in the snow and wasn't even cold. We dared him to because he wanted us to, but Nancy said once is enough, and we ate tacos, and Nancy didn't know how to run the microwave, but Brent said, 'If we can teach Daddy to run the microwave, we can teach you.' And we teached her how. Daddy, I wish you would go to Hawaii again, and Nancy and her dog would stay with us. Oh, we had the grandest time!"

"I'm glad you had a grand time, Bev." The doctor steered the Jeep into a parking space at the nursing home and made a mental note to check with Nancy about the dog in his bed and Brent's barefoot capers in the snow.

"Let's go see how all our friends in the nursing home are doing today. Remember to shake their hands and to speak up, because some of the old folks can't hear too well. Now, let me tie your hat."

With Bev's little hand in one of his and the satchel in the other, Dr. Lehman walked into the nursing home for a routine checkup on the residents there.

The wrinkled faces lit up with delighted smiles when they saw Dr. Lehman's little daughter. "Well, you brought your girl along, how nice," the patients crooned in their quivering voices, extending shaky hands to the child and watching her with fascination.

While the doctor held a stethoscope to their chests, Bev entertained the folks with her prattle and the made-up ditties which she sang to them. On that day, Sunday school choruses about David and Goliath alternated with songs about a brave little dog fighting groundhogs, and barefoot boys in the snow. "And the little dog ran around and around, and the groundhog came tumbling down!"

"Okay, thanks Bev. That's enough songs for now," the doctor said, turning to question a resident in a wheelchair. "So, who was the first president you can remember?" he asked, testing his patient's mental alertness.

"We-e-ell, I can remember when Cleveland ran for office." The dim eyes brightened. "The first Democrat president since the Civil War. Uncle Jumbo, his relatives called him. He often said, 'Honor lies in honest toil,' and I never forgot that."

"You can remember back to President Cleveland's presidency in the last two decades of the 1800s!" Dr. Lehman exclaimed. "Well, I declare. That was a long way back. I suppose you remember McKinley then, too?"

"Oh, yes," the man's face lit up and his humped form straightened as he looked up at the doctor. "Why sure, I remember McKinley. Our family went to watch the parade when he came to Canton! Quite the excitement, I tell you."

Dr. Lehman examined several lumps on the man's arm as he spoke. "That's interesting. You know, just the other night I just saw a documentary on McKinley and his entourage when he came to Canton after he was elected president. One of the guard's horses in the parade stumbled, and the rider broke his leg."

"That's true! I saw it!" the white-haired gentleman exclaimed, nearly falling out of his wheelchair in excitement. "I was right there when that happened and I saw that with my own eyes!"

"Well isn't that something!" the doctor remarked. "You actually saw the parade and the stumbling horse. A piece of history."

"Let's see," the patient began as Dr. Lehman rose to leave. "The last time you were here you were getting ready to go to Hawaii for a meeting, weren't you? Did you have a good trip?"

"Yes, pretty good, thanks," Dr. Lehman nodded, slipping his stethoscope into his satchel. "It was a very informative convention."

"And what did you do, little girl, when your daddy and mommy went to Hawaii?" the man asked turning to Beverly.

"Oh, me and the dog, we slept in Daddy's bed." The doctor winced as his daughter babbled on. "She's such a nice doggie and even catches groundhogs, and I slept with her, but Brent, he didn't want to sleep in his bed 'cause he's setting the world record for sleeping out of bed the longest."

Dr. Lehman grabbed his daughter's hand. "Uh, good night, Mr. Smith. Say good night to the nice gentleman, Beverly." His face reddened as the residents' chuckles faded in the distance.

As father and daughter walked out of the building, many smiling faces and waving hands followed them.

"Bring your daughter along again next time!"

"Good by, little girl! Come back and sing for us some more!"

"That music really knocked me, Dad," Bev announced as the two got into the car. "Did it knock you?"

"Yes, Beverly, it did. In fact, it almost knocked me over."

As the two drove back down the country road, the doctor asked, "Bev, what do you want to do this summer?"

"Oh, I s'pose take swimming lessons and go to Camp Loryville. Are we going again this year, Daddy?"

"So you like going to Laurelville. Yes, I suppose we'll go for music camp and the week for medical workers. Would you like to invite some children from the city to come stay with us for a week again this summer?"

"Yes! And we could show them what cows look like, 'cause they don't know, and show them how cows give milk and horses give cider, and they could see the goats at Nancy's, and we can take them to Sunday school."

"I want our children to see how folks in other parts of the world live," Dr. Lehman often told Phyllis. "I want to reach out to those who have less." Perhaps someday, he'd take his children to visit a developing country. Until then, maybe they could invite exchange students to stay in their home. Selfishness was not a part of his vocabulary, and he didn't want it to be a part of his children's, either. It looked as though he didn't need to worry about Bev. She was so generous, she'd even share her bed with a dog.

"Give to the world the best you have, and the best will come back to you," Dr. Lehman and Phyllis believed.

When Dr. Lehman walked into the office after the visit to the nursing home, Nancy was pulling charts for the office calls the following day.

"Bev told me this afternoon that they had the grandest time while we were in Hawaii, and she wants us to go back again," he remarked, leafing through the day's mail.

"I suppose she had lots of stories to tell." The receptionist glanced at him warily.

"Yes, she did. She told all the residents in the nursing home that she and the dog that caught groundhogs slept in my bed while I was gone."

Nancy laughed shakily and pulled another chart. "Actually, Doc, we didn't *bring* the dog to bed with us. She's just so used to sleeping with me that she'd hop in sometime during the night, and Bev found out, so she wanted to join us, too. I suppose you heard about Brent running around in the snow barefooted, too."

"Yes."

"He kept wanting me to dare him to run around the house in the snow in his bare feet. I really didn't think he'd do it, but he did and claimed he wasn't a bit cold. He wondered if he should do it again, but I told him I thought once was enough. You have good kids, Doc, really. Not a bit of a problem. I scarcely found anything out from Brenda. When she wasn't doing homework, she had her nose in a book. It was fun, really. Any time you want to head back to Hawaii, my dog and I will be glad to look after the children."

"No chance of that real soon," the doctor slit an envelope and pulled out a letter. "Phyllis has been dreaming of a trip to Hawaii for years, but I don't think she'll talk about going again for a long time."

"Why is that?"

"Well, there was a record rainfall on the island while we were there. In fact, it rained every single day. The only nice pictures we got were postcards. But that's life. You take what comes. There's no use getting upset over things that can't be changed."

"Like dogs in one's bed?"

"Yes, like dogs in my bed."

19.

COURT ORDER

D r. Lehman could hear the quiver of distress in the caller's voice when he answered the phone one spring Sunday afternoon.

"Syl Yoder here, Doc. We got us a problem. Don't know if you remember us or not. You were our doctor before we moved out here to Mill Creek a couple years back. I'm Sim's Sammy's Syl."

"Sure, Sam Yoder's son Syl, I remember you. What's the problem?" Dr. Lehman asked with warm concern.

"Well, I'm calling from the hospital. Our baby wasn't due yet, but they had to do an emergency C-section. Now this doctor out here in Mill Creek thinks the baby has to be sent to some hospital a couple hours away in Akron, and we don't want him to do it. We won't hardly be able to visit the baby. Especially my wife won't be able to, with looking after the other young'uns; and me, I've got to milk the cows. And we don't have no insurance, either, Doc. Do you think it would really be all that necessary to move the baby to that Akron hospital?"

"How early was the baby?"

"Around eight weeks, I think."

"And how much does he weigh?"

"Three pounds, three ounces. He's tiny, but he's just perfect, Doc, and such a plucky little guy."

"I see. And does he breathe on his own?"

"Yeah, he don't have tubes in his nose like some of them other babies do."

"Well that's a good sign. Technically, Syl, I think they should be able to keep him in the local facility, especially if he's breathing on his own." The doctor thought of the tiny babies at Barb's house surrounded with hot water bottles and fed with a medicine dropper, one droplet at a time. "But I couldn't give an accurate diagnosis without seeing the child," he added.

"Could you talk to the doctor or something?" The youthful voice was edged with desperation. "He says if we don't sign papers to let them move the baby, he'll get court orders to do it and that will give the state custody of the baby." The husky voice faded away.

"Hmmm. Sounds a little unreasonable. Would you like for me to come out?" Dr. Lehman glanced at Phyllis who was writing a letter. They had planned to attend a cantata that night, but he knew Phyllis would want him to go.

"Oh, that would be wonderful. I know I can trust your judgment, Doc."

"I'll be out in two or three hours."

"One more thing yet, Doc. Would you mind picking up Mom and Dad and bringing them along? I hate to ask you, but it would mean so much to have them here."

"I'll do that." He knew where Sam Yoder lived, having been there numerous times on house calls. As the doctor and the middle-aged Amish couple headed toward the distant city, Dr. Lehman weighed all the options.

"What do you think, Sam?" he asked the grandfather. "Should they sign papers for the baby to be transferred or should they wait and see what happens?"

"Well, as I see it," the elderly man drawled, "if God is in control of everything that happens, as we believe he is, then why should we try to change what he has allowed to take place? Besides, if heaven is our goal for our families, then why should we struggle so hard and strap ourselves so deep into debt to all stay together down here?"

Dr. Lehman couldn't help but smile. He knew the answer before he ever asked the question. Most of his Amish patients would have agreed. They often felt a dilemma about possibly tampering with God's will.

Early in his practice, Dr. Lehman struggled with how much he should insist on taking full advantage of the latest technology when it might cause more trauma and expense to the family. He liked Dr. Eberly's advice: "Do your best to explain the medical procedures available, then let the patients make the final decision. Once they've decided on the course of action they feel comfortable with, give them the best medical care you can within their chosen parameters." It was good advice, he thought, and he generally followed it. The times he didn't, he wished he had.

On one occasion, Dr. Lehman transferred a child against the wishes of the parents because, from his perspective, it seemed the best thing to do. The child lingered in the hospital for a month, then died, leaving the family with a $100,000 hospital bill they struggled for years to pay.

Parents were responsible for the outcome, and they must be allowed to make the medical decisions for their children, the doctor decided. He concluded that never again would he make those decisions for parents and force them to do something they didn't feel comfortable doing.

When Dr. Lehman and the grandparents walked into the hospital room, the tense lines on the young parents' faces melted into a relieved smile, and the young mother blotted away tears with a handkerchief. It had all been so traumatic for them—the baby coming weeks earlier than expected and finding out he'd have to stay in the hospital for a month or two. Now the doctor insisted on sending the child to a distant hospital. Just the thought of their little one being sent so far away was almost more than they could bear. But now, Dr. Lehman had come. His advice could be trusted, and the couple would not have to work through the situation alone.

"Nathaniel's tiny, but he's just so perfect," Syl explained with a proud smile, leading the way to the nursery. "He's got those long Yoder legs and the Troyer nose. But you'll have to see him yourself."

The four of them rolled up their sleeves and scrubbed their hands outside the nursery. Syl led the way among the maze of incubators until he came to the incubator labeled "Boy Yoder."

Dr. Lehman studied the tiny infant. Sure, he was small, but he had seen tinier infants. The little fellow's color was good, and he was breathing nicely without assistance.

The wee hands flailed the air, but when Syl thrust his large, callused hand into the incubator, the baby gripped his father's finger tightly and quieted. The infant looked up as if to ask, "Why don't you hold me?" The young man wiped a tear from his eye. Clearly, the little one already had a grip on his father's heart.

"What do you think, Doc?" the grandfather asked quietly when the nurses were occupied on the other side of the room.

"I see no reason why he wouldn't be just fine here," Dr. Lehman responded in a low tone. "The latest research continues to prove the benefits of interaction between preemies and their parents. Personally, I'd like to see the child stay where he can have as much interaction with you as possible. It's calming for babies to sense their parents are near, and they grow faster and do better, too. But, of course, I can't force another doctor to do something he's not comfortable doing."

"There's the doctor," Syl whispered, looking toward the door.

"Hello!" A friendly smile lit Dr. Lehman's face as he extended his hand to the newcomer. "I'm Dr. Lehman. I was the Yoders' family doctor when they lived in Mount Eaton."

The local doctor wore a wooden smile and his handshake was stiff.

"Cute little guy, isn't he," Dr. Lehman commented.

"Little is right," the physician snapped. "Too little. We must get him some specialized care fast. These folks," he said, glancing at Syl, "don't care enough about their son to sign the papers to have him transferred to Akron Children's Hospital."

"No, you don't understand!" the young father stammered, looking anxiously at Dr. Lehman for help.

"Sir," Dr. Lehman squared his shoulders and looked his counterpart in the eye. "Sir, I think you misunderstand. I believe the Yoders care very much for their child, and they feel it would be best for him to stay in a local hospital where they can interact with him. Since they don't have a car, they would have very little contact with their son if he were transferred to Akron. Research confirms that parental touch and interaction are vitally important in stimulating a premature baby's will to live. The child's breathing on his own," Dr. Lehman continued as the other physician folded his arms across his chest and narrowed his lips into a thin line. "What would be gained by transferring him to Akron Children's Hospital? The child's parents would like the baby to stay in this hospital. Can that be worked out?"

"Well, Dr. Lehman, as the doctor of this infant, I do not want to bear responsibility for this child dying. I will pursue a court order tomorrow if the parents refuse to sign to have him transferred." The doctor's gaze locked on Dr. Lehman for a moment.

Later the little group that gathered around Mrs. Yoder's bed was solemn. "Like I said, if I were your doctor, I'd leave the baby here," Dr. Lehman told the Yoders. "However, I can't force another doctor to operate according to standards he's not comfortable with. It's up to you. If you don't feel comfortable signing the papers to transfer the baby, you don't need to. There's a chance the judge won't give a court order, but if he does, I'm afraid there's nothing I can do. I wish you the best. Let me know what happens."

"Don't forget, Son, 'all things work together for good,'" Syl's father encouraged as he and his wife walked out of the room.

I hope so, Dr. Lehman thought as he drove home. But that doctor seemed awfully set on his decision.

Monday afternoon, Syl Yoder called Dr. Lehman again. "Well, they're taking our baby to Akron," he said brokenly. "The doctor got the court order and they took Nathaniel. He said we can expect him to be there for two months at least. I don't know how often we can get up there. Christine has to care for the other children, and I've got the chores. Then if we have to spend up to four hours round trip on the road and pay a driver to take us, Doc, how will we ever pay that hospital bill?"

The two months Nathaniel was hospitalized seemed endless for the Yoders, who occasionally hired a driver to take them to Akron to visit their son. It tore their hearts to leave their infant at the end of visiting hours, as they sensed the little one needed their presence even more than a full-term baby would have. And just as stressful was knowing that their wishes didn't count. Technically, the child belonged to the state.

The ordeal unnerved the Amish community when they saw how the judgment and wishes of the child's parents had been overruled—unnecessarily, they felt. The case gave them a greater distrust for the medical world. Were Dr. Lehman and his colleagues the only doctors who understood Amish culture, and the only ones they could trust?

When Nathaniel was four months old, Dr. Lehman received another call from the Yoders. "The baby's home now, Doc, but the state still has custody of him. There's going to be a hearing to determine whether we are fit parents or whether Nathaniel stays in custody of the state. I don't think we could stand it if they wouldn't give us custody. Christine's just exhausted, all that running we've been doing."

"I'll come out," Dr. Lehman offered. On the day of the hearing, he closed down his office and traveled to Mill Creek to attend the session.

"It has been my privilege to know Mr. and Mrs. Yoder and their parents for years," Dr. Lehman told the judge in his solemn, dignified manner. "I assure you that this couple will be responsible and competent parents to this child, and, in fact, the best parents this child could have. I have observed the dedicated care and bonding that has already taken place, and there's no question in my mind that it's in the child's best interests to be raised by the family into which he was born."

The young mother brushed tears from her eyes as the judge announced he was awarding custody to the parents.

"Doc, we Amish are known as 'the quiet in the land,'" the grandfather remarked on the way home from the hearing, "but sometimes we need a voice. Today you were that voice. Thank you."

It wasn't the first time Dr. Lehman was that voice, nor would it be the last. Later, Dr. Lehman received an urgent call asking him to come to the Tobe Beiler residence at once. He finished delivering a baby, and then headed for the Beiler home.

What's going on? he wondered, noticing a vehicle parked in front of the Amish farmhouse. The license plate revealed that the vehicle was from another county.

As Dr. Lehman lifted his hand to knock, the door burst open and there stood a wide-eyed woman, breathing heavily as she twisted her *kapp* strings.

"*Ach mei zeit*, Doc, I'm so glad you're here," Mrs. Beiler cried, her terror melting into confidence.

"Some *Englischers* are saying since I don't care for my baby good enough, they're taking him away. But, Doc, it's not true that I don't take care of Rudy! You know Rudy never was right in his head when he was born, and, oh Doc, Tobe's not even here! He's at the Kidron Auction, and I couldn't let them take my baby, and I didn't know what else to do, so I sent for you!" she finished breathlessly.

"Has someone notified your husband?" Dr. Lehman asked in a low tone.

"Yes, the hired girl ran to the neighbors. Thank the good Lord she was here," Mrs. Beiler exclaimed in a whisper, stepping aside. "Anyways, Doc, come inside."

"Hello, I'm Dr. Lehman, the Beilers' family doctor," he smiled amiably and extended his hand to the women sitting on the edge of the couch.

A tall woman stood and flashed her I.D. card at the doctor. "Helen Cain, from Children's Social Services, and Dana Wickman, my associate." The set of her face and cool glare of her eyes reminded Dr. Lehman of a challenged lioness guarding a fresh kill.

"On a complaint of child abuse and neglect, as reported by a nurse at a local hospital," the woman began, "and for the welfare of Rudy Beiler, we need to remove him from the hazardous environment of this home."

Mrs. Beiler eyed her doctor as he folded himself comfortably into the hickory rocker she offered, just as relaxed as if he were visiting with old friends. Did Dr. Lehman ever get ruffled?

"You say a nurse reported child abuse?" he asked, recalling the instructor of his Dale Carnegie course saying that people won't hear you until they feel heard themselves. "So, in what way did this nurse feel the Beilers abused their son?" Dr. Lehman questioned.

"The child was treated for a hernia at the hospital, Dr. Lehman," Ms. Cain's voice was as stiff as her posture.

"That's right, is there anything else?"

"Well, there were signs the child had been crying a lot."

"Okay, is that it?"

"Is that it? I would say that's plenty!" the social worker spat. "Constant crying is a sign of abuse or neglect or both. We have homes that would give this child the care and attention he needs."

"Were you aware that Rudy was born with physical and mental handicaps?" Dr. Lehman questioned with a hint of sternness.

"Well, no, the nurse hadn't mentioned that," Ms. Cain glanced at the child lying listlessly in Mrs. Beiler's arms, staring absently at the ceiling, emitting mournful little wails now and then.

"When I delivered Rudy, I could tell that there were problems. The child's disorders cause him to fuss and cry a lot. In addition, a child with his condition will not live much more than another year."

Ms. Cain's rigid shoulders wilted as the doctor continued.

"I know the Beilers quite well, and I've observed that they give Rudy the best care anyone possibly can. I assure you he is not being abused or neglected. As you can tell, he requires lots of care, but Mrs. Beiler is very patient, and Mr. Beiler has hired a girl to help his wife with her work so she can spend more time with Rudy."

The door slammed and Mr. Beiler strode into the room looking sternly at the intruders, like a ruffled rooster who had come to protect his flock.

Dr. Lehman quickly stood and introduced the women. "I think we've got a bit of a misunderstanding here, Tobe," he explained. "When Rudy was in the hospital with his hernia, a nurse reported to Children's Services that she thought he was being mistreated. I don't believe the nurse or our visitors here were aware of Rudy's condition, so I was just explaining it to them.

"And now, Ms. Cain," he continued, turning back to the women fidgeting uncomfortably on the edge of the couch and clutching their briefcases. "As I was saying, I can affirm that the Beilers have given their child the best care they can. What do you think about making me responsible for the health of this child? The Beilers could bring Rudy to my office once every week where I could examine him and then report back to you."

Ms. Cain looked at her companion, who shrugged. "I guess I don't see anything wrong with that," the woman conceded, standing to her feet and edging toward the door. "But once every week, Dr. Lehman, I'll be expecting a report from you," the social worker announced, handing Dr. Lehman her card. "Every week."

Dr. Lehman stood and shook her hand. "Thank you, Ms. Cain," he continued with a firm air of authority. "You'll be hearing from me. And as I said earlier, I cannot guarantee how long the child will live, considering the problems he was born with, but I will promise you, Ms. Cain, that as long as Rudy lives, he will receive the best care."

The social workers quickly agreed to the proposal and left. Dr. Lehman fulfilled his end of the deal, and eventually the mandatory weekly checkup was reduced to once a month, and eventually was dropped entirely.

Meanwhile, at Mill Creek, Syl and Christine Yoder waited apprehensively for the hospital bill for their premature infant, certain it would cost the price of a farm.

"How's Syl's baby?" Dr. Lehman asked the grandfather in his office a number of months later.

"Nathaniel's doing great, Doc, and so are Syl and Christine. Remember how I always quoted that Bible verse, 'All things work together for good'? Well, don't you know, they never had to pay a cent on that hospital bill."

"Well, that's wonderful! Some churches must have given pretty generous offerings to cover those bills."

"No, Doc. It wasn't that way at all. Since the baby was a ward of the state, the state got the bill!"

20.

JEEP DOCTOR

"Did you deliver any more 'Cheep' babies recently, Doc?" the Amishman asked as the Jeep pulled out of Barb's drifted driveway, and the snow swirled around the windshield.

"Well, no, I haven't delivered a baby in the Jeep for a while, but I did deliver one in the office some time ago," Dr. Lehman replied.

"Hey, that sounds like a cheap baby to me!" Harry slapped his knee, laughing heartily at his own joke. "Chust a $25 office call!"

"Well, not exactly," the doctor chuckled, "not exactly. There was one baby born in our clinic that had a much higher bill than the $25 office call, because we had to life flight that one."

"Ach du yammah, so the helicopter came out to your office?"

"That's right. It landed in the field behind the clinic back before my house was built," he said, thinking of Dr. Eberly's young patient who had come to the clinic for her aching back. "The first-time mother was not aware that she was in advanced labor. By the time she arrived at the office, there was no time to do anything but to deliver the pre-term infant right in the examining room. Yes," Dr. Lehman continued, "the baby was premature, and since we had no emergency squad in those days, they had to life flight the baby to Children's Hospital. No, that certainly wasn't a cheap baby at all," the doctor finished.

As the Jeep headed down Harrison Road on the way home from Barb's that snowy evening, the slightest touch on the Jeep's brakes sent the back end fish-tailing across the slippery road. Since Harry's farm was along this road, Dr. Lehman had offered to give the farmer a ride home after he delivered the man's infant at Barb's place. And Harry was quite the talker, the doctor discovered.

"Let's see, didn't you crash your 'Cheep' around here somewhere?" the passenger questioned when the Jeep slid around a corner.

"Oh, Harry," the doctor groaned. "How'd you hear about that? No one was supposed to know! Why, I parked the Jeep behind the clinic so no one would see it, and then as soon as I could slip away from the office, I parked it inside my garage."

"Ha! Lester told me about it. He was along that day when you hit that icy spot and flew into the ditch. That nurse of yours got a bad cut on her head, too, ain't?"

Dr. Lehman winced. "Uh, yes. Actually, Rebecca was knocked out for a bit. Nancy gave me a hard time about that one. 'What'd you do, Doc, beat her up?' she asked when I brought Rebecca in the back door with a bloody forehead. She almost always wore her seatbelt, but for some reason she didn't have it on that day."

"Yep, Lester said he was *vundahboah* surprised when you drove that 'Cheep' right outa that ditch and headed back for the clinic. It just climbed right outa there, he said. Why, I would've liked to see that myself."

"These Jeep Wagoneers are built tough," the doctor replied. "Someone ran into me a couple of years back and totaled her car, but the Jeep had barely a dent. I tell you, Harry, it's a good car for me. I can sleep well at night because, with the four-wheel drive, I know I can reach my patients if they need me."

As he turned the Jeep onto a snowy lane, the headlights illuminated drifts reaching the lower rung of the fence. "I can walk in, Doc," Harry offered. "I got my *schtiffel* on."

"No problem. The Jeep will get us through."

"Well, ain't that something," Harry remarked, stroking his beard as the Jeep charged through the deep snow. "This does almost as good as a horse and buggy getting through them drifts!"

"Yes, I don't' know what I'd do without it. I should have bought a Jeep sooner, but I didn't think I could afford it," the doctor said as Harry climbed out.

"You delivered too many cheap babies!" Harry laughed. "*Grohs dank*, Doc. Better stay outa those ditches. Everybody knows your 'Cheep', and the news would be all over town if you crash!"

"Believe me, I'll try my level best to keep this vehicle on the road," Dr. Lehman agreed, longing for a quiet evening with a book by the fire and a bowl of Phyllis' chili that was simmering on the stove.

As he drove out the lane, a dark figure appeared in the blowing snow directly in front of the Jeep, waving for him to stop. Icy flakes melted on the doctor's face as he rolled down his window.

"*Vee gehts*, Doc? Quite a storm we have here, ain't? Well, Doc, *Dawdi's* been havin' *vundahboah* pain in his gut. I was coming in from the barn and I saw your Jeep in Harry's lane. Would you mind looking in on *Dawdi* for a minute, Doc?"

"I'll be glad to stop by. Let's see, Amos, you live—"

"Next farm over."

"Hop in, let's go."

In front of the farmhouse up the road, the doctor wrapped a scarf around his neck, picked up his satchel, and followed Amos toward the lights of the *Dawdi haus*.

After shedding his coat and boots, Amos led the doctor back the hall. "Come on back to the *kammah*."

Upon examining the elderly man, Dr. Lehman discovered the man felt pain in his abdomen and that he had been spitting up blood. He turned to the family and announced, "I'm afraid he has a bleeding ulcer. He really needs to get to the hospital tonight."

"*Ach mei zeit*, the hospital? Tonight? But the storm warnings!"

"I'll take him in my Jeep," the doctor offered.

As Amos and his wife pulled on *Dawdi's* thermal underclothes for the trip, Dr. Lehman's radio buzzed.

"Waid Spidell wonders if you're going up to Doctors Hospital this evening," Phyllis said when he called her back on the two-way radio. "He doesn't trust driving to Massillon in his hearse on these roads, and he has a body that he needs to bring back to Mount Eaton tonight yet."

"A body! Tell him I'm heading there now, and I'll stop by in a couple of minutes to pick him up if he wants to ride along."

"What about the soup?"

"I'll eat it when I get back."

"But the roads—"

"Don't forget, I've got a Jeep. It'll get us through."

Dr. Lehman helped *Dawdi* climb into the back seat of the Jeep, wrapped a blanket around the elderly man, and the two headed down Harrison Road through the blowing snow to Mount Eaton.

"Supposed to be quite the storm," the funeral director announced, climbing into the passenger's seat and shutting the door behind a flurry of snow. "Our neighbor Lina is a nurse at Massillon Community Hospital, and she's afraid she won't make it in this blizzard."

"We'll stop and pick her up," Dr. Lehman announced, backing the Jeep around. Before long, the doctor, funeral director, patient, and nurse were all on their way to Massillon in the Jeep.

"What's this sheet of plastic for?" the nurse questioned, getting situated on the seat.

"Oh, just throw it in the back," Dr. Lehman replied. "I always keep it in here just in case."

"In case of what?"

"Oh, just in case I have to deliver a baby in my Jeep."

"A baby? You've got to be kidding!"

"He's not kidding," Mr. Spidell assured the nurse. "In fact, he's had to deliver quite a few babies in his vehicle, especially in the days before Mount Eaton had an emergency medical squad. He's gotten so good he can deliver them when the light turns red and keep on going when it turns green."

"Well, not always," the doctor protested as his passengers laughed.

"Tell us about the baby at the stoplight," *Dawdi* urged.

Dr. Lehman scratched his head. "Oh, I don't know."

"Sure, Doc, go ahead," Mr. Spidell encouraged. "I don't know I've heard all the details myself."

"Well, Lina," Dr. Lehman began after a moment. "It was like this. A patient come into my office for a routine checkup in the days before Mount Eaton had an emergency squad. She was having regular contractions, but I noticed on her chart that the baby was not due for several weeks. I told her I'd feel more comfortable doing the delivery at the hospital, since her baby was early. Seeing there wasn't time to wait for an ambulance, I helped her into the back seat of the Jeep.

"I drove as fast as I dared through downtown Massillon. Just a block or two from the square, the light turned red in front of me. As I brought the Jeep to a stop, I heard the woman say, 'It's coming!'

"I threw the transmission into park, turned around, delivered the baby, and wrapped it in a blanket. The light turned green and off we went! No one in the cars around us ever knew what happened in that short moment!"

"Wow, Dr. Lehman, you *are* good!" Lina laughed.

"This Jeep and I have had lots of adventures," he remarked, guiding the Wagoneer along the white, trackless road.

"I hope we don't have too exciting of an adventure tonight!" *Dawdi* worried, peering nervously at the drifting road ahead.

"The Jeep will get us through," he promised. "But I'm sure glad the roads weren't this bad on some of those runs I made racing against the clock."

"Like the case of the twins?" the funeral director asked. "I'm sure Lina would enjoy hearing that story, too, Doc."

"You're talking about the police escort?" Dr. Lehman questioned.

"That's the one."

"Let's hear it, Doc!"

"Well, if you insist," he remarked with a shy smile. "But I'd like to hear someone else's stories."

"We insist!"

"Well, Lina, my patient was expecting twins. When she called that afternoon, I could tell by the tone of her voice that things were about to happen. I knew the couple didn't have a car, and 911 didn't exist yet, so I rushed out to their house. The husband came home from work just as I drove in the lane. The patient was ready to give birth, but I didn't want to deliver her at home and risk the complications of delivering twins."

"Of course," the nurse agreed. "That was wise."

"Well, I knew there was no time to wait an hour for an ambulance, so I asked the husband to help his wife into the Jeep, and off we went. Along the way, we passed the Massillon post of the State Highway Patrol, so I pulled in and asked for a police escort, because I could tell things were getting serious and I had to hurry.

"The police radioed for all the traffic lights to be turned red in the city of Massillon, and then an officer escorted us through town with his siren blaring and lights flashing. Fifty-one minutes after I first spoke with the police, the babies were born—a girl and a boy, 10 minutes apart. The dad just stood there shaking his head in disbelief.

"That couple had an older set of twin boys in addition to three other sons and one other daughter!" Dr. Lehman chuckled.

The Jeep pulled up in front of Massillon Community Hospital and Dr. Lehman announced, "Okay, Lina, here you are!"

"I don't know how to thank you," the nurse declared, opening the door.

"Just take good care of your patients, and I'll be repaid," he replied.

A few minutes later, Dr. Lehman drove up to the emergency room of Doctors Hospital and helped *Dawdi* into a wheelchair that an orderly brought for him. After admitting the elderly man, he drove his Jeep around to the back of the building.

While the funeral director entered the morgue to locate the body, Dr. Lehman laid down the back seat of the Wagoneer. His colleague returned a few minutes later with several orderlies pushing a gurney draped with a white sheet. Carefully, the men eased the stretcher into the back of the Jeep, slammed the hatch shut, and the doctor and funeral director headed back to Mount Eaton with their unconventional cargo.

Dr. Lehman drove silently for a few moments, thinking of the silent passenger in the back. "This reminds me of the days Desvoignes' hearse served as the local ambulance," he finally said. "Before I had my Jeep, if I sent someone to the hospital who needed to lie down en route, I'd call Desvoignes. He'd send a driver out with the hearse, pick up my sick or injured patient, and take them to the hospital. I tried to warn my patients, so they wouldn't have a cardiac arrest when they saw the hearse coming up the lane and think I had already sent for the funeral director!"

"I'm glad Mount Eaton has an emergency squad now," Mr. Spidell said with a smile. "I wouldn't want to be responsible for sending any of your patients to my funeral home prematurely, Doc."

As Dr. Lehman saw the lights of Mount Eaton winking through the snow flurries, he told his friend, "If I may say it, hauling a corpse is not as noisy or messy as delivering a baby in my Jeep. But honestly, I'd rather deliver a howling infant in my Jeep than haul a corpse!"

As the two neared Mount Eaton, Dr. Lehman wondered about the dead man's life and how he passed his last moments. "I can still remember the feeling I had the first time I ever witnessed an autopsy," he remarked after a bit, "and the first cadaver dissection. But perhaps the reason the dissection is burned into my memory is because of what happened to one of my teammates that term."

"Sounds like you have another story up your sleeve," Mr. Spidell remarked.

"Yes, but that's a story for another night. We're nearly home and there's a bowl of chili and a couple tired children waiting up for me!"

As the years passed, Dr. Lehman replaced his Jeep with newer models every few years, commenting that it was one of the most important tools in his practice.

Dr. Lehman and his Jeeps saw so many adventures that the Jeep became his trademark as much as the Amish buggy was a trademark for many of his patients. In fact, Dr. Lehman became known as the "Jeep Doctor," or "Cheep Doctor," as some of his Pennsylvania German–speaking patients called him. When Dr. Lehman's children drove his Jeep years later, they'd say, "Dad, everyone waves when we drive the Jeep."

"Yes, and you'd better wave back when you drive my vehicle," he told his family. "I don't want my patients thinking I'm stuck-up. After all, that Jeep represents me!"

21.

MED SCHOOL
MEMORIES AND MISHAPS

"That bugs me," Dr. Lehman muttered.

"What bugs you?" his wife wondered.

"Oh, that letter I wrote in med school. When I hauled the body back to the funeral home tonight, it brought back memories of the autopsies and cadaver labs in my med school days. I got to thinking about a letter I wrote to my youth group describing a week of med school, and it bugs me that I can't remember where I filed it."

Phyllis returned a moment later with an envelope. "Is this what you want?"

"That's it!" he cried, reaching for the letter. He unfolded the yellowed sheets and a hundred memories seemed to tumble out of the folds: the overpowering formaldehyde odor of the cadaver lab, the lecture hall, the expulsion of a classmate, and the endless months of intense study. And then the little blunder that threatened to end all he had worked so hard to attain.

As he read the letter he had written as a med student, the typed lines seemed to whisk him back to CCOM's lecture hall that first day of med school. He could still see the dean standing in front of the 75 nervous, young students, solemnly announcing: "Never forget that for every one of you accepted to Chicago College of Osteopathic Medicine, there are five other applicants who would have liked your seats." Dr. Lehman vowed he would always be thankful he was chosen to fill one of those seats.

As weeks passed, the number of students began to dwindle under the rigorous schedule and intense demands of med school. Many of his classmates had the advantage of being a little older than he. In addition, most of the students were familiar with medical terms, having worked in hospitals or as medical technicians and pharmacists. Some students' parents were doctors. He, on the other hand, was the first generation off the farm, and he knew nothing about medicine, not even how to treat a cow for mastitis. He had, however, taken practically every biology course Eastern Mennonite University offered.

Elton witnessed his first autopsy in his first semester of med school. The corpse was a 21-year-old African–American male who had died of encephalitis, or infection of the brain, after picking at a small boil near his nose. The infection spread to the young man's head through his lymph system and killed him.

Soon after Elton arrived at CCOM, the students were divided into groups of four and each group was assigned its own cadaver. Elton and his three teammates named their male cadaver Murphy. Those first days, the overpowering stench of formaldehyde stung the students' nostrils and brought tears to their eyes, and the sights curdled their stomachs. But as the days passed, the scenes and smells became as customary to Elton as the odors of the old Lehman dairy barn near the square of Kidron.

"Families have donated their loved ones' bodies to use in our research," the lab professor explained. "You will treat the cadavers with respect." Carefully, he showed them how to begin cutting in the arm and shoulder area. Most difficult of all was cutting into the corpse's face.

Dr. Lehman still recalled the strong odor of formaldehyde as he looked at the yellowed type-written letter he had sent from med school. He nearly forgot about the letter describing a week at CCOM that Harlan Steffen, a youth pastor from Sonnenberg Mennonite Church, had asked him to write for his youth group. Steffen had copied the letter and sent it to the young men from church serving away from home in programs for conscientious objectors. Glancing over the discolored sheet, he read the note Steffen had jotted above his letter: "I'm sure all of us are proud and happy to have one of our boys pursue such a worthy vocation. We're with you, Elton, and wish you the Lord's blessing."

Below the note, Dr. Lehman recognized his own type-written letter composed the winter of 1961. In it he described his schedule and course work, studying physiology, parasites, diseases, and the therapeutic value of drugs. Classes started by 8 a.m. and finished by 4:30 p.m. Then he returned home to eat supper, read the day's mail, and study until 1:30 a.m. In spite of the rigorous schedule, he concluded: "The vast amount of material to learn and without the definite promise of reaching the goal at times gets quite discouraging and frustrating. But sincerely believing that the Lord has led me here, there isn't a thing in the world I would rather be doing now than being an osteopathic medical student at CCOM!"

He remembered the overwhelming pressures and demanding deadlines placed on the med students that led some to cut corners. "Dry labs" were common shortcuts students tried, which involved filling out the patient history after conducting only a partial examination, or without even examining the patient at all.

Running out of time, one of Elton's partners on the dissecting team did a dry lab. While filling out the history of a surgery patient, the student reported that the pulse of both feet was palpable and that both showed good color.

"I don't understand how you could get a palpable pulse and observe good color on both of this patient's feet," the instructor told the nervous student when he pulled him into his office. "Especially since one of the patient's legs was amputated! Young man," he continued sternly, "because of your cheating, you are dismissed from this school."

"Please, give me another chance!" the student pled. "Just one more chance!"

In spite of his pleas, the student was not readmitted. Even a lawsuit did not reverse his expulsion. Eventually, the expelled student studied podiatry at another school, and, ironically, spent the rest of his life doing the very job he'd been kicked out of med school for failing to do—examining feet!

Med school was taxing and rigorous, but there were no easy, legitimate shortcuts. So, Elton routinely studied until midnight or later every night. He took a study break Saturday afternoons and spent the evenings doing observation in an emergency room on the south side of Chicago.

Sunday mornings, Elton attended a local Mennonite church where the pastor often invited him home for lunch. By 3 o'clock Sunday afternoon, he hit the books again until midnight, wistfully thinking of friends having fun back home while he was tied to his books. How would I ever have survived the pressures of med school without the help of God? Dr. Lehman wondered.

"Where's your horse and buggy?" fellow students taunted when they learned of his Mennonite roots. At first Elton's fraternity brothers sharing the house regarded him warily, but they soon grew to respect him. Elton drew strength from the prayers of his mother, the encouragement of mentors, and his commitment to God. He kept in touch with his Mennonite roots through the *Gospel Herald,* a church periodical.

When the young med student first arrived in Chicago, Pastor Delton Frantz from Woodlawn Mennonite Church, 12 blocks from CCOM, invited Elton to attend church there. Since Elton had no car until his junior year of med school, he walked the 12 blocks. He enjoyed the multi–ethnic congregation that was active in the community.

Pastor Frantz and his wife adopted Elton on Sundays, inviting him home for lunch along with Vincent Harding, an African American who was completing graduate studies at the University of Chicago. Pastor Frantz and Vincent Harding became spiritual mentors to the young student those years. Elton never forgot the hospitality of the congregation and pastor, and was sorry to learn later that a city gang had set fire to the church.

The years there were no Mennonite congregations within driving distance, Elton met to worship with fellow Mennonite students. From these meetings, two new congregations formed. While studying at Ohio State University, Elton and other Mennonite students, including his roommates Don Wyse and David Miller, occasionally met together for Sunday services. Mennonite pastors and teachers, including H.S. Bender and John Drescher, traveling through the area encouraged the students to continue meeting and often held worship those Sundays. These meetings led to the development of Columbus Mennonite Church.

While Elton completed his internship in Akron, Ohio, Dr. and Mrs. Richard Yoder invited the Lehmans and other local Mennonites to their home Sunday evenings. This group eventually became Summit Mennonite Fellowship.

By Elton's senior year, he developed a knack for starting I-Vs. Often when he came to work, the previous shift of interns had left several I-Vs for him to start when he came on duty. If he couldn't start one, Elton found a senior nurse to assist him.

The lowest moment of his years in med school took place when he was on rotation at one of Detroit's largest hospitals. As a senior student, he was called to the fourth floor to administer a patient's intravenous medication.

"We need you to give Benadryl to this lady," the patient's private nurse announced, handing Elton the syringe.

"What's the dosage?" he questioned.

"Twenty-five milligrams."

The syringe looks awfully large! Elton thought as he slowly released the medication into the vein. Something didn't seem right. "How much Benadryl did you say you wanted?"

"Twenty-five milligrams," she repeated.

As Elton studied the empty syringe, he suddenly felt faint. That wasn't 25 milligrams, it was 25 cc's! he realized in horror.

Elton stared at the nurse. Thanks for ending my medical career! he wanted to shout. In one minute, all those sleepless nights and years of study drained away with the overdose of Benadryl you gave me to inject into your patient!

But he didn't say a word. Instead, he dialed the number for the senior resident. "I've just given a patient 25 cc's of Benadryl," he whispered.

The supervisor dashed into the room, surveyed the situation, and studied the patient thoughtfully. After a long moment, he said, "Well, Lehman, I suppose she'll get a good sleep out of it."

And that's exactly what happened. Nothing more was said, and Elton was not expelled from CCOM after all.

As Dr. Lehman placed the yellowed letter back into his file drawer, he thought of all the sacrifice, discipline, and study behind the diploma hanging on his office wall.

Some of my patients can't comprehend the investment of time and effort behind my degree, he mused, smiling as he recalled a recent conversation with a local farmer.

"How many years did you go to school?" Dr. Lehman had asked the farmer, trying to generate conversation during a delivery.

"Eight years," the farmer responded. "And you?"

"I went to school for 23 years," Dr. Lehman replied casually.

"Twenty-three years!" The farmer studied the doctor incredulously. Shaking his head, he sadly declared, "Boy, Doc, you must have been a slow learner!"

22.

HANG IN THERE, BARB!

As Dr. Lehman walked into Barb's house, the glow of the lantern illuminated a young man pacing the living room floor, awkwardly trying to soothe a shrieking infant in his arms.

"Your first one?" the doctor questioned amiably as he walked toward the curtained partitions.

"Oh no!" the man drew back in alarm.

"Oh, I'm sorry. So you're an experienced father then," he smiled and disappeared behind the curtains. Behind him, Dr. Lehman heard several muttered exclamations, but the midnight chimes muffled the young man's words.

"You made it after all!" Barb looked up from the patient's bedside, a relieved smile easing the lines on her weary face. "That Doc," she remarked to Dr. Byler. "I tell you, his Jeep knows its way out here by itself!"

Glancing around, Dr. Lehman noticed there were women in three of the four beds partitioned by curtains, and a fourth woman occupied the bed in the delivery room.

"Just in time!" Dr. Byler announced. "We delivered one of yours a few minutes ago, and now we'll let you take over this one!"

"I'm glad you were here to handle the delivery for my patient," Dr. Lehman told his colleague after the third baby arrived later that night. "Just a down payment on all you delivered when I was teaching Bible school in Minnesota, to say nothing of the times you covered for me while we were in Romania or Central America."

"Hey, I'm always glad to contribute to a worthwhile cause," Dr. Lehman countered, referring to Dr. Byler's occasional work with Christian Aid Ministries. "It looks like you've had quite a night here."

"Positively hectic," Dr. Byler looked up from the chart he was filling in and ran his fingers through his curly hair. "I came straight from church and had my co-pastor close the service. I even interrupted Liz's date to get her over here in time," he smiled significantly toward the nurse caring for one of the newborns.

"We just delivered one baby when another buggy comes flying in the lane. It was your patient, Doc, and she couldn't wait until you came. No sooner had we delivered her when the third couple walks in the door. We had some repair work to do after the second delivery, and Sarah was taking care of the first infant. The second baby just cried and cried.

"I asked Barb if there wasn't anyone else around to hold that crying child. Well, Liz reminded me that her boyfriend was sitting out in the car all this time waiting on her. They were having a date when I called, but he brought her over to help out. So we called Andy in to hold the baby for us so we could take care of the mother."

Dr. Lehman began to laugh. "Excuse me a minute. I've got something to take care of!" He strode into the living room and spotted Andy in a rocking chair with the newborn sound asleep on his shoulder.

"I hear you are Liz's friend," Dr. Lehman said.

"That's right," the young man eyed the doctor warily, "and this isn't my child," he was quick to add.

"I understand that now," Dr. Lehman smiled. "Sorry for the confusion. But you are doing a good job. Barb could sure use some help—"

"Oh, no, no! One night is enough. But I will say, Barb does have a hectic life, poor woman. I don't see how she survives: rocking babies half the night, cooking, cleaning, canning, and washing for all the women and her own family. I noticed a couple bushels of apples standing outside waiting to be canned."

Just then Barb appeared with several generous slices of fresh apple pie topped with scoops of ice cream. "You've earned it," she smiled, setting down the two slices of pie and taking the sleeping baby from Andy.

"I was just going to ask where Sarah's at. I haven't had my supper yet!" Dr. Lehman laughed, as Barb disappeared into the kitchen for several more pieces.

The young man picked up the china plate with the syrupy apple slices oozing between the golden crusts and shook his head in amazement. "And when did she have time to bake *this*?"

Somehow, it seemed Barb always found time to do the things that mattered, even if it meant depriving herself of sleep. But Barb wasn't as young as she once had been, and the stress was taking its toll.

"I can't go on like this forever," she confided in Dr. Lehman. "I'm wearing out. My legs hurt so bad at the end of a day that I can hardly walk. Everyone expects me to keep doing this, but, Doc, I can't go on forever."

After the doctors drove out the lane, Sarah rocked a fussy baby while Barb cleaned the rooms and rubbed backs. As one baby settled, the next began to cry. Finally Barb told Sarah to go to bed, and she'd rock the babies. "I need to unwind a little before I can sleep, anyway."

I'm too tired to write in my diary tonight, Sarah sighed wearily, collapsing across her bed. Maybe I'll just read a few pages instead, she decided, paging through her journal.

One woman has lots of boys and always brings a suitcase of denims along to sew buttons on while she is in labor, Sarah read.

. . . Today the man came who likes to ride Barb's son's wagon down Lytle's hill while he's waiting for his wife. It's a wonderful hill for coasting,

but I think he's having more fun outside than his wife is inside the house!

. . . Last night I told Barb I'd be on night duty till the other party comes. Had four babies. They were so fussy. Gave them all some of the red peacemaker medicine and by 12, Barb finally got up. She asks, "What's wrong with them babies?" "Well," I says, "nursing mothers need no more peanut butter pie!" And then Barb measured out the red medicine and they all dozed off.

. . . The basement is so full of sheets to dry; I wish it would be nice out. I want to iron these today yet, then wash enough to fill the lines again.

. . . A busy day. Seven ladies and babies. Had one lady on lounge and one in the labor bed and on the cot in kitchen and four in the big room. Only have five cribs so made one nest on table in the baby room and one on the cushioned chair. Lehman was out of town, but as soon as he got back he came out and loaded up two parties and took them home. Barb says it takes Dr. Lehman to get things done.

. . . Fannie 'n Annie, born Nov. 28, weigh 3-lbs. 13 oz., and 4 lbs. 4 oz. First feedings were water with dropper. Then Similac. They were getting 7 cc's, now today they take almost half an ounce. Still using droppers. On Isomil now. Barb rubs olive oil over abdomen and back every feeding . . . . Annie went home Dec. 17, and Fannie Dec. 19 . . . .

. . . Today we have five ladies and all have baby boys that weigh 8 lbs.!

. . . Not one mother has died here in all these years. Barb says somebody is watchin' over this place.

. . . Barb says her legs bother her so much, and she can't go on like this forever. The women keep begging, "Hang in there, Barb!" She's praying that God will give her strength to continue as long as God wants her to. But then what? What will the women do without Barb? Well, maybe Lehman will know what to do. He can get things done.

In spite of all the warnings, the news at the quilting bee some time later still came as a surprise. No one thought it would actually come to that.

When Mattie broke the news, every woman sitting around the quilting frame turned to stare at her in disbelief. No one spoke. Not a needle moved.

Anna held her needle in midair. Never mind that she had pricked her finger or that a droplet of blood dripped onto the brilliant colors of the Amish Flower Garden design. No one even bothered to scold the little girls who bumped the frame as they popped out from under the quilt to see what the disturbance was.

The women with their blue, green, and purple dresses and white-bonneted heads bending silently over the quilt resembled the drooping blossoms bordering the quilt. Slowly, the needles began to snake around the fabric flowers once again. A scissors snapped at a thread now and then.

"*Yah* well," a gray-haired, wrinkled grandmother tied the strings of her starched white prayer cap beneath her chin as she broke the silence. "So Bill Barb says she's not going to help deliver any more babies? Why, she must be 65 by now and has been doing this for around 45 years. They say she helped deliver 200 a year for the last several years. *Ach* my. Can't say that I blame her for wanting to quit."

"*O du yammah*, what in the world are our daughters supposed to do now?" A plump, motherly woman stabbed the fabric layers with her needle. "I was born at Barb's, my girls were all born at Barb's place, and now where's my Mary supposed to have her baby?"

No one spoke. No one had an answer.

For as long as some could remember, the Amish had delivered their babies in the peaceful, homelike atmosphere at Bill Barb's. There they knew what to expect and what was expected of them. The serenity and quiet surroundings contributed to easier, shorter labors. In contrast, the city hospitals seemed uncomfortably strange and bewildering with the intimidating technology and blaring televisions, which were foreign to their quiet, simple lifestyles.

Little else was discussed the rest of the afternoon around the quilt, and little else was discussed behind closed doors of Amish homes that night. In fact, the quandary of the respected midwife's retirement was the main topic of conversation among the Amish men at the sale barn the next morning. Between bidding on cattle and horses, the bearded men stood in clusters, solemnly discussing the dilemma of the retiring midwife, beards wagging and straw hats bobbing.

"*Yah* well, *vas danksht?*"

"Can't Barb teach someone else to take her place?"

"The women all claim there's no one like Barb. Besides, the state would probably shut anyone down who'd try to start something like that these days."

"Hospital's out, ain't it?" one young father ventured.

"*Unfahgleichlich!* The womenfolk would never stand for it. Nope, that's not the answer."

"*Yammah!* Hospital birthing would make a man poor real quick!" The father of a dozen children jingled the loose change in his pockets as he spoke. "How many of us can afford to spend a couple thousand every other year? Ain't no way."

"You don't suppose she could be persuaded to keep on?"

"They say after the Amish hospital plan didn't go through down in Columbus, Jonas told her, 'Barb, you know we tried our best to get an Amish hospital in here, and they killed the project. You just can't shut down on us. You fill such an important role in the community, and the people won't let you quit. If you shut your doors, they'll be pounding them down.'

"Barb just smiled and said, 'I can't last forever, Jonas. I've been helping deliver babies since I was 20, and now I'm 65. I think it's time to quit.'"

"*Yah* well, we've got a problem. Barb's quitting for sure. Says everyone begs her to wait and just deliver their baby, but she says she's wearing out and she just can't take it no more."

A balding, white-haired man leaned heavily on his cane and adjusted his wire-rimmed glasses. "I wonder what Lehman would have to say. You know, he's one doctor that really cares about us Amish folk. If anyone would know what to do, it would be Doc."

"Now you're talking!" Straw hats bobbed in agreement. If anyone would have an answer, Dr. Lehman would. Few men rated higher in their opinion than their doctor, except for, perhaps, their bishop.

"We'll talk to Doc about it next time we see him," several men agreed as they headed for their buggies.

The next weeks, when those men brought family members to the Mount Eaton clinic for checkups, sutures, or X-rays, they brought up the dilemma of Barb's retirement. Dr. Lehman mulled over the problem as he drove to the hospital or the nursing home and made house calls. If only Columbus legislators wouldn't have killed the dream for an Amish hospital, he thought. But they did.

It was such a good idea. The hospital would run like hospitals in Europe, where the family provided food and care for patients. There would have been a birthing wing like the hospital had in Cleveland. Oil lamps would light the homey rooms, and Mennonite nurses who understood the ways of Amish would provide care. The hospital would have been built and staffed according to state regulations and financed entirely by the Amish community, Dr. Finer had assured state legislators.

"You've got a good plan and an ideal location," state officials admitted, "but, unfortunately, state regulations have changed. The construction of such a facility would require a special certificate that would be impossible for you to acquire. The extensive regulations and expenses would make the project prohibitive."

Dr. Finer and Dr. Lehman had kindled a spark in the hearts of the Amish community, and it refused to die. Vanloads of Amish flocked to hearings to appeal the case. Several local hospitals, however, feared competition and complained about the project, pressuring officials to block the proposition. In Columbus, the verdict was given: there would be no Amish hospital.

That hospital would have been the perfect solution to Barb's retirement, Dr. Lehman thought as he drove to Barb's house one night. It would have been ideal—a birthing wing and Mennonite nurses. Dr. Lehman's face lit up as dozens of ideas flashed through his mind like bursts of lightning in a storm. *It's got to work!*

After the delivery that night, Barb set a generous slice of pie on the table as Dr. Lehman finished his paperwork by the light of the gas lamp. "Pecan pie! My favorite! Barb, you just can't retire."

"Doc, I've poured my life out for those mothers. If I'd have endless youth and energy, I'd go on forever, but I don't."

"I know, Barb. Do you have any suggestions?"

Barb sighed and sat down on the chair across from the doctor. Dark pouches sagged beneath her weary eyes. Time had creased her pleasant face and tinged her hair with silver.

"I don't suppose the state would let us have a set-up like this at someone else's house, would they?"

Dr. Lehman laid down his fork. "Barb, you know they've just looked the other way because you are doing a good work and because you've been doing it so long, but if anyone else would start up at their house—well, they wouldn't allow it. I've been doing some thinking, though. I'd like to check into the possibility of having a special building constructed for a birthing center. It could be staffed with nurses and—"

"*Mei zeit,* Doc, that's it! That's the answer!" The fatigue on Barb's face seemed to vanish and her eyes glowed with excitement. "And they could build an apartment attached to the birthing center so the staff would have a place to relax. Oh, Doc, it's a great idea. You understand and care about us Amish like few folks do," Barb said, getting to her feet.

"You understand how for generations we Amish have lived simple lives without all the gadgets of technology. You understand our beliefs about insurance, thriftiness, and stewardship. Doc, you know how we feel about trusting that God is in control of every circumstance. You understand us, Doc, and our people appreciate you for it. Talk to Jonas D. Yoder, Doc, he could give you lots of ideas. He's a builder."

"He's just the man to talk to," Dr. Lehman agreed, slicing off another bite of golden brown pecan pie. "Try to hang in there, and we'll see what we can do."

As the Jeep drove out the lane, Barb thought, if anyone can do it, Doc and Jonas can.

The next day, as Dr. Lehman drove across Mount Eaton to Jonas D. Yoder's home, he thought about the unusual Amishman who engineered and constructed sophisticated office complexes. In addition to being an entrepreneur, Jonas had a broader range of experiences than many Amish contemporaries. Not too many Amishmen traveled to Alaska or parachuted out of an airplane. Jonas had done both.

Jonas had hired a chauffeur to take his family to Alaska by motor home one summer. Like many plain folk, Jonas was involved in disaster aid, cleaning up after floods and hurricanes. In Florida, while helping with reconstruction projects after a hurricane, Jonas surprised his wife one evening by arriving home floating from the sky in a parachute. He told her he'd be home at 6 o'clock and that she should be waiting in the yard for him. Strapped to a professional parachutist, the Amishman landed several feet from where his wife sat on her lawn chair and nearly sent her into cardiac arrest.

One of the activities Jonas found most rewarding was participating in prison ministry. To him, life was more than constructing grand buildings or eating shoofly pie and sleeping under hand-made quilts. Jonas believed in serving God by serving others.

The Amish entrepreneur quickly supported the project. "It's exactly what our people need," he agreed. "And I know our folks would pitch in with money and labor. Why, if every Amish family in Wayne, Holmes, and Tuscarawas counties gives $100, we'd be able to build quite a complex!"

Together, Jonas and Dr. Lehman walked around the selected five-acre plot across the road from the builder's home in Mount Eaton. Scarcely a two-minute drive from the doctor's house and office, the setting was peaceful, surrounded on two sides by fields and pastureland. It would be a perfect location for a medical center.

"Are there any other birthing centers in Ohio?" Jonas asked. "Are any precedents set?"

Dr. Lehman shook his head. "There are no free-standing birthing centers anywhere in the state. We'll have to pioneer our way through the project. But something has to be done. If Barb closes down, it means going back to delivering home births. Dr. Byler and I can't oversee all home deliveries in the area. We can't be everywhere at once."

"I'm willing to check into the possibilities of building a center," Jonas told the doctor. "But first I'd like to chat with Barb one more time and see if I can't persuade her to let the mothers keep coming to her house."

That same week Jonas stopped by Barb's house to talk to her about the project. "Barb," he said, "if you want to keep having the women come to your house, we won't do a thing, but if you're ready to quit, we'll do what it takes to get another set-up going."

"I'm quitting, Jonas,"

"Okay, Barb, you deserve to retire. And whatever it takes, we'll do it!'"

Jonas didn't realize it would take lobbying at the state capital. But he did it. He hired a driver and traveled to Columbus time after time to meet with the maternity division of the public health department, where he kindly but firmly outlined what his people wanted. "There's a real need for a set-up like this, and if it doesn't pass, you can expect busloads of Amish to arrive on your doorstep to plead their cause," he warned. "Busloads."

The idea of a free-standing birthing center was a new concept to the department. However, Mary Ellen Miller, a nurse in charge of the division, saw the advantage of getting births out of the homes and into a setting under the supervision of doctors and nurses. So she lobbied for the cause.

"I think it's a wonderful alternative and will serve the Amish community well," she told Jonas. But the state health commissioner wasn't convinced and endlessly checked each detail with his attorney.

The builder kept traveling back to the capital, meeting with Miller and the health commissioner. Each time, he stressed his commitment to follow building codes and staff the facility with registered nurses. In an emergency, the Mount Eaton squad could deliver a patient to Doctors Hospital in 17 minutes—the same amount of time needed to assemble a C-section team at the hospital. The doctor and builder had thought of every angle. Finally, after much delay, the health commissioner agreed to the plans. Because the building was a birthing center and not a hospital, the state wouldn't require a certificate of need.

"So we have your permission to build a free-standing birthing center?" Dr. Lehman questioned. "Will you please put that in writing?" People came and went in government positions, the doctor knew, and he didn't want to risk beginning work on such a major project without getting the health commissioner's word in writing.

"Jonas! I've got it!" he told the builder in the spring of 1984. "I'm holding the health commissioner's letter in my hand. When can we start?"

It had been two long years of meetings, negotiations, prayers, pleas, and miles of red tape, but at last the Amish would have their own birthing center.

True to their promise, the Amish and Mennonites of the community rallied to the cause. Every Amish and Mennonite church in Holmes, Wayne, and Tuscarawas counties whose members planned to use the center asked each family to donate $100. The fund drive raised $250,000, and construction began on the Mount Eaton Care Center, as the new facility was named. Not a cent of federal, state, or county tax money was used to construct this building.

A board of five non-Amish and two Amishmen, including Barb's son, assisted the builder in designing plans and raising funds. Dr. Lehman drew up a list of medical specifications he knew the state would require. The structure would be designed to meet state regulations and fire codes, and a registered nurse would be on duty around the clock. The state would be permitted to inspect the building annually; a flat fee of $275 would be charged for up to a 72-hour stay after delivery; and doctors would furnish the medicines they dispensed, as well as their personal equipment. High-risk patients with previous C-sections, high blood pressure, high sugar, or those carrying twins would not deliver at the Care Center but at a hospital, instead.

In November 1984, construction began. When the builders hit rock at the site, the project took more time and finances than planned, but the Care Center was built on solid rock, on the second-highest populated spot in the state of Ohio.

In October 1985, Mary Ellen Miller and other officials from Columbus inspected the structure and approved it. On November 11, around 1,000 people attended the open house for the Mount Eaton Care Center.

"You may close your doors now, Barb," Dr. Lehman told the midwife, "but we want you to come work with us at the new birthing center."

Dr. Lehman had asked the state to recognize Barb's years of experience and allow her to serve as an authorized staff member. To Dr. Lehman's relief, the state agreed.

At an Amish quilting some time later, the women discussed the new Care Center. "You know," Mattie remarked, "if Barb had never decided to quit, we wouldn't have a nice, new birthing building. Reminds me of the verse about everything working out for good to those that love God. Now, who do you think will be the first to use that new Care Center?"

No one guessed that the baby who should have been the first infant born at the Care Center would be born in a car, instead.

23.

Doc's Amish Birthing Center

A chilling wind chased a kaleidoscope of colored leaves across the fields and whistled through the golden shocks of corn. Behind the silhouetted horse and buggy approaching the village of Mount Eaton, deepening hues of lavender and pink melted into the twilight. The young driver tucked a heavy blanket around his companion. "Warm enough?" he questioned, flipping on the external battery lamps.

"We're good and warm, Ben." The rosy-cheeked woman brushed the stray curls back under her bonnet and studied the baby quilt hanging in the display window of Spector's Dry Goods store. I wonder if I chose the right color, she mused, her thoughts going to the baby quilt tucked in her suitcase. Maybe it should have been blue, she thought, gently rubbing the mound that was once her slender waist.

With a light tug at the reins in Ben's work-callused hands, the spirited steed drew to a stop as one of the village's two traffic lights turned red. Waiting for the light to change, Ben glanced at the Mount Eaton business establishments illuminated in the last glow of twilight. Spidell Funeral Home and the village bank stood ahead to the left, with Mount Eaton Clinic behind them. Lengthening shadows stretched beyond Hilltop Market, the hardware store, gas station, fire station, Mount Eaton Elevator, and the Wagon Wheel Restaurant. Here and there, a few buggy horses stood tethered to the hitching posts that bordered most establishments.

"Did you hear Dr. Lehman say why folks don't use turning signals in Mount Eaton?" Ben asked.

"No, why is that?"

"Because everyone knows where everyone else is going, so no one needs turning signals around here!" Ben laughed, slapping his knee in delight.

"Well, I sure hope not everyone knows where we're headed tonight!" Anna replied, blushing slightly as the traffic light turned green. A smile lingered on Ben's face as he flicked the reins and his horse trotted briskly down Route 241 past the brick Mount Eaton School toward the rolling hills in the distance. Just out of town, a neatly-lettered sign announced, "Mount Eaton Care Center," with a bold arrow pointing left.

"This must have been where he did it."

"Where who did what?"

"Where the driver took the wrong turn the night the first baby should have arrived at the Care Center," Ben said, stroking his dark beard thoughtfully. "Never did make it, they say. Baby was born in the car that night."

"Oh dear, they were so close!" Anna shivered in spite of the heavy robe. The buggy pulled left onto the Care Center's black-topped drive.

"Oh, I do wonder what Doc's Care Center is like," she said, gazing up at the large brick structure built into the hill several hundred feet from the road. "It sure looks different than Barb's house."

"It's awfully nice," Ben promised. "They've got nine nice big rooms for the women, they say. They all have steel doors instead of curtains, Anna, and each room even has its own bathroom and refrigerator! Think of it! And then there's a big room for the nurses, Jonas Yoder told me, and some offices and even a nice lounge. Downstairs in the walkout basement, there's a room with washers and dryers. No clothes lines, Anna. Then there's a big room for meetings and even a room where a driver can sleep while he's waiting. I tell you, Doc and Jonas thought of everything! And then, they have rooms for nurses to live and, of course, there's Bill and Barb's apartment."

"It must be quite the place. I can't wait to see it. I'm just so glad Barb's still helping," Anna murmured. "I don't know if I could have a baby without her."

"You can be glad Barb and Bill moved back," her husband told her.

"Moved back?"

"Yes, hadn't you heard? They were so lonely for the grand-children so they moved back to the homeplace some time ago. They weren't there long till they decided to come back to the Care Center apartment three days a week. Bill said he needed a break from those six dozen grandchildren now and then!"

"Oh, I do hope Barb's here tonight," Anna exclaimed as the buggy drove up to the sheltered entry. Anxious to get inside, she picked up the bag with the quilt and handmade baby clothes and handed them to Ben. As Ben unloaded her bags, Anna gazed through the sparkling glass doors to the grandmotherly woman walking briskly down the hall towards them. A white prayer *kapp* covered her graying hair and her slate-blue dress nearly brushed the tops of her black shoes. Kind eyes looked out from the wire-rimmed glasses. Barb!

Ben clutched his hat and led his horse to the buggy shed where the stork weathervane quivered in the wind.

Flinging the door open against the wind, Barb reached for Anna's bags. "Come in! Did you have a cold ride? Feels like it could snow."

Anna assured the midwife that they had kept warm, then she let her eyes sweep around the clean, orderly room. To her left was a homey kitchen area with a refrigerator, sink, several microwaves, and a round wooden table and chairs. Sandwiched between two chairs stood a coffee table stacked with interesting books and copies of the *Reader's Digest, The Budget, Farm and Ranch,* and other periodicals. To the right, several black jackets hung from a coat rack.

The shrill cry of a newborn floated up the hallway. "Are there many here tonight?" Anna asked, following Barb through a set of double doors leading into a long, spacious corridor.

"We have two babies in here right now and another mother waiting." Barb paused at the nurses' station.

"Anna Troyer is here, Susie," the grandmotherly woman informed one nurse pulling a tiny gown over the head of a wailing newborn. Anna gazed wistfully at the tiny infant in the pink, handmade gown.

Dr. Eberly's former nurse turned and flashed a warm smile. "We'll be dressing your baby next!"

"Oh, I hope so!" The shy smile on Anna's flushed face broadened as she read the sign above the counter where the baby lay. "We shall not all sleep, but we shall all be changed," the hand-lettered poster read. A hickory rocker and an empty wooden crib stood to one side of the counter.

As the sharp tightening returned, Anna rested lightly against the counter between the hall and the nurses' station until she could breathe again.

"How are your contractions? Still coming?" Barb asked as they walked down the hall.

"Yeah, still coming all right. Four or five minutes apart, mostly."

The glass door slammed behind him as an icy blast followed Ben into the building. Halfway down the wide corridor, Barb paused and opened the door labeled "4."

"Here you are!" she said, switching on the light.

Anna sighed contentedly at the cozy, spacious room. The lamps on the ivory walls glowed warmly over the recliner, bed, and crib. To her left, she noticed a clothes closet, a sink and spacious counter beneath a wide mirror, a small refrigerator, and a restroom complete with a shower. A clean, handmade gown hung on the hook on the door and a window overlooked a dark meadow. Ben eyed the comfortable recliner in the corner, while Anna noticed the small patchwork quilt and tiny hand-sewn gown folded neatly at the foot of the handcrafted crib.

"If you'd rather not use the electric lamps, we have kerosene lanterns on the walls of Rooms 3 and 5," Barb offered.

"Thanks," Ben replied, hanging his straw hat on a hook, "but the electric lights don't bother us none."

"Fine. Now you just take your time and settle in," Barb encouraged, shutting the blinds against the darkness. "You can put your food in the fridge, take a shower if you like, Anna, and get changed into the gown. Then you can push this call button, and Susie'll be in to check on you." Barb flashed a motherly smile and the door clicked shut behind her.

"Wow, Anna, this must be as nice as a motel!" Ben remarked, surveying the clean, comfortable surroundings.

While his wife got settled, he unpacked the meals she prepared and froze in advance. If these meals didn't satisfy his hunger, he had been told the Care Center's kitchen refrigerator and cupboards were well stocked with frozen meals and canned soups. Juices and snacks were also available, and a large coffeepot of steaming water stood ready for a tea bag or packet of instant coffee.

When Susie knocked at the door of Room 4 a few minutes later, she found Anna settled comfortably in bed, glancing through a baby name book while Ben reclined in the comfortable chair and read a newspaper.

"Your contractions are still coming regularly?" the nurse questioned.

"They sure are!" the young woman replied.

"Let's get a heartbeat," Susie announced.

The blub, blub, blub of the Doppler filled the room. "We've got an active one in there! Let's check and see if we'll have a baby tonight!" Susie suggested.

"Say! Almost six centimeters already!" The nurse made a notation on her clipboard. "I better call Dr. Lehman and let him know."

Across town beyond Spector's Store, the bank, and Dr. Lehman's office, a lane threaded between two houses to a sprawling house on a knoll. Beyond the house, the beacon of Akron–Canton Airport 30 miles north flashed faintly across the night sky. In the dining room of the home, the Lehman family sat around the table, enjoying the last morsels of tasty pumpkin pie.

"There's nothing like fresh rhubarb pie in the spring," Elton began, "strawberry pie in the summer . . . "

"And pumpkin pie in the fall!" Beverly finished for her father.

"That's right, there's nothing like a good piece of pie," Elton remarked. "Do you have flute lessons tonight, Bev?"

"Yep, Dad, better run. Mom's going to *Messiah* practice and Brent's got a meeting. Guess you'll have the house to yourself!"

"We had a hectic day at the office, so I don't think I'll mind a quiet evening by the fire," he replied.

Brent and Joon Kim, the Korean exchange student boarding with the Lehmans, excused themselves to leave for a class meeting at Central Christian High. As president of the class, Brent didn't want to be late.

"It's below freezing and it's starting to snow," Phyllis' concerned eyes followed the boys. "Are you sure you want to ride that cycle tonight? I'll drop you off on the way to practice if you want."

"No thanks, Mom, we'll be fine. See ya."

After throwing another log on the fire, the doctor settled into the recliner and began leafing through *Postgraduate Medicine*, wondering how soon the phone would ring.

"Let's go, Bev. Don't forget your flute!" Phyllis called, buttoning her coat and picking up her *Messiah* score. "So long, Elton. Enjoy your quiet—"

The ringing telephone cut her short.

So much for a quiet evening!

The caller was his daughter from Eastern Mennonite University. "How are you? Good to hear your voice. How's that biology project coming for Professor Roman J. Miller?" he asked.

After hanging up the phone a few minutes later, Elton propped up his feet and picked up the *Wooster Daily Record*. As he scanned the headlines, the phone rang again. Reaching for the phone, Dr. Lehman knew he would not be spending a quiet evening by the fire.

While driving across town, he thought of how the Care Center had made a difference in his life. Barb and the nurses could oversee the patients until delivery was imminent, and then in two minutes, he could be at the new facility. When several women were laboring simultaneously, they could all be monitored under the same roof.

Driving out to Barb's had racked up some 22 thousand miles annually on his Jeep. Now, he averaged only 15–16 thousand miles each year.

As Dr. Lehman approached the illuminated building on the hill, he thought the facilities seemed like a dream come true—offering most of the conveniences of a hospital and all the comforts of home.

"She's coming along nicely, Doc," Barb informed him, looking up from the desk at the nurses' station. "We should have a baby before long. I'll set up in Room 4 while you pull on your scrubs."

"You doing okay?" Barb wondered as she entered Anna's room with a glass of ice chips for her patient.

"They are coming pretty hard, she says," Ben informed the midwife as he rubbed his wife's back.

"Just relax. Breathe slow and easy," Barb encouraged. "That's good. The doctor'll be in here in a minute to see how you are doing."

That was Barb. She left the women alone if they didn't want to be disturbed, but when she saw they needed encouragement, she was at their side, cheering them on. As the midwife talked, she placed a package of sterile instruments and a stack of newspapers on the counter beside the sink.

After a brisk knock, the doctor strode into the room. "How are we doing here?" he asked, looking from Anna to Barb and nodding to Ben. "She's at seven centimeters already," he announced a moment later. "How far apart are your contractions?"

"Oh, about every three or four minutes."

"And how long do they last?"

"A good minute, I'd say."

"You're coming along well, Anna. Things could go fast now."

Anna sank back into her pillow, shut her eyes, and concentrated on relaxing and breathing with the constricting pains.

"Hard day, Doc?" Ben asked.

"Not too bad. Had a boy come in today who mutilated his hand in a harvester. Then I had to leave the office this afternoon for a delivery, so that made things a little more hectic."

"A baby born during office hours? Does that happen often, Doc? When are most of the babies born anyway, at night or day?"

"Well, we can find that out," Dr. Lehman replied, pulling a little black book out of his pocket and flipping through the pages. "We did a study of my first thousand deliveries and found that most babies were born between 10 and 11 o'clock at night. A later study of all the babies I've delivered showed that 29 percent of the babies were delivered from 7 a.m. to 3 p.m. Thirty-two percent were delivered from 3 to 11 p.m., and 38 percent were born between 11 p.m. and 7 a.m."

"And what time suits you the best, Doc?"

"Technically," the doctor replied, "there is no perfect time to be called out on a delivery. During the day, I'm needed in the office. In the evening, I like to be with my family. If I'm not with my family, I've got board meetings to attend. But if I could choose, it would be between 9 and 11 at night, before I go to bed. But, of course, babies don't understand that!"

"I imagine you get called out at a lot of times when it doesn't really suit you, but you go anyhow. Do you like your job, Doc?"

"Yes, Ben, I really do. Delivering babies is a large part of my practice, and a fun part, because 95 percent of the time everything goes well and you have a happy mother and father."

"Say, is the story about the baby that chose its own name true?" Ben asked, leaning forward expectantly.

"Well, yes, in a way."

"So how did it happen, Doc?"

The doctor glanced at the clock on the wall above the closet. He had phone calls to make and paperwork to do, but that could wait. From her nest of pillows, Anna watched Dr. Lehman settle into a folding chair. A story would be a welcome diversion. The pains were harder now and closer together.

The lamp's soft glow warmed the spacious room. The men lounging comfortably gave the room a homey feel. Through the glass sides of the tiny, handcrafted crib, Anna could see the pink and green squares of a handmade comforter. Soon her baby would lie there and she would know what it looked like, if it had dark hair or none at all, and whether it was a boy or a girl.

"Come, baby, come," she whispered into the pillow.

The doctor combed his fingers through his dark hair. "It was the couple's first baby and both parents wanted to name the baby after a different grandfather. They couldn't decide what to name him, so the new father fished a Hilltop Market receipt out of his pocket and tore it in half. He wrote 'Jacob' on the back of one slip of paper and 'Levi' on the back of the other. Then he placed one piece of paper in each of the baby's fists.

"'We'll let the baby decide which name he wants', the father said. 'Whichever name he hangs onto the longest is the name we'll give him.'"

Ben grinned at Anna, who managed a wooden smile. Damp curls framed her flushed face. He almost felt guilty for enjoying the evening, but he sensed that the story helped pass the time for her.

"It so happened that the wind slammed the door shut and the frightened baby opened both fists at the same time with the reflex typical of newborns and dropped both names," the doctor finished with a chuckle. "The nurse told the father that the baby must not have liked either of the names."

Ben laughed heartily. "Then what, Doc? What'd they name him?"

"Well, they tried it again. This time the baby hung onto the paper that read 'Levi', so that's the name they gave him!" Dr. Lehman laughed with Ben and then stood to his feet. "I think it's time we check this young lady again. How are you doing, Anna? Are your contractions coming closer and lasting longer?"

"Yes!"

"Are you having one now?" he asked.

She managed a muffled groan.

"Barb, let's adjust this birthing bed. We'll soon have a baby."

Susie stuck her head in the doorway. "Doc, come quick! Dr. Byler's patient just arrived and she's all set to go. And I got two different heartbeats!"

"Oh, come on!" he exclaimed, but the nurse was gone. Hurrying from the room, he called over his shoulder, "Take it easy, Anna. We'll be back before long. Try to wait."

"If the baby's coming, you let me know," Barb said, fanning the woman's flushed face. "We can't make a baby wait!" Her eyes twinkled knowingly at Anna as if to say, "The boys don't know all the rules to this game."

"I'm walking across the hall for a minute to see if they need help," Barb said softly a moment later. "One of us will be right back; ring if you need us."

"Anna, *liebe*, you're so brave." Attentively, Ben wiped her flushed face with a cool, damp cloth.

"Anna," Susie slipped into the room and her voice was soft and soothing as it penetrated the pain that seemed to grip the woman. "The doctor wants me to get a heartbeat again."

The steady gurgling of the Doppler reminded Anna that her baby would arrive eventually. "Anna, your baby is going to be here in a couple of minutes. Breathe in your nose and out your mouth. That's it. Slow and easy, slow and easy," the nurse murmured softly, looking down at Anna with caring, compassionate eyes. "Okay, now, relax . . . let yourself go limp . . . sink down into the mattress . . . relaxing all the way down to your toes . . . like Flopsy Mopsy . . . or Raggedy Ann." Her voice was calm and steady like the continual gentle lapping of waves.

A newborn's wail filtered through the walls from the next room. Moments later, Dr. Lehman and Barb swept into the room just in time to catch Anna's baby.

"A girl!" Dr. Lehman announced triumphantly above the sound of suctioning and intermittent squawking of the infant. "And we've got two little boys across the hall!"

Anna's eyes grew misty as she watched Susie dry the infant and wrap the chubby little body in a soft blanket, her round, red face showing above the flannel blanket. A little girl. Her own perfect baby.

"Congratulations!" the nurse handed the baby to Ben. "Show her to Anna," she suggested, bustling out of the room to see how the twins were faring.

When Barb had finished assisting the doctor, she took the infant and laid her on Anna's chest and covered them both with a blanket. "Here's your little girl! Give her some love, and then we'll weigh her and clean her up." Barb patted the young mother's shoulder and whispered, "You did great, Anna."

The mother gazed lovingly at the miracle in her arms, and the previous hour seemed to evaporate.

"Does she have a name?" Dr. Lehman asked.

"Well, we hadn't quite decided."

"Do you have an old grocery list in one of your pockets?" Dr. Lehman questioned with a twinkle in his eyes.

"Oh, no, no thanks, Doc! I think we've got a name." Turning to his wife, Ben asked, "You still like the name Ruth Anna?"

She nodded. "It fits her. She'll be Ruthie for short."

"Come, Ruthie," the nurse cooed, scooping up the little bundle. "We're going to find out how much you weigh, then we'll bring you right back to Mommy."

"Nine pounds, seven ounces!" the nurse announced, returning with the infant a moment later.

"Nine-and-a-half pounds! How much bigger do they come?" Ben asked.

"Well, we delivered one boy here that weighed 13 pounds."

"Thirteen pounds! He was half grown!"

The doctor carefully examined the baby. "You've got a fine daughter," he announced as he scrubbed his hands. "Have a good night. I'll be over in the morning to check on you."

"He is a wonderfully good doctor," Ben told his wife after they were alone in the room. "He takes time to talk and makes you feel special. I guess that's one reason everyone likes him. He treats us Amish with respect, too."

A short time later, Susie opened the door after a brisk knock. "I'll be glad to heat something up for you, then you can eat while I bathe the baby," she offered.

"That sounds wonderful. There's a container of chicken soup in the little fridge you can warm up, and you can toast two pieces of bread if you don't mind."

Before long, Susie returned with a tray holding homemade chicken soup, buttered toast, and fruit juice for two. After setting down the tray, the nurse reached for the baby. "Come, little Ruthie, we'll wash you up and get you dressed while Mommy and Daddy have some supper."

Anna's eyes followed the nurse tenderly cuddling the baby as she carried her out of the room. She has that same motherly, compassionate touch as Barb, Anna realized. I sure hope if Barb ever retires that Susie's on duty when I come back the next time.

The warm soup refreshed the couple as they discussed what their little boys would say when they saw their sister in the morning. Ben stifled a yawn when Barb knocked at the door and pushed the bassinet into the room. "The baby's ready to see her mamma," she announced.

Anna pushed back her tray and eagerly reached for the newborn dressed in a tiny gown and wrapped in a pink flannel blanket and small quilt. The baby's large, dark eyes surveyed their surroundings, and the tiny lips sucked contentedly on a little fist.

"Would you like to stay the night, Ben?" Barb asked as Anna pressed her lips against the tiny head. "We'll be glad to roll a cot in for you. Dr. Lehman said it's snowing out."

"Sounds great," Ben agreed, stifling another yawn.

When Susie rolled a cot into the room a moment later, Ben was listening to the howling wind outside. "Say, what do you do if the electric goes out?" he wondered.

"Oh, that's not a problem," the nurse said, placing a blanket on the cot. "Jonas Yoder lives just across the road, and if that happens, they bring oil lamps and thermoses of hot water, and heat up meals in their gas oven. No," Susie assured him, "storms aren't a problem here. Even when we were snowed in with every room full and the roads drifted shut so that no one could come or go, Doc and his Jeep could still get through. And when we were running low on groceries, he offered to drive up to Hilltop Market and buy sandwich fixings and ice cream bars. One thing about the Care Center is that Doc's always your neighbor, and you know he'll be there to help. Like one of our nurses who got her car stuck in the ditch on the way to work. Doc wouldn't let us call the tow truck, but hooked a chain to his Jeep and pulled her out himself. Yes, if there's a problem, Doc will take care of it," Susie finished.

"Now, if the baby gets fussy and you need me to watch her so you can get some sleep, just give me a call," Susie offered a moment later.

After turning out the lights, Ben and Anna talked of their dreams for their new little daughter. When the baby whimpered, her daddy was at her side, crooning comforting words in her ear, picking her up, and rocking her. If he couldn't comfort her, he laid the little bundle beside her mother.

"It's just so peaceful here," Anna whispered contentedly after they settled in to sleep.

And the price sure beats a hospital bill! her husband thought. Only $275 for a three-day stay!

If Ruthie had been Dr. Lehman's 4,000th delivery, the delivery would have been free. One fortunate couple managed to have the 2,000th baby Dr. Lehman delivered, and the 3,000th one, so they had two free deliveries.

In the office up the hall, the doctor finished his paperwork and put on his coat. Barb was heading for the basement stairway when he met her in the hallway. "You aren't working too hard, are you?" he asked, studying the elderly woman with concern.

"*Ach* my, Doc," she laughed. "I don't have anything to do anymore. All I do is encourage the women and rock babies. Why, the nurses look after the cleaning, laundry, and food, and take care of the babies in the night. They do everything!"

"Everything except make pies!" Dr. Lehman replied with a chuckle. But there'd be a slice of pie waiting at home, and he'd be there in less time than it took to warm the Jeep.

24.

Zebra-Striped Toast and Contagious Contractions

A black-velvet darkness settled over Mount Eaton. One by one, the stars flickered on like tiny night-lights scattered across the dark sky, and windows darkened in the homes across the hills. But south of town, a light glowed brightly in a window on the far end of the Mount Eaton Care Center. In the nurses' station, a nurse laid a sleeping infant into the crib and tucked the soft quilt tightly around the newborn. Not yet, Florence told herself as she looked longingly at the journal on the counter. Not until my work is done.

"We record interesting statistics in this journal," one nurse had told her. "And we also write in any unusual and humorous Care Center stories. Take a look at it sometime." But Florence had other duties to look after before she could read.

As she placed the instruments from the recent delivery into the autoclave, Florence thought about how different Mount Eaton was from her home on the prairies of Manitoba. Mount Eaton, with its hills, buggies, and 25 mile-per-hour speed zone, was a contrast to the endless expanse of the Manitoba plains, where one's speed was less regulated. Not so in Mount Eaton, she had discovered to her chagrin. The very memory grated like a fingernail against a chalkboard.

She could still see herself buzzing down the black-topped lane of the Care Center, trying to get her letter to the post office before the mail went out for the day. *I wish Dad were here,* she thought longingly, glancing at the familiar address on the envelope lying on the seat of the car. *Everywhere I turn, I see that Steiner boy eyeing me. Now, if Dad were here, he could help me size up this guy in no time.*

Yes, there were so many things to write home about, and letters took so long to get to Manitoba. This note just had to get into the post office before the mail went out today.

When Florence reached the square of Mount Eaton, only a stone's throw from the post office, she noticed the flashing lights of the police cruiser. The shrieking siren seemed to announce to the entire village that the new nurse in town was about to receive a traffic ticket.

"Do you know why I pulled you over?" the stern-faced officer glared down at the nurse.

"Uh, well . . . I . . . I suppose you're wondering about my out-of-state license plate?"

"No. Do you know how fast you were going?" the officer demanded.

"I . . . well, I'm not sure. I suppose around 30."

"Thirty-one miles an hour! And this is a school zone! May I see your driver's license, please." Then he wrote her up, asked her to appear in mayor's court to contest the ticket, or mail in the $70 fine.

Mayor's court! the girl realized in horror. *Dr. Lehman is the village mayor, and he presides over the court! Never!*

Anger and humiliation welled up in the young nurse as she drove away. *I should have just walked that quarter-of-a-mile to the post office,* she fumed. After hurling the letter down the mail chute, Florence drove past the clinic. Seeing Nancy's car there, she pulled in on impulse. *I've got to talk to someone,* she thought. At home she would have talked to Mom and Dad, and they would have given her advice.

"He slaps me with a fine of $70!" Florence cried in indignation after she poured out the story to the receptionist. "Or else I can go to court and contest it in front of Dr. Lehman, and I'm not about to do that!"

"Talk to Doc," Nancy encouraged. "Explain the situation."

"Never. I'll pay the fine before I do that."

"Talk to him," Nancy countered. "I'd do that if I were you. You're new in town and you didn't know what the speed limits are. Doc's got a kind heart, and he's easy to talk to."

"He's too busy, I can't bother him. The other night, Jonas Yoder's wife said she was sweeping the floor at the Care Center when Doc popped out of the lounge, his hair all messed up like he had just woken up. She said he ran down the hall, dashed into a room, and a minute later came walking back with a sheepish smile. 'I must have dreamt the baby was coming,' he said. Poor Doc, he's so busy that he has to work in his sleep. No, I couldn't bother him."

"Florence, Doc's never too busy for people who need him," Nancy insisted.

So, Florence gathered up her courage and talked to Dr. Lehman about the fine. He was kind and sympathetic like Nancy had said. "I can see that must have been very frustrating for you, especially just having arrived in town and not being used to 25 mile-per-hour speed limits. But with all the buggies and children on bikes, we are trying to keep Mount Eaton a safe place to live. Do you think you were actually exceeding the speed limit?"

"Why, yes, I guess I was," Florence admitted with a hint of a smile.

"Well, in that case, it wouldn't work too well for me to tell the officer I'm canceling your fine, would it?"

And so, Florence wrote out a check for $70. Even remembering the incident, the nurse found herself slapping the receiving blankets onto the table as she folded them. Seventy dollars would have purchased two good pairs of shoes.

And then the brown eyes and boyish grin of that muscular farm boy kept haunting her, too. Such problems! she fretted. What'll I do if he asks me out? I hardly know him!

I better stop worrying about fines and boys and check on my patient, Florence chided herself as she tossed a load of baby clothes into the washer before heading up the steps to the main floor. She opened a door softly and glanced around the dark room. The dim glow of the nightlight illuminated a young woman tossing restlessly on her bed. "How are you doing, Martha?"

"Oh, I don't know. It seems like the contractions have slowed down again. And I don't want another dose of castor oil if I can help it! I told Joe he can take the next dose!"

Florence laughed softly at her patient's sense of humor. "We had one woman who put castor oil *on* her stomach, because that's where it was needed after all, and she thought it worked! Some babies just take a long time to come, don't they?"

And others come faster than you want them to, she thought, walking up the hall. Like the night Alice was on duty. Alice had described the scene with such vivid detail that Florence could picture it perfectly. A van drove up to the entrance in the middle of the night, and Alice knew that that meant business, because no one had called ahead to notify her of the arrival. When she observed a well-rounded woman struggling to climb down from the van seat, she knew the situation was urgent. She grabbed a wheelchair and dashed down the hall to the entrance to help the husband ease the distended woman from the vehicle into the chair. As she ran down the hall pushing the wheelchair ahead of her, the nurse observed the patient's graying hair. She's had a dozen children already and she'll go fast, Alice realized in alarm. There was no time to waste, and certainly no time to call a doctor.

Barb! I've got to call Barb!

At the nurses' station, Alice lunged across the counter, snatched the phone, stabbed at the numbers to Barb's basement apartment, and yelled into the mouthpiece: "Barb, get up here! I need you *now!*"

With the husband's help, Alice eased the woman into a bed. "She's ready to go!" Alice realized in dismay.

Dashing down the stairs, she met Barb, who was pulling on her *kapp* and pinning her dress as she came. "Get up here quick!" Alice cried, grabbing Barb by the elbow and yanking her up the stairs. Bursting through the upstairs door, Alice heard the wail of a newborn.

Running into the patient's room, the women discovered the father nervously holding the baby. "Not much different than calving!" he laughed shakily.

Alice yanked open a drawer and grabbed several instruments and handed them to Barb, who clamped and cut the cord. As Alice checked the baby and wrapped her in a blanket, the midwife examined the mother.

"Call Dr. Byler," Barb ordered tersely from the mother's bedside. "We've got another baby coming and it's breech."

Dr. Byler, who lived only a mile away, arrived in time to deliver the twin. Since the woman had delivered a dozen other babies, the breech baby came almost as easily as its twin.

But that was not the closest call. One of Dr. Lehman's patients didn't even make it inside the Care Center doors, the nurses had said. Lois was the only nurse on duty that winter night when a car sped up the lane, the door slammed, and a wide-eyed man dashed up to the nurses' station. "You better get out there fast," he gasped. "My Amish neighbor lady is having her baby in the back seat of my car!"

Not one to panic, Lois picked up the phone and dialed Dr. Lehman's number. *I need to call Doc,* the nurse thought. *If I leave the building, the other women in labor and the newborns will be unattended.*

The call woke Dr. Lehman, who promised to come immediately. The nurse grabbed a kit containing a suction syringe, scissors, and clamps from the counter, as well as the plastic-backed pad and rubber gloves stored beside the kit. She rushed out the door past the driver pacing nervously in the lounge.

As Lois yanked open the back door of the car, she saw the husband leaning over the front seat, speaking encouragingly in Pennsylvania German to his wife on the back seat. The driver was right. The baby was definitely coming. Lois caught the infant, wrapped it in a blue, plastic-backed pad, suctioned its nose, clamped and cut the cord, and tried to shield the baby from the cold air blowing in through the open door behind her.

Glancing up at the nervous father, the nurse said, "Can you turn up the heat? And listen, I forgot a blanket. Can you please get one off the shelf in the supply room on this side of the nurses' station?"

He's shook, Lois realized as the father dashed back to the car, blanket in hand. This baby needs to get inside, but I don't want him walking around with it. He's so nervous he may drop it. "Listen," she said, "I want you to take the baby inside, sit down, and hold it close to keep it warm." The father followed the nurse's orders, and Lois climbed into the car, waiting with the mother until the headlights of Dr. Lehman's Jeep pulled alongside a moment later.

"Bring the delivery table to the front door," Dr. Lehman said calmly and opened the car door to check his patient. Lois pushed the delivery table to the door, helped him lift the young mother onto it, and wheeled her to an empty room.

Yes, Florence thought. Some babies come faster than you care for them to come, and others need a lot of patience. Like Martha's baby. Maybe it's turned a little, and then when it rotates, things will go fast. I'd better keep an eye on her.

A cry from the nursery sent her up the hall. In a glass-sided crib, a tiny, dark head bobbed and little arms flailed under the soft quilt. Tenderly, the nurse scooped up the bundle and changed her diaper. Placing the tiny arms against the little body, she wrapped the little one tightly in her flannel blanket. Newborns loved that security, she knew. The baby quieted in her arms but gazed around with large eyes like shiny glass beads.

In the hickory rocker with the baby in her arms, the nurse savored the peaceful, quiet atmosphere at the Care Center. Other nurses told her of hospital nurseries they worked in where the noise level was often so high that it seemed the wall tiles would crack. As Florence rocked the baby, her eyes fell on the book lying on the shelf. Ah, now I can read while I rock this little one, she sighed contentedly as she opened the journal.

Some Records We Have Set, the first page was titled. *The smallest baby born at the Care Center: 2 pounds, 6 ounces; 10-25-88, Martha Schlabach; Mom, Katie Schlabach (Mrs. Levi Jr.). The largest baby born at the Care Center: 13 pounds, 22 inches; 11-15-96, Derrick Tyler Wengerd; Mom, Fannie Wengerd (Mrs. Ferman).*

Turning the page, the nurse continued to read: *We had one lady who was pregnant 26 times—seven miscarriages, 19 children.* Florence remembered Dr. Lehman telling that story. *We had one woman who had three sets of twins and four single births: 10 children in nine years.*

Dr. Lehman kept his own small book of interesting facts, which he carried in his pocket, Florence knew. He told her that he delivered an average of 187 babies a year. It took five years until he began to average 100 deliveries a year. In his first year of practice, he delivered 28 babies. In 1992, he delivered the most babies in one year—281. In 1993, he had 275 deliveries, and in 1994, 278. The last 61 days of 1996, he had 59 deliveries. Over his career, Dr. Lehman also delivered 72 sets of twins and one set of triplets.

"For a number of families, I've delivered two babies in one year," she had heard Dr. Lehman say. "One in January and another in December—but not every year, of course!"

No wonder Doc is so busy he has to work in his sleep, Florence thought, flipping through the section of humorous incidents that occurred at the Care Center.

Such as the zebra-striped toast. A nurse walked into the kitchen one morning to find an Amishman contentedly browning his bread on the wonderful new gadget called a toaster. Carefully, he laid the two slices of bread across the top of the four-slice toaster. He pressed the lever down and observed that the coils down in the belly of the appliance heated up. What a slick contraption! After a few seconds, the man lifted the corner of one slice to see that it was nicely brown-and-white striped. Hmm. These gadgets make fancy bread. He flipped the slices, waited a bit, and picked up his zebra-striped bread. Strange, he thought. He liked all of his bread toasted, not just parts of it. Oh well, some people must like it this way. Not too efficient, though.

The nurse picked up a piece of bread, adjusted the temperature control from five to three, and dropped the slice into one of the slots. "If you toast your bread *inside* the toaster instead of on top of it," she suggested, "you can do four slices at once, both sides at one time, and it won't be striped like a zebra!"

The Amishman smiled, thinking that the *Englischer* who invented this contraption wasn't so foolish after all. Not bad. Pretty efficient, too. Four slices at once!

Florence flipped through the pages until she found the story about the young couple who came without calling. She remembered hearing about that one. A shy, young couple had timidly peered around the window at the nursing station. No one had called. Who could this be? the nurse wondered.

"What can I do for you?" she asked kindly.

"We are having a baby," the young man announced.

"Must be their first. They sure do look young," she thought, observing the girlish face and the man's thin beard.

"Have you had any contractions?" the nurse asked the woman who peered out from under a black bonnet and held a black shawl tightly around her ample form.

The young couple looked at each other questioningly.

"Have you had any pains?" the nurse tried again.

"No."

"Did your water break?"

"Uhhhh . . . I . . . I don't think so," the girl stammered, blushing slightly.

"Then why did you come?" the nurse asked as gently as she could.

The young man drew himself up to his full height and pushed back his shoulders, "Well, the due date is today, so we came to have the baby! That's why!"

"Oh, I'm sorry, but it doesn't work that way. You must wait until her pains start, and then time them. When the pains are hard and several minutes apart, or if her water breaks, then you call us here at the Care Center, and we'll tell you if it's time to come or not."

The woman blinked back tears.

The nurse noticed her disappointment. "Listen, it won't be long. The pains will start soon. Maybe today, maybe tomorrow, probably before the week is up. But you don't want to stay here and wait that long. Go home and rest, and when the pains start, time them and call us."

"See you soon!" the nurse called as the young couple walked out the door.

"That was certainly not typical," Dr. Lehman agreed when the nurse shared the story with him. "But it's not the first time I've heard of that happening, either. An engineer brought his wife to the hospital some time ago because it was her due date."

"An engineer?"

"Yes, an engineer," he nodded. "He kept insisting that this was the day his baby was due and this was the day it would arrive. The nurses could not get through to him that babies don't necessarily arrive on their due dates. In fact, they finally had to ask the doctor to talk to the engineer."

"I can hardly believe that."

"Well, you know, with an engineer everything is predictable, exact, and precise. It's almost easier to understand why an engineer would think that way than a farmer."

The Care Center staff discovered that, more often than not,

the farmers were so thoroughly "educated" by their experiences that some would have felt quite at home delivering their own baby, and most were at least knowledgeable about the process. They had delivered hundreds of calves, rotating them in utero and even pulling them out, if necessary. And, big calves were harder to deliver in a cold, dark barn than tiny babies in a warm, well-lit Care Center. But, their children were far more valuable than calves, and that was the difference. No one could argue that.

One farmer, who lived 90 minutes from Mount Eaton, wanted the nurse to teach him how to check his wife so he wouldn't have to bring her to the Care Center unnecessarily. Three times he had paid a driver 50 hard-earned dollars to bring his wife to the Care Center, and three times they returned without a baby: false labor. Fifty dollars each time! This false labor was expensive and time consuming!

As the couple prepared to leave after the third time, the farmer turned to the nurse and said, "I'd like you to teach me how to check my wife so I can tell when she's ready to go. That way we won't waste any more time and money on false runs."

"Oh, that would take too long," the nurse replied, trying to discourage the father.

"*Ach*, I could learn!" the farmer insisted. "I've delivered lots of calves, and I know I could learn how to check her! I know just when to call the vet for the cows! I know I could learn!"

"Listen, there is a big difference between checking a cow and checking a woman. Most medical people spend a long time learning those things." The nurse could be stubborn, too! "Just bring her when her contractions are getting hard."

Not long afterward, the couple showed up at the Care Center for the fourth time. The woman barely made it to her room when the baby arrived, and the doctor missed the delivery entirely.

Glancing down, Florence saw that the baby slept serenely in her arms. "You just wanted to be close to someone, didn't you," the nurse cooed, touching her lips to the downy head.

I've learned a lot about the Amish folks by working here, the nurse thought as she cuddled the baby close. By and large, they are a widely-read, self-educated people, although there are exceptions. Because many Amish are more comfortable speaking Pennsylvania German than English, an occasional misused word, or even an incorrect syllable, could provide a humorous result.

Mary recorded a story of the time a patient's husband stopped by the window to ask, "Did the patient that Dr. Lehman was seducing last night have her baby?"

The nurse looked at him with horror. "Dr. Lehman's not that kind of man. He'd never try to seduce any woman, and certainly not a patient!"

"Well, he seduced her, and I don't think there's anything wrong with him giving her medicine to start her pains!" the man was indignant. "Why, we sometimes seduce cows if their labor doesn't continue."

Mary began to laugh. "*Inducing*! Dr. Lehman was *inducing* the patient, not seducing her!"

The farmer's face reddened as he hastily agreed, "*Ach*, yes, yes, inducing. He was inducing her!"

Another day, a nurse checked on a patient and asked about her contractions.

"Oh my," the expectant mother sighed, lowering her voice to a whisper. "They are getting quite contagious."

The nurse jumped back in mock horror. "*What*! Your contractions are becoming contagious? I think I'd better leave!"

"Oh please don't leave. They . . . ohhh . . . they are coming all the time."

"Continuous! Your contractions are continuous! Well that's good, that means you'll soon have your baby," the nurse patted the woman's arm encouragingly. "But I'm glad they aren't becoming contagious. Someone needs to do the work around here!"

The Amish are industrious, helpful folk, Florence had observed. One farmer couldn't bear to sit around and do nothing while he waited for his wife's labor to progress, so he went and cleaned out the Care Center barn.

On another occasion, when one of the nurses spotted a snake coiled near the cornfield bordering the Care Center property, a patient's husband went out to investigate. The farmer wanted to kill it the way he killed all snakes, by stepping on its head. But the nurse was concerned the snake would bite him. So, to appease the nurse, the Amishman crushed the snake with a shovel instead of the heel of his shoe.

And when Kathy accidentally locked herself into the bathroom adjoining the nurses' station, she was extremely thankful that the Amish men were as handy at taking things apart as they were at constructing them. Nothing causes panic like being locked behind a sturdy door when a baby in the next room is about to be born. As the Care Center nurse, it was Kathy's job to care for the baby and mother after delivery, and here she was, ridiculously locked in a little cubicle. In desperation, she pounded frantically on the bathroom wall. Fortunately, another nurse on duty heard the commotion and came running.

"You can be thankful we were across the wall," the nurse's colleague told her through the door. "If we had been at the other end of the hall, we would have never heard you. Just hang in there. I'll see if anyone knows how to take this door apart."

"You are going to have to take the pins out of the hinges," the prospective father instructed Kathy, sliding a screwdriver under the door a moment later. Once the nurse had removed the pins, the muscular Amishman shoved in the door and freed the nurse from her short imprisonment, just in time to help deliver the baby.

Florence closed the book suddenly. Speaking of delivering babies, I'd better check Martha! The woman was wide awake. A quick check revealed it was time to call Dr. Lehman. Minutes later, Florence heard the doctor's Jeep climbing the hill. He washed up, pulled on his scrubs, and walked into Martha's room in time to deliver her baby.

Twenty minutes later, he looked up from the form he was filling out. "By the way, Florence, last Sunday afternoon when I was taking a nap, a young man called me and asked some questions about you."

"So, what did he want to know?" she asked, gripping the edge of the counter.

"Well, for one thing, he asked for your personal phone number."

"And what did you tell him?"

"I had to admit I didn't know what it was, or if you even had one. Actually, I'm embarrassed to say I couldn't even give him your last name. I told him I thought you hailed from Manitoba somewhere."

"And what did he say?"

"He sounded kind of disappointed. Here this doctor couldn't even relay pertinent information about one of his nurses! I suppose a person's performance is more important to me than their last name or where they come from. But anyway, I guess I didn't strike out completely, because I gave him an address where he could reach you."

"Right! You gave him the clinic address, and all the nurses saw the letter and teased me about my secret admirer. I declared I didn't have one, as far as I was concerned!"

"Ah, that was fast. So he already sent a letter, did he? Well, I'd encourage you not to keep him waiting, but to answer soon. He comes from good stock, Florence, from a long line of Swiss farmers. And those Swiss are industrious folk, tidy and pleasant. Yes, I've known the Steiner family for years. In fact his brother introduced me to the kerosene remedy when he injured his hand in a farm accident. And his cousin was born during the blizzard the time I rode the fire engine to the house because the roads were closed.

"Yes, between those two Steiner families, there were around 17 boys, so they kept us busy stitching up one farm accident after another. Really, Florence, this Steiner boy seems to be a nice young man. Don't make him wait too long."

As he left, he laid a package on her desk. Must be an early Christmas gift, Florence figured, shaking and squeezing the soft packet. It feels like a pair of socks, she thought. As she ripped it open, a wad of one-dollar bills fell out.

"What in the world!" Quickly she counted them. Sure enough, there were exactly $70! *Oh, Doc!*

A year-and-a-half later, Florence received a card from Dr. Lehman saying:

Dear Florence,

Your "special day" would have come sooner if you had answered that special letter sooner, as I urged you to. As a wedding gift, I'm giving you writing paper, envelopes, and stamps to assist you in answering future letters sooner. I'm also giving you a flashlight, which you should have had to assist you on your detective work as to whom that letter came from—which would have made your special day come sooner, too! This is my last advice, and I'll turn you over to Oren!

Best wishes,
You're a great nurse!
Dr. Lehman

If only every day would be filled with the happy moments, smiles, and laughter that so often characterized life at the Mount Eaton Care Center. But deliveries were only part of a country doctor's duties. As a family practitioner, Dr. Lehman served patients from birth—until death.

25.

THE MYSTERIOUS CASE OF "LITTLE BOY BLUE"

D r. Lehman studied the face in the picture of "Little Boy Blue" in the *Reader's Digest*. He scanned the soft, straight hair, the parted lips and round face, eyes closed as if in sleep. He never dreamed that he had seen this child before, nor that the boy was a patient of his. Never.

The magazine described the bitterly cold Christmas Eve when the body of the boy was found—alone in deep weeds bordering a field.

How had this child, who looked to be about nine years old, come there? Who would abandon such a small body, dressed in a baby blue sleeper on a night when the wind-chill dipped to 40 below zero? Did his death signal some larger threat? Were more people at risk of injury or death at the hand of a killer whose motives were as yet unknown?

The poignant irony of this peaceful-looking child, dead on the Eve of the holiday honoring another child's birth, only deepened the mystery and the horror.[7]

Perhaps it was his experience as coroner that sent Dr. Lehman scanning the article again for clues to the child's death. The dark bruises on the neck were caused by freezing and not by strangling, as had earlier been speculated. The skin was torn from the face by wild animals and not from torture. The body showed no signs of abuse or mistreatment, the article said. But there was no clue as to what caused the child's death.

If foul play was involved, then why wasn't the body better hidden? Dr. Lehman wondered. Was the boy deposited at the roadside by a relative after dying of natural causes?

Three months after the discovery, the body still had not been identified, nor did his fingerprints match any in the files of missing children. Though the cause of death was still a mystery, a pathologist had ruled that the child likely died of natural causes. "Little Boy Blue," as the child in the blue sleeper was called, was released for burial around Easter. But no one claimed the body. Local folks and others as far away as Kansas donated a lot, vault, and casket for the boy that the community had named Matthew, meaning gift of God.

Some 450 people attended the funeral for the abandoned child, where the pastor told them that those who left the child beside the road may have been fearful of the law or could have been confused or sick. He said that God did not ask the audience to know the hearts of those who abandoned the child, but rather, God wanted them to search their own hearts.

Pastor Samuelson guessed that whoever had deposited the body in the roadside weeds had done so in deep sadness. His clue? The child's hand had been placed over his heart. The officiating minister tried to comfort his audience by imagining the tender reasoning which may have led to such an action.[8]

In closing, the pastor read a well-known children's prayer:

Now I lay me down to sleep,
I pray thee, Lord, my soul to keep.
If I should die before I wake,
I pray thee, Lord, my soul to take.
Amen.

Eventually, a donated granite headstone marked the child's grave: "Little Boy abandoned, found near Chester, Neb., Dec. 24, 1985." A space was left for the child's real name if the mystery were ever solved. At the base of the gravestone read: "Whom we have called Matthew, which means Gift of God." Flowers, teddy bears, and other gifts decorated the graveside. Across the country, the story of the abandoned child touched people's hearts, and money poured in to help cover the funeral and burial expenses for the child who seemed to have been forsaken.

Before closing the magazine, Dr. Lehman turned back to the photo and thoughtfully studied the mystery child once again. After laying aside the magazine, he couldn't dismiss the unusual case from his mind. The fact that the child in the new blue sleeper was clean, his hair neatly trimmed, and his nails carefully manicured indicated he was well cared for. So, why did no one claim the body? How did he die? Who laid the boy in the snowy field near Thayer, Nebraska, and placed his left hand over his heart? He recalled that the Swartzentruber Amish place a hand over the heart of their dead before burial.

Two weeks later, Sheriff Young from Thayer, Nebraska, called Dr. Lehman. "I'm investigating the Little Boy Blue case, and I'd like to ask you a few questions. I understand that you were Danny Stutzman's doctor, is that correct?"

"Danny Stutzman! Why yes, he was a patient of mine a few years back before his father moved out of state . . . ." Dr. Lehman's voice died away as the implications struck his heart. Danny! Oh please, Lord, not Danny!

"Do you have a copy of his fingerprints on file?" the sheriff questioned. "Some of Eli Stutzman's acquaintances suspect the abandoned child may be his son Danny," the sheriff continued. "Friends of Eli's in Wyoming sent me pictures of Danny after they read the story of Little Boy Blue in *Reader's Digest*, and thought the picture of the child resembled Stutzman."

"Let me check with the woman in whose home the child was delivered," Dr. Lehman offered, hoping the suspicions would prove false. "But Barb generally sends the fingerprints home with the mothers, and Danny's mother died in a mysterious barn fire."

After hanging up the phone, Dr. Lehman returned to the photo in the *Reader's Digest* story and scrutinized the picture of the boy once again. It just might be Danny, he thought, studying the straight, sandy-colored hair and the round face of the child in the blue sleeper who appeared to be slumbering peacefully. The face does vaguely resemble Eli's, and I can see a similarity to Ida, too, but it's been so long since Eli and Danny left the community.

As Dr. Lehman gazed at the picture, his thoughts traveled back to the first time he had seen Danny—at the delivery out at Barb's house on September 7, 1976. Barb had called saying Mrs. Stutzman had arrived and that her labor seemed to progress awfully fast for a first-time mother, so he rushed out to the Hostetler home. Bill's horses frolicking in the pasture and Eli Stutzman's buggy horse standing placidly at the hitching post gave no hint of the tragedies that lay ahead for the young family inside.

As he opened the door, the high-pitched cry of a newborn quickened the doctor's steps. Pulling back the curtain of Barb's delivery room, his eyes swept the chamber. Barb was placing a red-faced, squalling infant into the arms of a pleasant-faced woman.

"A two-hour labor," Barb beamed. "How do you like that for a first timer?"

"Almost unheard of," Dr. Lehman replied, opening his satchel as he surveyed the room.

Blonde hair framed the new mother's appealing face and soft hazel eyes. A lean, solidly-built young man sat quietly on a chair near the bed. His brown hair was trimmed in bangs above his eyebrows and fell evenly below his ears in a typical Swartzentruber haircut. Intensely blue, the eyes in the narrow, bearded face shone with unusual interest as they followed the doctor's movements.

One would never have imagined that the schoolteacher in suspenders and home-sewn clothing had once owned a car. Nor would one have guessed that the shy Amishman with the winning ways had once been a clean-shaven hospital orderly.

"Howdy, Doc," the young man smiled warmly.

"Congratulations, Eli! So, you have a son, do you? Have you decided on a name for the little fellow?"

"We're calling him Danny," Eli replied with a proud smile. "Danny Stutzman."

I hope for Ida and for the child's sake that this man has stabilized, Dr. Lehman thought, recalling the times Eli's father, a Swartzentruber Amish bishop, had called him out to the Stutzman home to tend to the teenager, who appeared to suffer nervous breakdowns. More than once, Dr. Lehman had prescribed medication for Eli, who cried inconsolably during those times.

There were whispered reports that Eli had done his *rumshpringa*, buying a car, drinking, and more. Numerous Amish youth "sowed their wild oats," but many of those eventually settled down to join the church and marry in the faith.

A number of Amish parents strongly opposed *rumshpringa*. "If we sow wild oats, we'll reap a bitter harvest," they declared, believing youthful sins created habits that made it difficult to adhere to the church's standards when a person wanted to settle down. This seemed to be the case with Eli.

To marry Ida, he sold his car, got rid of his "English" clothes, grew his hair and beard to regulation length, and joined the church. From their earliest courtship days, the youth with the brilliant blue eyes and charming personality had captured Ida's heart. She heard rumors about Eli's wild life but loved him anyway. Surely, with a caring wife, Eli would settle down and be a good husband and father, she reasoned.

Dr. Lehman was pleasantly surprised when the Stutzmans brought Danny to the office for baby shots several months later. He had never vaccinated any other Swartzentruber Amish children before. Eli must be more progressive than his fellow church members, and he must care deeply about Danny to break protocol for what he believed was best for his son, Dr. Lehman thought. And now they had a second child on the way. Perhaps the Stutzman home would be a happy one, after all.

The following summer, headlines about a barn fire in the *Wooster Daily Record* caught Dr. Lehman's attention. Did the barn belong to one of my patients? he wondered, quickly scanning the article.

Eli Stutzman. The name struck him like a dart. The article said the burned barn belonged to Eli Stutzman, whose wife Ida had *died* in the barn fire. He read the line again. There must be a mistake! Quickly, he devoured the rest of the article for clues to the tragedy. "I don't understand," he sighed.

Phyllis glanced at her husband's furrowed eyebrows and frowning face. "What don't you understand?"

"This article about the barn fire. It seems odd Ida died in the barn fire. It says here that Eli claimed the barn was struck by lightning in the afternoon. He says he doused the flames all evening, but the fire must have smoldered into the night. When his wife woke him at midnight saying the barn was on fire, he ran to the upper barn to see what he could salvage while Ida rushed into the milk house to try to save the milk cans. Later, Eli reported that he found his wife lying on her back near the milk house, dead, under the milk vats she had supposedly been trying to save.

"Strange. If Ida was overcome by smoke, why would she fall on her back if she had been pushing the vats? She would have fallen forward. I wonder what Dr. Questel found."

"It was a heart attack," the senior coroner replied matter-of-factly when Dr. Lehman asked several days later about the cause of death.

"A heart attack?" Dr. Lehman questioned. "How did you come up with that?"

"Stutzman said his wife had a weak heart ever since she had rheumatic fever, so it figures that the woman died of a heart attack with the excitement of the fire and the strain of moving the milk vats."

"There must be a misunderstanding," Dr. Lehman said. Ida has been a patient of mine ever since she was a teenager, and she's always had a strong heart!"

"Something doesn't add up," Dr. Questel mused.

"Yes well, perhaps Eli got things mixed up in the stress of the fire. I hope that's what happened. But how did she get those bruises on her face if she had a heart attack and fell over backwards? It's a very strange case."

The Amish community came together and built a new barn for Eli Stutzman, Dr. Lehman learned. They donated not only labor but the materials, as well, since they felt sorry for the man who seemed emotionally unhinged at the loss of his wife and barn. It didn't suit the Amish too well that Eli drew up plans for a barn better designed to hold race horses than for the functions of a traditional Amish dairy. The unconventional barn plans were one of the first indications, however, that Eli's heart no longer was with his Amish kinsfolk.

In addition to the support Eli received from Ida's family and from the Amish community, a neighbor family tried to help him and his motherless child. When they baby-sat for Danny, they observed that he was always very clean and well cared for. Yet, the child seemed frightened, and they often saw men hanging around the Stutzman home, partying and drinking.

After a trip to Florida in 1978, Eli bought a car and modernized the house and barn, installing electricity and modern appliances on the farm. He trimmed his Swartzentruber hairstyle short, shaved his beard, and bought clothing to replace his home-sewn wardrobe.

Then in 1982, Eli sold the 83-acre farm and moved to Colorado, where he and a partner bought a horse farm. After selling the horse farm two years later, Eli and his son moved to Texas, where he found a job as a carpenter. A friend, Glen Pritchett, eventually moved in with them. When Pritchett's body was found in a ditch with a bullet hole in his head in May 1985, Eli was a likely suspect. Eli moved on again when police questioned his son about the relationship between the two men.

Eli then left Danny with friends in Lyman, Wyoming, saying he wanted to work on clearing his name. Six months later, one week before Christmas 1985, Eli picked up his son in Wyoming, explaining that he was taking the child to see his grandparents near Apple Creek, Ohio. But the child never arrived. The night before Christmas, an abandoned body was found in a Nebraska cornfield.

And now Sheriff Young wanted Danny's newborn footprints. After the sheriff's call, Dr. Lehman walked across the street to Mayor's Court and thought about Eli and Danny. Is it possible? Could Danny really be Little Boy Blue? I can hardly imagine—Eli was always so caring and concerned about Danny. Surely not.

As the Mayor's Court convened, Dr. Lehman addressed a young traffic offender who had driven his buggy around a stopped school bus that had its lights flashing. The youth held a Florida driver's license, the doctor was aware, so the offender knew better than to pass a stopped school bus.

He doesn't have an Ohio license, so I can't take his driver's license away for violating the law. What penalty can I give him? Dr. Lehman thought.

"What were you thinking when you passed the school bus with its flashing lights?" he questioned.

"About deer hunting," the youth replied.

Ah, that's the answer. I can take away his hunting license, Dr. Lehman thought. "Have you shot a deer this season?" Dr. Lehman questioned.

"Yep, I got mine," he replied.

I guess I'll have to fine him, he decided.

"Your fine will be—" Dr. Lehman began. Suddenly, he recognized the face of the man accompanying the young traffic offender. That fellow was a friend of Eli Stutzman!

Dr. Lehman pulled the man aside after the court session ended and showed him the picture of Little Boy Blue.

"Why, that's Danny Stutzman!" the man exclaimed. "I'm sure of it!"

Meanwhile, Ida's relatives had been doing their own detective work. In July 1986, the late Mrs. Stutzman's father Amos Gingerich received a letter from Eli stating that Danny had been killed in a car accident in Lyman, Wyoming, and was buried there. Shocked by the news and still suspicious about Ida's death, her father Amos and brother Andy took a bus west to see Danny's grave and to investigate the story. The Gingerichs found no grave nor could they locate any records of an accident involving Danny. Nor did Eli's Wyoming friends know anything of an accident or of Danny's death. They said Eli picked the boy up at their place days before Christmas to take his son back to Ohio to visit his grandparents over Christmas. After the holidays, Stutzman had written that he was employed at a carpenter shop in Ohio, and that Danny was happily enrolled in a Mennonite school nearby.

Though distraught by Danny's death and the uncertainties surrounding it, Ida's family comforted each other saying it was for the best. Danny was safe in heaven with his mother where he would be free of his father's influences.

One piece at a time, the clues came together. An acquaintance of Eli reported to the sheriff that he had received a letter from Eli before the holidays saying Danny might not be with him when he arrived. Stutzman's '75 Gremlin had been seen in the Thayer, Nebraska, vicinity the day before the body was found. In addition, some speculated that Danny may have known too much about Pritchett's murder, for which Eli was wanted by the police.

News articles reporting the mysterious case mentioned that Dr. Lehman was the Stutzman family doctor. When reporters called Dr. Lehman to question him about Eli, Dr. Lehman told them how Eli made sure his son had the full line of vaccines, which was almost unheard of among Swartzentruber Amish. Several articles reported Dr. Questel's misgivings about the ruling of Ida's cause of death. "I always wondered if we missed the boat on that one," he said, adding that he now believed he should have sent Mrs. Stutzman's body to a crime lab for a "meticulous autopsy."[9]

In December 1987, palm prints taken from one of Danny's report cards proved that Little Boy Blue was indeed Danny Stutzman. A warrant went out for Eli's arrest. Detectives traced him through return addresses on letters he had written relatives. He was arrested at a trailer park in Texas, taken in for questioning regarding the death and abandonment of his son, and charged with a felony of child abuse.

Arriving in Thayer, Nebraska, Eli asked to see his son's grave. "I'm glad it's finally out in the open," he said. "I feel I have caused people pain and grief, and I'm sorry. I will not deny that I have handled the situation with Danny's death the wrong way, and I beg forgiveness. I'm guilty of lies, but I did not abuse or kill my son."[10]

Eli pled guilty to abandoning a body and failing to report a death. At first, Eli's answers in the court session were unemotional and expressionless. Then, when asked whether he had killed his son, he began to weep. "No! He was sick!"

Eli said that when he picked Danny up in Wyoming and started out for Ohio, his son was sick, and when Eli gave him medicine, he just got worse. At a rest stop, the boy put on the new blue sleeper Eli had given him for Christmas and then lay down with a blanket on some luggage in the back and seemed to fall asleep, the father explained.

The boy was unusually quiet for some time and didn't respond when spoken to, so Eli said he pulled over and checked on him. When he couldn't waken the boy, he panicked, he said, and didn't know what to do. Remembering his training as an orderly, he gave the child CPR. Then he said he stayed and prayed with the child several hours before placing him in the snow where God could find him.

Dr. Lehman followed the newspaper articles about the Stutzman case. Some articles reported that in Wyoming, Danny was being treated for haemophilus, a form of influenza that can cause two fatal diseases, meningitis and epiglottis. Meningitis causes inflammation of the brain and spinal tissues, while epiglottis is a swelling of the air passages, causing suffocation. Was this illness the cause of Danny's death? some wondered.

One attorney pursued the lead that Eli's Gremlin had a leaky exhaust and that the child died of carbon monoxide poisoning, since the autopsy showed a slightly elevated carbon monoxide level. Yet, authorities felt that the level found in the body was not high enough to be fatal. Eli's attorney quoted from a pathologist's ruling that the child died from natural causes.

But if the child had died of natural causes, why did the father abandon the body and lie to his relatives about the death? folks wondered. Eli explained that he didn't want to face his family and friends.

Roommates and acquaintances were puzzled over the death, describing Eli as kind and loving with his son, saying he never struck him.

In January 1988, Dr. Lehman read the newspaper account reporting that Stutzman, 37, had pled guilty to misdemeanor charges of abandoning a body and concealing a death, and was sentenced to 18 months in jail. Another article reported that Stutzman underwent psychiatric evaluations to determine if he should be sent to prison. The psychiatrists diagnosed Eli as a socio-psychopath.

Eighteen months after the initial sentencing, newspaper articles announced: "Stutzman Given 40 Years in Killing of Albert Pritchett, A Former Employee and Roommate."[11] Photographs showed 38-year-old Stutzman with a neat haircut, a mustache, and a suit and tie.

"My client maintains his innocence, and we will appeal," Stutzman's attorney declared.[12]

After Eli was jailed, Dr. and Mrs. Lehman flew to Texas to visit the doctor's sister Jenelle.

"We'll be close to where Eli Stutzman is incarcerated," Dr.

Lehman told Phyllis. "I want to see if I can get permission to see him." As he drove up to the gate of the penitentiary, he thought of the charmingly shy Amish youth he had known.

The man with the short brown hair parted neatly at the side bore little resemblance to the Eli that Dr. Lehman recalled. Only the brilliant blue eyes and the crisp facial features called to mind the former Amishman, whose lean face now appeared hardened.

"How are you, Eli?" Dr. Lehman asked, his eyes and voice brimming with concern for his former patient.

"I feel really good," Eli shared, obviously happy to see the doctor. "They tell me I have AIDS but I can't believe it, because I feel great."

"Eli," Dr. Lehman asked gently after a few moments, "they say you killed Danny. Did you do it?"

"No, Doc. I didn't kill my boy."

"Then why did you lay him in the snow?"

"It was such a beautiful night," Eli said, gazing thoughtfully at the ceiling. "The moon was shining down on the snow, and I just laid him out where God could find him."

Eli's troubled face told the doctor that he still lacked the peace and happiness he had searched for and that possibly had cost the lives of those dearest to him in the process.

For the next number of years, Dr. Lehman's sister and her husband regularly visited Eli in prison. Eventually, he was released to a halfway house with orders to stay in the state of Texas.

Every December, when Dr. Lehman opened an envelope postmarked in Texas and read the homemade Christmas card from Eli, he prayed his former patient would come to know the Prince of Peace, who came to set captives free.

26.

THE PUZZLE OF THE PERPLEXING PAINS

"Doc, Tina says her stomach hurts again," Nancy announced after placing the phone on hold.

"Tina says *what?*" The doctor whirled around to face the receptionist. "Don't tell me her stomach is bothering her again! She was here twice yesterday and almost every other day last week. The tests don't find a thing wrong." Dr. Lehman scratched his head thoughtfully. "Does she sound like she's in pain?"

"No, she doesn't have that tortured tone to her voice, but—"

"One can never be sure. Try and work her in this afternoon, if you can," he replied. "Sometimes patients need a loving touch, kind word, or a listening ear more than they need a prescription."

Dr. Lehman walked back to his office shaking his head at the puzzle. After flipping through his reference books for a few moments, he snapped them shut again with a sigh. Lord, I need wisdom for this case, he prayed. Help me find out what's wrong with Tina!

Between phone calls and setting up new appointments, Nancy's thoughts, too, kept going back to the elderly woman with the mysterious stomach pains. We can't keep letting her come in every day or two, she thought. But on the other hand, we can't afford not to. What if there really is a problem? she worried, thinking of the story Alice told her years ago.

"One morning early in the practice," Alice had said, "we had an elderly woman who called complaining of chest pains. It was one of those hectic days, but we managed to work her into the afternoon schedule. The patient died before she got into the office. After that, none of us wanted to take any chances. Nancy, if patients claim to be in pain, then let them come."

Alice is right, Nancy thought, opening the door to the waiting room. But I just wish we could solve the mystery of those chronic stomach pains!

She scanned the room already filling with patients holding black bonnets or hats on their laps. In the corner, an "English" lady read a story to an Amish boy in a small hickory rocker. Nancy knew the child didn't understand the English words, but he sat politely, anyway.

"Okay, Paul, we're ready for you," Nancy called, spotting the youth she was looking for. Showing the teenager to a room, she requested, "Please put a urine sample into a cup in the restroom."

Are there any more tests I should be running on Tina? Dr. Lehman wondered as he walked into an examining room where Alice had prepped an elderly patient for office surgery. The area around the sebaceous cyst had been shaved. After numbing the site, he lifted the scalpel and slit a narrow incision across the top of the golf-ball-sized bulge, careful not to cut too deep to puncture the cyst.

"We don't want to destroy the capsule," Dr. Lehman explained, "or we'll have a lot of thick cheesy stuff all over the place." Carefully he lifted out the intact cyst and then began to stitch shut the incision.

"What makes the cyst grow?" the patient asked.

"We don't always know," he replied, stitching as he spoke. "But most sebaceous cysts are caused by a plugged duct."

Just as he knotted the last suture, Nancy popped into the room. "Doc, we've got a burn victim out here. It looks like he'll need the squad and some morphine."

After calling the squad as Dr. Lehman had instructed, Nancy couldn't concentrate on her deskwork. The names on the envelopes she was trying to address blurred until all she could see was that poor patient quivering from shock and pain. The memory of her mother's accident flashed in her mind: the roaster with the turkey and sizzling broth spilling down over her mother's side, the terrible pain, the hospital stay, and then Dr. Lehman's kindness. He let her off work for two weeks with pay and stopped by the house regularly after her mother was released and didn't charge a cent.

I've got to go back there and see if I can help that poor man, she decided, hurrying back the hall. As she entered the room, one of the nurses injected the patient with morphine. Another held ice packs to the scorched, blistered torso. Grabbing a couple of packs, Nancy held them against the reddened skin until the ambulance arrived. She couldn't help but notice the terrible burns, and that every hair had been burned off his chest.

"I was throwing gas on a trash pile, trying to get the junk to burn," the patient explained. "All of a sudden the whole gas can just exploded, and there were flames all around me."

As the medics carried the stretcher out to the loading dock, Nancy heard the front door creak open.

"What do you have there?" Dr. Lehman asked as his flustered receptionist entered the lab with a plastic cup dispenser brimming with yellow liquid.

"A urine sample. It's my fault. The cup dispenser was empty so the poor chap thought I wanted him to use the cup *dispenser*."

"And what are you going to do about it?"

"I'm going to buy a new cup dispenser. One with holes in it."

"And we'll have to make sure that it stays stocked with cups, too," the doctor advised. "And perhaps screw it securely to the wall. If only all our dilemmas were so easy to solve."

Nancy heard the front door creak open and turned around to see a spry, elderly woman totter into the waiting room with a large smile wreathing her wrinkled face. "Why hello, Tina!" Nancy greeted warmly. "Don't you look nice today! Do you have a new dress?"

The wrinkled face glowed as Tina hobbled to her seat, leaning on her daughter's arm. "I'm just fine, except for that nasty tummy ache," she sighed, patting her neatly permed curls and adjusting her necklace.

"There's our Tina!" Alice bubbled, giving the old lady a warm hug and then guiding her into an examining room. I could almost record her vitals with my eyes shut! Alice smiled to herself, jotting the last notations.

Who's coming now? Nancy wondered as a young man limped painfully into the waiting room. His arm dangled at his side and beads of sweat stood out on the tense lines of his youthful face. Nancy shook her head, thinking, Buddy, you're wasting your time here. You should've gone straight to the hospital.

"Whatever did you do?" she questioned.

"I was playing . . . ball at the ball field up the road . . . ," he grimaced. "My shoulder's out of place or broken . . . I've never had such pain in my life," the youth groaned, his pale face contorting in agony.

"I'm afraid you'll have to go to the emergency room. I don't think there's anything Dr. Lehman can do to help you."

"Oh, please! I was sure—"

"I know. Everyone seems to think that Dr. Lehman can fix anything, but, unfortunately, he can't."

"What do we have here?" Dr. Lehman asked, looking over Nancy's shoulder and assessing the situation. "Bring him back to the X-ray table and I'll see what I can do for him."

Wasted time, Doc, Nancy thought. Opening the waiting room door for the patient, she noted that he cradled the dangling limb with his other arm, cringing every step of the way.

In the X-ray room, Dr. Lehman and his nurse helped ease the moaning boy onto the low table. The doctor gently examined the youth's shoulder and asked questions about the accident. Resting his forehead on his hand for a moment, he tried to decide the best course of action.

"I'm going to do something a bit unconventional here," he announced, slipping off his shoe. "But I believe it will save you a trip to the emergency room."

"Just do it, Doc," the ball player urged. "This thing hurts so bad, I don't care what you do."

As Dr. Lehman gently lifted the injured limb, Nancy stepped closer. I've got to see this, she thought. Carefully, Dr. Lehman placed his stockinged foot into the hollow of the boy's armpit. Gently, he lifted the useless limb and gave the arm a quick yank. With a pop, the shoulder snapped into place.

"Well, of all things!" Nancy laughed, heading for her desk. "Well, Doc, what are you gonna teach us next?"

Maybe someone could teach me how to diagnose stomach problems, the doctor thought, hurrying to the room where Tina waited.

"Well, how's Tina today?" the doctor asked, walking into the room and patting the elderly patient's shoulder.

"Oh, I'm pretty good, except for that aching stomach again!" she laughed in her quivery voice.

"If we can ever take care of that stomach, I think you'll live to be 100, as perky and as healthy as you are," Alice observed with a laugh.

"My wife's grandmother was 103," Dr. Lehman said, scanning the clipboard. "When she turned 100, she decided it was time to cancel the subscription to *Prevention Magazine!*"

The three laughed together. Then as the doctor examined the patient, he became increasingly perplexed. He could find nothing abnormal, and yet she complained of pain every week. He asked all the same questions he asked every week, and any other pertinent question he could think of in addition, trying to diagnose Tina's perplexing pains.

"Well, Tina, I can't seem to find anything unusual. If those stomach pains continue, we'll have to run some more tests. I'll give you something for indigestion. If that doesn't help and if the pain persists for several days, let us know," he said, helping the elderly woman down from the table. "So long, Tina! Take care of yourself!"

That afternoon, Dr. Lehman saw routine cases, from an infant with diaper rash and a child with a fever to an elderly patient who needed his ingrown toenails removed. He wouldn't see 89 patients like he occasionally did during flu season, but with all the unscheduled cases arriving, the day was more than full. Still, he moved from room to room with calm and dignified efficiency, listening carefully to each patient's problems.

Emerging from an examination room, Dr. Lehman spotted his son standing in the hall as if he were waiting for him.

"What's up, Brent? Is there something you need?"

"Yes, I was just thinking, I need some pills."

"Pills! What's wrong, Son?"

"I need some pills to make me grow taller."

"Some pills for *what?*"

"To make me grow taller."

"Well, Brent, I haven't run across any pills like that yet, but if I do, I'll let you know. But Son," he added, resting a hand on his son's shoulder, "it's not the size of a man that makes him great; it's the size of his heart."

Brent knew what having a big heart meant. Mother was always saying Dad had a big heart—having a nurse pick up an elderly patient who had no way to get to the clinic, leaving the busy office when an elderly neighbor called to say she couldn't wake her husband, or asking Brenda to carry a plate of food down to the home of another elderly patient. Dad's heart must have been stretched by all the people he cared about, Brent thought, heading for his bike.

Nancy was brooding over Tina again when she looked up to see Levi Troyer standing in front of her window along with his small son. "He fell down the *hoy loch* and hurt both his hands and one leg," the father explained. "Thought maybe Doc should have a look at him."

"You must have had quite a fall," Dr. Lehman observed in the X-ray room as he gently examined an injured limb.

"He went headfirst," Levi said, shaking his head. "Why, I told Marvin he could have killed himself falling a dozen feet onto the concrete!"

"Accidents like that happen with little boys," Nurse Chris sympathized. "Nurse Karen's son broke his wrist tussling with a neighbor boy, and she had to call Doc in after hours on a Saturday evening. Things like that happen."

"*Yah vell, so gehts*," Levi agreed as Chris read the X-ray. "That's just the way it goes sometimes. Do you get many broken bones in here?"

"We see a fair amount," the doctor replied. "In the winter, we see a number of fractures from sledding and ice skating accidents. In the summer, youngsters fall off a hay wagon, out of a tree, or off a horse or fence, or down a hay hole."

"I suppose!"

"What kind of breaks do you see on the X-ray?" Dr. Lehman asked, turning to his nurse.

"I don't think they're Smith," Chris replied, handing Dr. Lehman the large black film. "They look like Lehman breaks to me," she said.

"You mean my boy's gonna be lame?" Levi demanded. "He'll be crippled?"

"Oh no, definitely not," Dr. Lehman assured the father, looking up from the X-ray he was studying. "Calling a break a

Lehman break is the nurse's way of saying it's a break I can handle in this office. Actually, his leg isn't broken, but both of his wrists are. The bones are not shattered, however. If they were, we'd have to send your boy up to Doctors Hospital for Dr. Smith to operate on, so you can be thankful they were Lehman breaks instead of Smiths."

"*Ich saag!*" Levi agreed, leaning back in his chair with a sigh. "It will cost enough without surgery yet, too. It's good his leg isn't broken. I didn't figure it was, the way he could walk on it some."

"You can't always go by that. We had one girl come in who had walked on her injured leg for 10 days thinking it must not be broken because she could walk on it, but it was."

"Well, I just hope them wrists heal up real good."

"My brother broke both of his bones in his wrist when he was playing basketball," Chris shared, giving the child a dose of Tylenol with codeine. "And they healed up real well."

"Now, we're going to have to stretch your arm out to get the bones back in place," Dr. Lehman explained to the young patient. "It will hurt for a little, and then it will be over and we can put a cast on it to keep it in place until it heals. Are you ready?"

The child nodded bravely and the doctor gripped the hand at the wrist while Chris took hold of the arm just below the elbow. Both pulled in opposite directions until the bones slipped back in place. The child winced as pain shot through his arm, but he stoically bit his lip and didn't cry out. Carefully, Dr. Lehman laid the arm on the X-ray table and took another set of X-rays to make sure the bones were in place.

When he was certain the bones were properly aligned, the doctor took a length of gauze-like padding and dipped it into a bucket of warm water. Gently, he wound the wet, spongy mass around the broken limb, smoothing it out as he went. Then he treated the second broken wrist while the plaster/gauze mixture on the first one hardened into a cast.

"Six weeks with casts on both arms!" Levi sighed as he led the way to the receptionist's desk. "*Yah* well, I suppose you'll learn to stay away from those *hoy lochs*, Marvin."

Week after week, Tina's daughter brought her to the office, almost irritated with the puzzling pains. And week after week, it was the same. The doctor found no cause for her discomfort. What is Tina's problem? they kept wondering.

"A nurse from the nursing home called about Tina," Nancy announced one afternoon.

The doctor glanced up with a trace of weariness in his eyes. "She wants another appointment?"

"She was asking for one, so the nurse asked if she'd like to see Dr. Mitchell. But no, she had to come to Mount Eaton Clinic. The nurse asked her why she always complains of stomachaches and asks to go to Dr. Lehman's office. 'Well,' she admitted, 'it's not really that my stomach hurts. But when I go to Dr. Lehman's office, they make me feel special.'"

"Oh, Tina," Dr. Lehman laughed. "What next?"

"And by the way, Doc," Nancy added. "Levi is in the waiting room with Marvin."

"Marvin? He was doing great last week when we took the casts off his arm," Dr. Lehman said with a concerned expression. "What's the problem?"

"Marvin was playing tag in the hay loft and fell down the hay hole again. He hurt his wrist."

27.

A Jewish *Kippah* for Doc

"Dr. Lehman, will you teach me how to do a circumcision?" the caller asked.

"You want me to *teach* you to do *what*?"

"A circumcision. You see, we are Messianic Jews. My wife is expecting a baby, and if it's a boy, we'd like to have him circumcised on the eighth day after his birth. Our rabbi is getting older and doesn't do circumcisions anymore."

"If that's the case, Mr. Dayan, why don't you just bring your son to my office on the eighth day, and I'll be glad to do the circ for you," Dr. Lehman offered.

"You mean you'd do it?"

"Sure, I would!"

"That's great." Daniel Dayan's voice died away. "But the only thing is, we always have a *Brit Milah*, a special service, and then a celebration afterwards."

"Well, in that case, I'd be glad to come to your synagogue."

"You mean you'd drive an hour-and-a-half?"

"Of course!"

"Oh, that'd be fantastic! But, Doc . . . . " Dr. Lehman heard the excitement in Daniel's voice die away. "How much do you charge for something like that?"

The two agreed on a fee, and Mr. Dayan promised to call Dr. Lehman as soon as the baby arrived to schedule a time for the ceremony.

"What are you going to do next, Elton Lehman?" Phyllis asked when he told her about the Jewish ceremony.

"No telling," he laughed. "I just go wherever I'm needed."

That was Dr. Lehman. He wanted to live a life of service, witness, and ministry. Even on vacations, he preferred activities that were educational and inspirational over those that offered simply pleasure. Every summer, the Lehmans attended Music Week at Laurelville Mennonite Church Center. Often, vacations coincided with church conventions, including one held in India. During spring breaks, there were family excursions to the Cleveland Rain Forest, a museum, or the state capital. Summer trips included a tour of the western United States.

Perhaps the most memorable of all the Lehman trips took place the summer that Elton and Phyllis took their children to South America. There they visited his sister Geri and her family, who were missionaries in Bolivia, as well as Phyllis' niece Bonnie and her husband Galen Stutzman, serving with Wycliffe in Lomalinda, Colombia.

In Lomalinda, the Lehmans visited the memorial for Chet Bitterman, the Wycliffe missionary who was kidnapped from his wife and young children, held for ransom, and murdered. Brent and his sisters rode motorbikes over the same mountainous trails Chet had traveled, while Elton visited the mission hospital. The trip to South America broadened their perspectives and provided adventures that exceeded those they'd find on a cruise ship or ski slope.

The medical needs Dr. Lehman had seen in South America revived a longing he could never quite release: to serve on a medical mission. "I want my children to be service oriented," he frequently said. "That's what life is all about, serving others as we would serve Christ."

The Lehman family decided that one way they could serve others was to host foreign exchange students in their home. Beyond the satisfaction that came from serving others, hosting exchange students had its own unique rewards. Brenda and her fiancé Randy Benner, a pre-med student, traveled to China with a group of students from Eastern Mennonite University. In a layover in Japan, Brenda called an exchange student who had stayed in the Lehman home. The Japanese friend happened to have the day off work and gave Brenda and Randy a native's tour of the city. And when Korea hosted the Olympics, the father of a Korean exchange student, Joon Kim, had official connections and offered seats to the Lehmans.

The family's philosophy of service figured into the children's choice of major in college. Brenda considered following her father's steps to the medical field, but eventually trained as an accountant instead. Following her mother's example, she also volunteered at thrift stores that generated profits for missions.

Having caught a glimpse of the poverty and urgent medical needs in South America, Brent enrolled in med school, hoping to serve in a developing country. During his fourth year of med school, he spent eight weeks in Zambia.

After graduating from Central Christian High School as her other siblings had done, Beverly put her heart into working in youth camps and her musical gifts in playing guitar around campfires.

Through the years, Phyllis had set an example in serving others by helping out at the Amish and Mennonite Heritage Center in Berlin, Ohio, assisting the Red Cross, helping at the Mennonite Central Committee benefit auctions, giving music lessons, directing a junior choir, and doing other charitable work.

Dr. Lehman and his family fervently believed Christ's words, "Inasmuch as ye have done it unto the least of these . . . ye have done it unto me."[13] Out of that same philosophy, Dr. Lehman agreed to drive an hour-and-a-half to help the young Messianic Jewish couple. Serving at the special ceremony, he knew, would be far more rewarding than even his favorite pastime of tooling around with his antique cars.

Several weeks passed and the nervous prospective father called again. "Uh, Dr. Lehman, it would mean so much to my wife and me if our rabbi could hold the baby on the Elijah chair while you do the circ. This ceremony is rich with symbolism. We have a special board we lay our babies on for the ceremony, and if the rabbi could hold him on the special chair, it would be so meaningful."

"Sure," he agreed. "I don't see a problem with that at all."

Daniel called again several weeks later. "Doc, I was just thinking. Would there be some way I could snip the final bit of tissue? This whole event is so symbolic to us."

"I don't believe I see a problem with that," Dr. Lehman answered.

The next time Daniel called, he said, "Dr. Lehman, the due date for this baby is getting closer, and I keep thinking about this *Brit Milah*. I think I forgot to ask if you'd mind wearing a *kippah*."

"A what?"

"A *kippah*, a skull cap. Every man in our *shul*, or synagogue, must wear one during the service as a reminder of the *shechinah* glory of God above our heads."

The doctor chuckled as he pictured himself wearing a little round crocheted cap. "Well, I suppose I could do that for one day."

"Take me with you!" Phyllis said when he told her the newest twist. "I've got to see that."

"Just watch. After all this fuss, the baby will be a girl," the doctor predicted.

Soon the call came. "Dr. Lehman, we have our boy. The eighth day would be next *Shabbat*, next Saturday, a week from tomorrow. Is it going to fit into your schedule to come and do the circ on that day?"

"I'll be there," the doctor promised.

"Since we are Messianic Jews, we have *shul* both on *Shabbat* and on Sunday, so we'll have a short service before the *Brit Milah*," the father explained.

"Do you want to hand me my instruments when I do the circ?" Dr. Lehman asked his wife.

"Oh, Elton, I've been out of the office so long, I'd be sure to forget something in front of all those people. Why don't we ask one of the nurses to go along and do that?"

Early on Saturday morning, Dr. Lehman, Phyllis, and Nancy set out for the circumcision ceremony. For a time, all they could talk about was the *Brit Milah*.

"What's this special service going to be like?" Nancy wondered.

"We have no idea!" Phyllis laughed. "We do know that all the men, including Elton, will wear special caps! We've been to Amish services, but we've never been to a Messianic Jewish service."

"You and your family have been to South America, India, Europe—basically all over the world—but you've never been to a Jewish service!" Nancy laughed.

The 90-minute ride passed quickly and before they knew it, Dr. Lehman was pulling into a parking space.

"I can't forget the camera," Phyllis said, reaching for the case. "I've got to get a picture of Elton wearing that skull cap!"

"*Shabbat shalom!*" members of the congregation greeted Dr. and Mrs. Lehman and the nurse. "Peace of the Sabbath!" The Dayans, their rabbi, and his wife welcomed the doctor like an arriving celebrity and placed a *kippah* on his head.

As the service began, joyful singing, prayers, and meditations in Hebrew and English burst forth. Then the stooped, gray-haired rabbi spoke briefly, referring to the *Tanakh*, or Old Testament, as well as the New Covenant.

The parents carried the baby into the room and the congregation welcomed in unison: "Blessed is he who comes in God's name!"

"Blessed are You, *Adonai*, our God, ruler of the Universe who creates the fruit of the vine," the congregation chorused, and a goblet of wine circulated through the group. The aged rabbi dipped a gauze-like cloth into the wine and placed it on the baby's lips for him to suck.

"That's to help the baby with the pain," the rabbi's wife whispered to Phyllis.

Holding his tiny son, Daniel Dayan told the congregation how *Adonai* remembers a covenant forever, and how God made a covenant with Abraham and Sarah. And now Daniel and his wife Deborah were ready to perform this ritual of circumcision.

With dignified stateliness, the rabbi sank into a richly-upholstered red armchair known as Elijah's chair. The Dayans placed the infant on a pillow in the rabbi's lap and the rabbi proclaimed loudly: "Blessed are You, *Adonai* our God, ruler of the Universe, who has made us holy with commandments and commanded us concerning circumcision."

Dr. Lehman took his cue, knelt in front of the rabbi holding the child in the magnificent chair, and began to perform the circumcision, remembering that the father wanted to participate in the final step of the ritual. Suddenly, the young father leaned forward and whispered in the doctor's ear, "I can't do it! Just finish it yourself."

When the circ was finished, the parents pronounced a blessing, and the congregation bowed their heads as a prayer of blessing was offered for the boy, requesting speedy healing for the child and a petition that his father would have the privilege of raising and educating him. The prayer ended with, "May his hands and his heart be faithful in serving God. And let us all say, Amen."

With a final prayer and blessing, the child was named Yosef Daniel Dayan, and the celebration began. A photographer snapped pictures of Dr. Lehman with the baby. Then the Dayans and the rabbi and his wife accompanied the doctor, Phyllis, and Nancy to the festive tables.

"*L'Chaim!*" friends called to the Dayans and their tiny son. "*Mazel-tov!*"

As the Lehmans and Nancy sampled the lavish spread of dainty sandwiches and exquisite hors d'oeuvres, friends and family members of the Dayans shook the doctor's hand and chatted with the trio, thanking them for coming.

"You know, there are lots of similarities between the Amish and Jewish people," Dr. Lehman observed on the way home. "Both value close family ties and respect for elders, for example."

Several years later, when he hosted a Jewish colleague and three visitors from Israel, Dr. Lehman realized that he was not the only one who observed parallels between the two religious groups.

"I just can't get over the similarities between the Amish lifestyle and life on a *kibbutz*," the Israeli sociology professor marveled when Dr. Lehman took his guests to visit several Amish businesses and arranged for them to have dinner in a Swartzentruber Amish home. "In fact, I find the resemblance between the two groups so fascinating that I'd like to come back and do a study on the Amish! I'd like to learn how they keep their young folks in the faith."

As Dr. Lehman, Phyllis, and Nancy approached Mount Eaton on the way home from the Jewish *Brit Milah*, Phyllis remarked, "Oh, by the way, I was told the local urologist gets around $600 to do a circ at a service like that. Someone wondered what you charged, Elton, guessing you'd get twice that much with the distance we came, but I told them I didn't know."

"Well, Phyllis," the doctor said. "Dr. Finer, the Jewish doctor up at Doctors Hospital, did an awful lot for my Amish patients— starting a bus route and a house to accommodate Amish whose family members are in the hospital, giving discounts on cash payments, and even trying to launch an Amish hospital. None of those services directly benefited him. Now if I can help one of his kinfolk, I'll reap the same reward he did—the joy of serving others."

"So, how much did you charge?" Phyllis asked.

"Seventy-five dollars," the doctor replied with a smile. "After all, there's more to life than money. Winston Churchill once said, 'We make a living by what we earn, but we make a life by what we give.'"

28.

FIVE SMALL WHITE CROSSES

This must be the saddest day of my entire practice, Dr. Lehman thought, recording "May 13, 1993," into his journal. *Ten Amish children struck by a car while walking home from a birthday party . . . Five killed instantly, and most of the other five in critical condition. All patients of mine.*

How can I leave town now? he thought, glancing at the memo on his calendar: "May 14, Eastern Mennonite University President's Partnership Council Meeting."

For months he had looked forward to that meeting, but now all he could think about was his patients and their families at Akron Children's Hospital. Sure, the wounded were receiving good care by skilled surgeons. But after years of treating their fractures, lacerations, concussions, and viruses, it was difficult knowing he could do nothing to help them in the greatest medical crisis these patients ever experienced.

Like prickly burrs, thoughts of the shattered paradise along Harrison Road clung to his heart as he drove to Virginia. Even while meeting on campus, he couldn't shake the thoughts of the tragedy. During the meeting's open-share time, Dr. Lehman requested prayer for the five surviving children and their families.

"We saw the story of the accident on the news," fellow board members shared. "It's making national headlines."

What can I tell Roy and Erma, David and Ada, and Mel and Lizzie at the viewing tonight? he kept wondering as he drove home from the meeting.

Approaching Mount Eaton, he could almost see the accident site along Harrison Road. For more than 25 years, he had driven Harrison to Barb's house, passing the intersection of Criswell where the three homes stood on opposite corners of the crossroad. He could envision the well-kept yards, weedless vegetable gardens, brilliant flowerbeds, and tidy farmsteads along the peaceful country road. In his mind's eye, he could see the bridge, the fields, and the ditch.

On top of the hill, the Weaver and Kurtz families lived near *Dawdi* Troyer's house. Both Roy and David were skilled carpenters, Dr. Lehman knew, and men of common sense. Their wives, Erma and Ada, with their smiling eyes, pleasant faces, and friendly ways looked so similar that many folks couldn't tell the sisters apart.

Just past the intersection and over the knoll stood a well-kept farmette, the home of Melvin Troyer, the husky, no-nonsense businessman and his wife Lizzie.

I wonder which children from those three families were killed? the doctor thought as he headed toward Mount Eaton that afternoon. He thought of the routine office visits, emergencies, and the happy scenes surrounding the deliveries at Barb's and at the Care Center. It was not more than two years since he last delivered one of their children at the Care Center.

I don't know if I ever saw a happier father than Roy Weaver when his son was born, he reflected. *I can still see the glow on his face as he looked down at his newborn son, the first after four daughters.* That little boy was the sunshine in that home. Even the neighbors took it hard when he was hospitalized with a respiratory virus. But surely, the doctor thought, little Ivan wouldn't have been at the birthday party. After all, he's only two.

Dr. Lehman tried to mentally reconstruct the accident, trying to figure out just where the car had struck the children and where they would have landed. But the actual scene of the tragedy was far more heart-rending than any scenario he could have imagined.

It was a lovely spring afternoon that day in May when Lizzie Troyer stood at her living room window, watching the column of youngsters walk down the hill to the Swartzentruber family home, a quarter-mile below the intersection. How excited her daughters had been about the neighborhood birthday party! Since school was out for the summer, celebrating the girls' birthdays provided a special opportunity for the friends to get together again.

I'm glad David's son Marlin walked down to the party with the girls, Lizzie thought. Seven is a little young for such excursions. The children always stay off the road and walk on the left side, but even so. . . .

The girls spent the afternoon playing games, eating special treats, and opening birthday presents. Around 3:30, Lizzie's 13-year-old daughter Barbara mowed the last strip of yard, and then she and her friends Lori Weaver and Neva Kurtz walked down to the Swartzentruber home to escort the little girls home from the party. Little Ivan Weaver would not be left behind, nor would the girls think of going without the neighborhood darling. His mother Erma Weaver hitched the horse to the buggy and rode to Fredericksburg to pick up Roy, where her husband's workday on the carpentry crew had ended.

The buggy rocked gently as Roy climbed inside and sat on the seat beside his wife. "Where is Ivan?" Roy asked, taking the reins. "Where's my boy?" Holding the brown-haired toddler with the big brown eyes was the highlight of coming home, but tonight the buggy was noticeably still of the boyish chatter.

"Oh, he wanted to walk down with Lori, Barbie, and Neva to bring the little girls home from the party for Frieda's and Elsie's birthdays," Erma explained. "He seemed to think the girls would save a treat for him from the party."

A short time later, the Weavers spotted the girls walking in a column of twos in the grass along the road. The girls had remembered to walk on the left side of the road as they had been trained, and well off to the side.

"Let's stop and get Ivan!" Roy suggested when he spotted his small son walking hand-in-hand with the big girls alongside Harrison Road.

Ivan shook his little head when asked if he wanted to go home in the buggy, remembering the candies in the girls' pockets. So Roy snapped the reins and the horse trotted up the hill, while the little boy with the straw hat marched happily down the road with the laughing party of girls.

Minutes later, a pickup with a Colorado license plate drove slowly down Harrison Road from the direction of Mount Eaton toward Fredericksburg. Gazing out the windows, the two tourists eagerly soaked up the open fields, quaint farms with their windmills, grazing cattle, well-kept flower gardens, and weedless rows of sprouting vegetable plants. What an idyllic paradise!

Now and then, the couple snatched a glimpse of the quaint folks in straw hats and bonnets peering out from their carriages. If only they could get a closer look at some of those Amish.

Cresting the hill at the intersection of Harrison and Criswell, the sightseers spied a scene surpassing their greatest hopes. The driver braked as the couple gazed at the column of girls in white caps and long dresses walking toward them, two-by-two, along the side of the road. A steep ditch bordered the road, so the driver parked his pickup right on the road and waited for the group to approach.

Gazing intently at the column of youngsters, the tourists watched the laughing girls break into single file to cross the bridge and then regroup in pairs. One of the taller girls held the hand of an adorable toddler wearing a miniature straw hat over his wheat-colored bangs. How absolutely adorable!

Meanwhile, Ada Kurtz kept glancing out the kitchen window as she washed the few dishes that had accumulated over the afternoon. It's almost 4 o'clock, she worried. The girls should have been back by now. Neva knows she's supposed to start supper while I milk the cow. David will soon be home from work.

Near the barn, her son Marlin looked up to see a red car dart across the double yellow line, fly around a feed truck, and careen over the hill.

Cresting the knoll, the red 1993 Pontiac Lemans swerved to miss the tourist's pickup truck parked on the road. As his tires spat gravel on the left berm of the road, the teenage driver overcorrected and lost control, hurtling toward the happy group of children walking toward him on the grass to the right of the road.

"Mom!" Marlin Kurtz yelled, the door slamming behind him. "You should have seen that red car. It was going awfully fast and almost lost control in front of our house!"

Just down the hill, Lizzie Troyer heard the screeching tires. *The girls!* she thought, dashing to the living room window.

For an awful instant, bodies, birthday presents, shoes, and a tiny hat exploded into the air as the red Pontiac barreled through the column of children—tossing bodies over telephone wires, across the ditch, and beyond the creek. The car flipped over the embankment and a creek, landing on its roof in a hay field, pinning a child beneath it. A small girl dangled by the hair of her loosened braids from a barbed-wire fence. Two other bodies lay beyond the car, over 100 feet from the point of impact.

For a long moment, a dreadful silence paralyzed the countryside. Nothing seemed to move except for the tires spinning in the air like the flailing legs of an overturned beetle.

But Lizzie was already running, propelled by the adrenaline surge of horror. She didn't see the dazed teenager crawl out of the overturned car, or the tourists leap from their truck, or Sarah Swartzentruber dashing out her lane. All she saw were the smudges of color splattered across the hay field like mistaken blots on an artist's canvas.

From the kitchen window of the farmhouse at the crossroad, Ada Kurtz saw Lizzie's slender form flying down the road, her *kapp* strings streaming behind her.

The children!

Ada dropped the tea towel and ran from the house, recognizing Elsie's screams as she dashed down the hill. "Mommaaaa! Mommaaa! Momma!" Every anguished shriek shot a surge of energy through the mother's body and fueled the pounding feet.

"The children were hit!" Lizzie's son shouted to Roy Weaver, who was putting his horse out to pasture. A pang of terror gripped the Amishman's heart. All of his children were in the group. All five of them! In a flash, he sprinted across the field, leaped across the fence, and bolted wildly down the road, his frizzy auburn hair and beard streaming from his face. *Ivan! Lori . . . Wilma . . . Ruby . . . Frieda!*

Glancing out the window, Erma Weaver saw her husband racing toward the direction from which the children were returning. *No!* her heart cried as she dashed out the door and down the road behind him. *No! No! NO!*

Running as he had never run before, Roy searched the dreadful scene below him. Where were the children? Two stood in the grass along the ditch, but where were the other eight? And where was the little boy with the straw hat?

A teenager paced the road and an out-of-state pickup stood near the bridge. The wheels of an overturned car protruded from the hay field. An arm beckoned from one of the bodies in the field, but the other scattered forms lay still.

Lori Weaver blinked her eyes and looked around her, wondering why she lay on the grass near the creek, and why she felt as though she had just awoken from a long nap. Glancing dazedly about, her eyes focused on the sprawled form of one of her friends. And then she remembered—the red car. *Ivan!* There he was in a little crumpled heap. Quickly, she scooped up her little brother. Why was he so limp? "Oh, Ivan! *Veck uff!* Wake up, Ivan!" Lovingly, she cradled the head that dangled awkwardly from the little neck.

Approaching the bridge, Lizzie slid down the embankment toward the splotch of color along the creek, where her 10-year-old daughter Ruby lay, limbs and braids all askew like a forgotten rag doll. *"Please, pleeease!"* Lizzie pleaded, lifting the corner of her daughter's jacket from the girl's face. Instantly, she dropped the jacket back over the pale face and unseeing eyes. But that short glimpse branded into her memory the haunting expression on the precious features.

Tears blurred her eyes as she glanced up at her neighbor Sara Swartzentruber cradling the limp form of Roy's small son in her arms.

Oh, Ivan, you dear little broken doll.

"You don't blame me for inviting the children over, do you, Lizzie?" Sarah pleaded, glancing around the field at the bodies of little girls that, minutes earlier, had been playing so happily at the party celebrating two of their birthdays.

"Oh, no, of course not," Lizzie murmured, her eyes desperately searching the hayfield for Barbara and little Susan.

As Ada dashed through the hayfield, she saw the tourists untangling her daughter's hair from the fence. "Mommaaaa! Mommmaaaaa!" Elsie screamed, propelling Ada to run faster. "I'm coming!" the mother cried, sprinting through the hay that tried to trip and snare her. "I'm coming!"

"Momma is here, everything is all right now," she whispered in Pennsylvania German. Ada Kurtz soothed the girl as she dropped to her daughter's side, careful not to bump the leg that jutted out at an awkward angle. What an awful ending to a birthday party for a little girl who had just turned seven!

As his feet pounded the blacktop, Roy's eyes were glued to the little form in Sara's arms. *Ivan, don't die!*

As he reached out his arms for his limp, little son, an unseen knife seemed to gouge away part of Roy's bleeding heart. His hand brushed the soft hair that fell away from the sweet baby face as he desperately searched the sightless eyes and still chest for the faintest signs of life, even the slightest movement. Ivan! My precious son! his heart cried in anguish as he pressed the dear bundle to his chest. *My only son!*

The wail of sirens filled the air as a rescue vehicle screeched to a stop several feet away. A paramedic threw open his door and dashed to the scene.

"How bad is it?" he shouted to Roy. "Shall I call for help?"

"It's bad," Roy shook his head sorrowfully. "Real bad. There are bodies all over the place."

Gently, he handed the precious son to a paramedic and ran through the field searching for his daughters, hoping desperately that something could be done to revive the boy and that the girls would be all right.

Sitting in the grass were Lori and Ruby—but Wilma and Frieda? There were two bodies beyond the car, he remembered. Running past the car lying on its roof in the alfalfa field, Roy spotted two bodies lying face down. One had brown hair and the other blonde. Wilma! Frieda! My little songbirds!

Two paramedics ran over and dropped to their knees beside the still bodies of the sisters, checking for a pulse.

"Those . . . are my daughters," Roy's throat seemed to strangle his voice. "Are . . . are they . . . ."

"I'm sorry," the medic's pain-filled gaze dropped in discomfort. "I'm sorry, but they're gone. And the little boy—he's gone, too."

The scene began to spin. From every direction, sirens shrieked at Roy and flashing lights stabbed the peaceful countryside. If only he could turn back time to the quiet little Eden the community had been when he rode home from work several minutes before. If only he could go back and undo that decision to let little Ivan walk with the girls! If only . . . if only . . . .

"All that comes into our lives has been allowed by God," Roy could hear the preacher say. "And God will bring an ultimate good from everything he allows to happen."

With leaden feet, he trudged to the roadside where his wife stood waiting with Lori and Ruby and the still form of their son. Roy's eyes met his wife's questioning ones. Dropping his gaze, he whispered, "Three of ours . . . are *gone.*"

Erma sobbed quietly as the paramedics draped blankets over her children's bodies. The scene in front of her eyes seemed surreal. Surely the horrid flashing lights would vanish, the girls would come skipping and singing across the fields, and Ivan would stretch out his little arms to her once again.

But the flashing lights did not fade away. The girls did not come laughing and skipping through the hay field. And the little arms under the sheet didn't move. Tomorrow's birthday would never come for the little girl who had celebrated today.

Paramedics carried away the injured on white-sheeted stretchers, easing Barbara and Susan Troyer, as well as Elsie Kurtz, into the waiting ambulances. "Go ahead," a medic nodded to Ada, as her daughter cried for her mamma from the ambulance. "You can ride along." Ada glanced down at her barn dress and worn shoes as she climbed inside.

A little after 4:30, David Kurtz's driver dropped him off at his driveway after a day of installing kitchen cabinets. As he stepped out of the vehicle, he heard the sirens and saw the flashing lights beyond the hill. "Something awful must have happened down the road," he remarked to himself as a car pulled off the side of the road in front of the Kurtz home. The driver rolled down his window, shouting, "Your children were hit by a car! Jump in, I'll take you down to the site."

David arrived on the scene just as an ambulance was about to leave for Wooster Hospital with the last survivor, Ruby Weaver, accompanied by her grandmother. Though Ruby's legs were so bruised that she wouldn't be able to walk until after the funeral, she'd return home in several hours. Three of her siblings would come home in hearses.

At a paramedic's invitation, David Kurtz climbed into the ambulance with Ruby. As the ambulance sped away, he glanced out the rear windows at the overturned car under which the body of his 13-year-old daughter Neva was pinned. Black, squiggly lines crisscrossing the solid yellow lines, little shoes, and shreds of wrapping paper told the sad story.

Surely by some miracle, the hospital staff will revive some of the victims, the parents hoped as they rode to the hospital in the several ambulances. Surely. . . .

But at the hospital, the parents were escorted to the morgue to identify the bodies. The walk seemed like the longest trek the parents had ever taken, and yet it was one they wished would never end.

The scene within the stark, cool walls of the morgue seemed to wring the blood from their aching hearts. Five gurneys stood side-by-side, bearing the mangled remains of four girls and one small boy. And there, on those steel gurneys, lay the broken dreams of three families.

Sighs, muffled sobs, and whispered endearments echoed through the cool corridor as mothers fingered flaxen strands they would never braid again, touched the cold hands, and traced the lips that could not fill the house with music ever again.

Why couldn't the teenager have driven more responsibly? the fathers wondered as they studied the still faces of their precious children. Why did the tourists stop on the road? What a tragic, needless waste. How frightened the girls must have been as they watched the car bearing down on them. Did the children suffer?

"They're not here," someone whispered. "They are safe in the arms of Jesus."

Strained smiles lit the tear-stained faces. "Ah, yes, of course. They're so much better off. We must remember that."

If only the mourners could have heard the angelic voices floating from the skies, but it would be months before the parents would hear the story.

In the hospital lobby, Ada Kurtz recognized the young driver of the red car. "Are you hurt?" she asked with concern.

Startled, the youth looked into the kind, moist eyes of the pleasant-faced Amish woman. How could she care about him, he wondered vaguely. "I have a couple of scratches, but I think I'll be okay," he called over his shoulder as the sheriff hustled him down the hall.

"Was he drinking?" everyone wondered.

"No, the boy wasn't drunk," a sheriff informed the parents. "He was simply driving too fast and lost control. He had no driver's license and the car belonged to a girlfriend he knew only by first name. He said he was kicked out of his home when he was 15."

"Poor boy. He didn't have a chance," the Amish folk whispered.

There was little time to grieve over the dead, for the critically injured survivors needed their families' support. Wooster Hospital was not equipped to handle the severe injuries the children suffered, and they needed to be transferred to Akron Children's Hospital. As Elsie Kurtz was wheeled out to the helicopter, her parents were told they could not accompany her. The child's injuries were too critical.

Melvin Troyer, who was called home from a business trip, arrived at Wooster just as Susan was about to be airlifted to Akron

Children's Hospital. "I'm going with my daughter," he announced in his no-nonsense manner and climbed into the ambulance transporting his daughter to the heli-pad. The helicopter seemed to go straight up and then straight down again, landing gently at Akron Children's Hospital grounds, where a waiting ambulance transported the passengers to the hospital doors. To the other parents traveling in the Wooster Hospital chaplain's car, the trip seemed endless.

The night, too, seemed endless for those whose hearts were torn between injured children's bedsides and the rest of their families at home. The Wooster chaplain stayed supportively with the families through the night, making sure they had coins to purchase snacks and drinks from the vending machines. Around 3 o'clock Friday morning, several of the parents returned home to their families, while others stayed at the bedsides of their daughters.

As Friday morning dawned, neighbors and friends bringing casseroles, cakes, and condolences arrived at the three homes at the intersection of Harrison Road and Criswell. Neighbor men milked cows and fed livestock for the grieving families. Neighborhood women quietly scrubbed floors and windows to prepare the homes for the viewing hours, and plucked chickens to prepare food for the funerals that everyone knew would be enormous. Relatives used neighbors' phones to communicate with the victims' parents at the hospital to complete funeral arrangements.

That afternoon, several hearses drove slowly down Harrison Road. After unloading the hand-made, pine caskets, Mr. Spidell, the Mount Eaton funeral director, quietly explained to the families that the necks of the children had been broken. "Their deaths were instantaneous and basically painless," he assured the parents.

As the hearses disappeared down the road, news flashed across the countryside that the coffins had arrived. A long procession of buggies and bikes strung along the roads lined with columns of black-clad mourners walking toward the intersection.

When Dr. Lehman drove his Jeep into the neighborhood that evening, a line of people, four abreast, snaked up the road beyond the intersection of Criswell and Harrison, almost as far as one could see. Rows of cars, buggies, and vans filled every pasture and field as police directed traffic at the intersection.

"There's Doc!" one usher whispered to another as Dr. Lehman approached the line of mourners. "He shouldn't have to stand in line. What if someone needs him while he is waiting here?" Respectfully, the bearded usher approached Dr. Lehman and led him to the head of the line of mourners.

Roy Weaver glanced up as his doctor walked into the room. A smile lit his weary face as he whispered to Erma: "Look! There comes Dr. Lehman!"

Seeing Dr. Lehman momentarily soothed Roy's heart, as it usually did when he saw their family doctor.

Lord! What does one say at a time like this? Elton wondered, scanning the three hand-hewn caskets. Why, Lord? he longed to ask as he gazed down at the girls dressed in pure white shrouds and *kapps* and at the cherubic toddler robed in a miniature shroud. As he studied the angelic faces cradled on the white pillows, he recalled the happy memories surrounding each of their deliveries—the worried office calls for Wilma's concussion and Ivan's case of pyloric stenosis. In every medical dilemma the Weaver family had faced, Dr. Lehman always had a prescription or a remedy to suggest. But tonight there was nothing he could offer, not even words.

Sometimes, a caring, compassionate touch comforts more than the spoken word, he remembered. "I'm so sorry." The doctor's eyes gazed compassionately into Roy's and his strong hands enfolded the clammy one of the bereaved father.

The Amishman's eyes followed the doctor to the door. He cared enough to come! The doctor's loving concern lit a warm glow in his heart, like the lighting of a kerosene lamp on a stormy night.

The clock struck 10 as the last mourners filed past the coffins. "Over 2,000 people came through tonight," a bystander observed. "It's good the families nibbled on sandwiches while the people filed through or the line would still be going!"

"We don't have to worry about many people coming tomorrow," Roy told his wife as he blew out the lantern, "because there aren't many more people."

But there were. Vanloads of Amish friends and relatives came from across the country to what was the largest Amish gathering in recent history.

Soon after 6 o'clock Saturday morning, people began arriving. Neighbors and friends from miles around brought pies, cakes, and casseroles to the three homes. Thoughtful neighbors froze surplus baked goods and casseroles for the families to use later between hospital visits. Amish boys carried wagonloads of benches into the barns and shops. Others hauled boxes of grocery supplies for the following day. That day, between 5,000 and 6,000 people signed the visitation register.

The Kurtz and Troyer families shuttled between their homes flooded with thousands of friends and relatives, and Akron Children's Hospital, where the lives of their daughters hung by mere threads.

On May 16, funeral services were held for the five victims at six separate locations. Since no one house or barn could accommodate the huge crowd anticipated, services were held in all three of the families' homes, as well as in the Kurtzes' barn and in two of the families' shop buildings, which had been swept and lined with rows of benches.

Two or three ministers preached in German at every location, including several pastors who had traveled hundreds of miles for the service. Black-clad men sat on backless benches to one side of the buildings, while rows of women in white prayer coverings, black dresses, capes, and aprons lined the opposite side of the rooms. From time to time, the women dabbed their handkerchiefs to their eyes. Children sat erect and still on the backless benches, sensing the solemnity of the services.

At 10:45, ministers pronounced benedictions in all six buildings. Pallbearers carried the five coffins to a tent behind *Dawdi* Troyer's house, where around 2,000 people viewed the bodies one final time. Then the pallbearers closed the lids and lifted the small, hand-crafted coffins into long buggies specially designed for this purpose. The procession to the graveyard began. Endless lines of carriages stretched both directions on Harrison Road as the body of Ruby Troyer was taken north to the Troyer Cemetery for burial, and the Weaver and Kurtz cousins were transported to a graveyard to the south.

Harrison Road had been blocked off for the day to permit the Amish to move unhindered from house to house, to the graveyard, and back and forth from the accident site.

News photographers hunkered on every hill. A television photographer clung to the top of the Kurtzes' windmill, hoping for prime shots.

With mild annoyance, the Amish dodged the *Englischers* intruding into their mourning and snapping pictures all around them. When a reporter questioned *Dawdi* Troyer, he replied calmly but firmly, "We don't appreciate these goings on."

"Oh, I'm sorry, I'm sorry," the reporter apologized, backing away.

"I guess one has to realize they're just trying to do their job," *Dawdi* told his children.

"These people are private and don't want the cameras up in their faces," sheriffs tried to explain to the newspaper and television photographers. "They don't believe in photographs. It's all part of their teachings on humility."

"We can't chase the media away," the sheriff told the Amish folk, "but we will keep them from getting any closer."

Though the cameras did intrude on the funeral, they also connected the little Amish patients at the hospital with the memorial services for their sisters, which they were unable to attend. As the nurses showed Elsie Kurtz and Barbara and Susan Troyer the funeral procession on the screens in their room, the girls watched intently, recognizing their parents' buggies as they led the processions following the horse-drawn hearses.

"There goes Roy's surrey!" Barbara exclaimed as the long line of carriages wound over the hills. "But I can't see Lori!"

"I was in the back seat with *Dawdi* and *Mommi,*" Lori assured Barbara later.

After the burial, church friends served lunch to the families and all the guests. Ever efficient, the Amish had figured a way to serve hundreds of guests in almost no time at all. Youth formed relay lines, passing plates of ham and cheese sandwiches, noodles, potato salad, Jell-O with fruit, cake, and coffee to guests just as fast as they could take them.

Scores of friends and relatives who had traveled great distances to comfort the families pressed around them with final words of encouragement, so that it was nearly 3 o'clock when some family members finally sat down to eat lunch. As they ate, more friends lined up in front of the couples with last words of consolation, until the Kurtzes and Troyers left to visit their daughters in the hospital.

After forcing down a few bites, Roy walked down toward the milk house where a stranger cornered him.

"Mr. Weaver, I'm the chaplain from Wayne County Jail," the man explained. "I just came from seeing the driver who hit your children. He asked me to stop by and tell you how awfully sorry he is. In fact," the chaplain continued, "he feels so terrible that he's been threatening to take his life, and we've put him under special observation all night."

Roy clenched and unclenched his fists and the muscles at the sides of his face pulsed with tension. Then, taking a deep breath, he looked the man in the eye and whispered hoarsely, "Tell him we forgive him." A pained smile crinkled the weary lines on his bearded face as he added, "We don't hold anything against the driver."

"Oh, thank you!" The chaplain wrapped the startled Amishman in a big hug. "That's wonderful. The boy'll be so relieved."

Forgiveness is painful, Roy thought walking slowly toward the barn. It means I give up the right to demand revenge for the innocent lives that were taken. But on the other hand, forgiveness is healing. It frees me from the tormenting chains of bitterness.

"You're sure you don't want to press charges?" a sheriff asked the fathers.

"We can't do that," Mel, Roy, and David replied. "The Bible teaches us to turn the other cheek."

Monday, many of the local newspapers committed their entire front page to the story of the five Amish children. A headline in the *Beacon Journal* read: "'God Doesn't Make Mistakes.'" Beneath the quotation was the picture of four Amish girls dressed in black with white *kapps* climbing the hill above pairs of black skid marks scrawled across the yellow lines, like the scribbling of a child's magic marker. Another headline announced: "No Hatred, Only Pity for Man Who Drove Car."

The driver was charged with five counts of vehicular homicide, failure to control, driving left of center, and driving without an operator's license, the *Daily Record* reported under headlines saying, "Thousands Mourn Deaths of Five Accident Victims Sunday." The same paper quoted an area resident as explaining that the Amish "feel that people die when God calls them. If it's your time, then God takes you."[14]

Two weeks later, the *Daily Record* carried another story titled: "Amish Deacon: 'We're not Angry at the Guy; We Feel Sorry for Him.'" The writer quoted the area Amish deacon as saying, "A guy came in here and said the guy ought to be hung. Well, that's not the way we feel. We all feel real sorry for him. We hear he wasn't brought up in a family."[15]

The deacon explained further how the Amish don't believe in revenge but in following the Lord's Prayer, which teaches them to forgive enemies. The deacon said that the cohesiveness of the Amish communities assisted them in handling their grief, saying it was much easier because "everybody shares, everybody helps." God allowed the accident, the deacon said, but it was not his will.

Every time Dr. Lehman drove along Harrison Road, he slowed his Jeep and studied the five small crosses encircled in tiny rose wreaths near the bridge.

Occasionally, the doctor talked with the families in his office or in the homes when he stopped by. Twice after the accident, Mel Troyer brought Susan to Mount Eaton Clinic when she fractured her right wrist on two different occasions. When her brother accidentally sliced his hand with his hunting knife, the Troyers brought him to Dr. Lehman for stitches.

One evening when Dr. Lehman stopped by Mel's house, all the families had gathered to share about the details of the accident. It was exactly eight years since the day of the funeral.

"Not a day goes by that I don't think of the children," Roy confessed. "Before, our house was filled with singing," his voice grew soft. "And now, it's so quiet. And I don't have a little boy to help me with the chores. Family gatherings are so hard for us because we're reminded of what we're missing, but it's that singing I miss most of all."

"So, how do you survive?" Dr. Lehman wondered. As their family doctor, he was concerned not only for his patients' physical injuries, but for their emotional wounds as well.

"We remember where they are," Mel said after a moment. "We remember they are well taken care of, and then we can sleep."

Roy and David nodded in agreement. "That's right."

"You have got to think on the bright side," Mel added. "And the poems—they help, too," he remarked, removing a verse from the wall that was framed in memory of the children. It read:

I am standing on the seashore.
A ship spreads her sails to the morning breeze
And starts for the ocean.
I stand there watching her till she fades on the horizon
And someone at my side says, "She is gone."
Gone where?
The loss of sight is in me not in her.
Just at that moment when someone says, "She is gone,"
There are others who are watching her coming.
Other voices take up the glad shout: "Here she comes!"
And this is dying.

"I think I've read that poem a hundred times," Lizzie admitted.

As Dr. Lehman listened, the Troyers, Weavers, Kurtzes, and *Dawdi* Troyers rehearsed the story of the accident, the funerals, and their journey through grief.

"It is such a release to talk about it," Roy admitted. The doctor nodded, knowing a listening ear was one of the best therapies for grief that a doctor could prescribe.

"The girls went through a lot of suffering while recuperating," Dr. Lehman said.

"They sure did," David agreed. "Elsie had terrible pain when the doctor tried to loosen the stabilizing rods on her leg with his craftsman tools—and then he discovered he had tightened the screw instead of loosening it! I told him I work with tools all the time and I'd loosen it when we got home. I planned to stabilize it with a vise grip when I tightened it, but Elsie screamed awfully when I tried. She felt it the whole way through her leg, she said."

A blond-haired preschooler rested her head on Erma's lap as the evening aged, and the doctor said, "It seems like yesterday that I delivered that little one."

"She's five already," Roy remarked. "She was born three years after the accident. I tell you one thing, Doc, when I'd see you walk into the Care Center, my heart rate always went down. Every time. There was something calming about your presence. And the night you came to the viewing, I said to my wife, 'There comes Lehman!' I never forgot that."

As Dr. Lehman glanced around the room at the familiar faces illuminated in the glow of the lamplight, he sensed a warmth, a belonging. It was as though he was part of the family, a respected and needed elder brother. And because they seemed like part of his family, he, too, felt their loss.

"Have you heard anything from the driver of the car?" Dr. Lehman asked after a bit. "What's happening with him?"

"He's still in prison," Mel replied. "I suppose he's up for parole soon. His sentence was for 7-15 years."

"He wrote us each a card soon after it happened, saying how sorry he was," David added.

"My dad said a group of Amish had a Bible study in the prison where the driver was incarcerated," Roy began. "He came up to them afterward and introduced himself as the one who had killed the five Amish children. He said he felt bad about it and wanted to talk to us families when he got out of jail."

"Didn't a lawyer come out here to try to get you to sue him?" Dr. Lehman questioned.

"Yes," Mel nodded. He could still see Roy, David, and *Dawdi* around the table, listening politely to the attorney's offer. "You folks have had a terrible loss and accumulated exorbitant medical bills because of one young man's carelessness," the lawyer had said. "I'd like to help you get what you deserve."

Roy, David, Melvin, and *Dawdi* stared at the table in silence. Each thought of the anguish that had ripped their homes apart:

the five empty beds; the homes robbed of laughter, chatter, and song; Lori's sleepless nights and nightmares of a red, speeding car; little Susan's surgery—three weeks of traction and five months in a body cast—so traumatized that she couldn't be left alone for a minute, even when asleep; little Elsie's screws and stabilizing rods worn on her legs all summer, and the holes around the rods that had to be cleaned twice a day. And then Barbara with the hairline fractures in her pelvis, who, like Elsie and Susan, had to learn to walk all over again.

The driver had been careless, after all.

But then the three fathers recalled the love that had poured in from the community: the grocery bills for the funeral meal that an anonymous donor had paid; the $7,500 bill for the helicopter flight that arrived stamped "paid in full"; the pharmacist who never let *Dawdi* pay for Elsie's prescriptions; the storekeepers who refused to charge a cent for anything Roy needed to purchase; the 1,700 cards that flooded each of their mailboxes, many addressed to "Weaver, Kurtz, and Troyer families, Amish Country, Ohio" from hundreds of caring people all across the United States; the money that poured into an account at the Fredericksburg bank that had paid every cent of their expenses; and, yes, the retired fire chief Herb Spencer and his daughter who transported the girls to therapy every week, treated them with ice cream cones on the way home, and refused to take a cent for their efforts.

"Doc," Melvin said, leaning forward on his chair. "I looked at Roy and David sitting across the table, and I knew their answer. And so I turned to that lawyer and said, 'Sir, we told that young driver that we forgave him, so how can we sue him? And tell me, what would the hundreds of folks who helped pay our expenses think if we turned around and sued the driver?'"

"Besides," David put in, "the Bible teaches us to love and forgive those who wrong us."

"After all," Roy added, "it wouldn't bring the children back."

They are absolutely right, Dr. Lehman thought as he traveled home. And their forgiveness, painful though it may be, is like stitches binding the wound and keeping out the infection of bitterness, allowing them to heal.

As he stepped inside the foyer of his house, Dr. Lehman's eyes fell on a framed sketch from *The Martyrs' Mirror* titled, "The Other Cheek."

He stood there for a moment, gazing at the drawing of Dirk Willems pulling his pursuer out of the icy river. Dirk, who was wanted by authorities for his belief in adult baptism, could have escaped when his pursuer fell through the ice. Instead, he returned, pulled him out and paid with his life by burning at the stake on May 16, 1529.

May 16! Why, that's today's date and the day my five patients were buried, he realized. The spirit of the Anabaptist forebearers lives on in the hearts of my Amish patients who chose, in the midst of their tragedy, to forgive the one who caused them so much grief. Only by God's grace can people respond with love and forgiveness instead of bitterness and revenge.

Several weeks after the memorable visit with the three families, Dr. Lehman heard the story of the heavenly music. "We didn't tell anyone for the longest time," Henry and Emma Miller said. "It was just too special. And we didn't know if anyone would believe us."

The Millers, neighbors to the three families, had spent the evening of the tragedy with the bereaved relatives. The sun had set and a blanket of darkness had settled over the countryside by the time Henry and Emma started the quarter-mile hike to their home. Their hearts were heavy and their downcast eyes blurred with tears as the couple walked slowly, thoughtfully along the roadside. Quietly, they pieced together the tragic details they had heard that evening. Scarcely 200 feet from the intersection, Emma stopped and listened. Her eyes met Henry's, whose eyes also filled with wonder. Together, the two looked up into the sparkling pinpricks of light sprinkled through the blackness above, listening intently.

There it was again—soft, sweet strains of music floating down from somewhere far overhead, rising to a crescendo and then fading away into the night. The couple hardly dared to breathe, not wanting to miss a note of the joyful, angelic strains, unlike any music they had ever heard before.

"Angels," Emma whispered in awe, drying her shining eyes with the corner of her handkerchief. "The music of angels."

Several hundred feet away, Roy's father Jonas Weaver sat alone in the yard of the Kurtz homestead, reliving the events of the day. The rest of the mourners had returned to their homes or gone into the house, but Jonas sat alone in the darkness. Too weary and sad to get out of his chair, the grandfather had stayed outside to be alone with his thoughts in the privacy of darkness. A deep ache burrowed in his heart as he thought of Roy's little girls skipping through the house, joyfully filling the rooms with song. He thought of dear little Ivan, the empty beds in three homes tonight, and of the terrible grief crushing the families' hearts. The great sorrow was almost more than his worn heart could endure.

And then he heard it, too. Clear and bright, the notes floated down from the sky like nothing he had ever heard before. He tilted his gray, bearded head to one side, but he couldn't quite make out the distant words—just sweet, melodic harmony drifting down from somewhere far above. And suddenly he knew that while there were tears and muffled sobs in the three homes that night, somewhere beyond the clouds, angels were singing, welcoming the dear little children home. And Roy's little songbirds were singing again.

29.

No Million Dollar Work-Up

"Is it a Lehman or a Smith?" Dr. Lehman muttered sleepily, picking up the phone.

"It's neither; it's a Mullet," the caller drawled.

"Oh, hello," the doctor sputtered, blinking awake and regaining his deep, distinctive tone. "Hello, Dr. Lehman speaking."

He squinted at the red, glowing numerals on the alarm clock: 3:20. Had it really been two hours since he collapsed into bed? Around 11:30 the previous evening, he was called to the office to X-ray a child's leg that fractured while jumping on the trampoline. He determined that the break was a "Lehman" and not a "Smith," because it was one he could care for. Then, as he was casting the leg, a call came from the Care Center saying a patient was ready to deliver and a baby was arriving. It seemed he slept for only a few moments before the phone jerked him out of that first deep slumber.

"Hey, Doc, Melvin Mullet here. We got a problem with the wife," the caller announced. "She can't move her arm and leg, and she's kind of layin' there and I thought I'd better give you a ring. Anything you can do for her?"

Dr. Lehman was wide awake in seconds. Uh oh. That sounds like a stroke.

"Let's see," he thought out loud. "She's bedfast."

"No, she's lying very loose in bed."

"Okay, she's lying very loose, but she can't get out of bed."

"You got it, Doc."

"Let's see, you moved up to Oak Ridge. I'd say that's a good hour-and-a-half drive." What shall I do? the doctor wondered. I have office hours in the morning.

"The boys and I really don't want to see *Mommi* go to the hospital and get the million dollar work-up," Melvin's voice trembled with emotion. "Unless you think it would do her some good."

Dr. Lehman closed his weary eyes and thought for a moment. "Look, Melvin, I'll tell you what. I've got office hours this morning, but I'll come down to your place before the office opens. I'll check out your wife, and then we can discuss what would be the best options for her."

"*Ach*, Doc, you're the best," the elderly man sighed. "I hated to call you, but . . . ."

I'd have time to sleep a few winks yet before I leave, he thought, replacing the phone on the hook and sinking back into his pillow. Every muscle in his body ached with weariness, but his mind was in gear and he couldn't shift it into neutral.

"Where are you going now?" Phyllis mumbled sleepily when she heard her husband stirring.

"Up to Oak Ridge to check on a stroke victim," he replied.

"Oh, Elton, you're driving all that way to make a *house call?*"

"That's right."

Alice met the doctor at the clinic where he collected the I-V supplies he thought he might need. "So, how old is this Mrs. Mullet?" the nurse wondered as the Jeep headed out on the dark, country road.

"Eighty-six, I believe," Dr. Lehman replied, noting the glow of a kerosene lantern in the window of an occasional house or barn.

"So she's lived a full life."

"She has, and I'm afraid there's little that can be done besides making the woman comfortable."

"Doc, you go the second and third miles to accommodate your patients," the nurse declared with a sleepy yawn.

"I just treat them the way I'd want to be treated," he replied. Alice's head nodded and the doctor drove in silence, thinking how grateful he'd be to spend his last hours surrounded by familiar scenes and faces.

Most of Dr. Lehman's house calls in recent years were made to accommodate the elderly, prescribing meds, catheterizing invalids, setting up I-Vs, and performing procedures for those too feeble to visit his office. As he drove, he remembered the house call he had made the night before to the *Dawdi haus* attached to one end of a spacious farmhouse. In the *Dawdi haus*, the elderly patient's daughter led Dr. Lehman and his nurse Chris to the spotless *kammah* where the elderly patient lay. As they walked into the room, Katie lay on her side, gazing out into the shaded, neatly trimmed yard where her grandchildren were trying to teach a tiny baby goat to drink from a bottle. Katie's granddaughter glanced up from the Psalm she was reading to her grandmother as she gently fanned the aged woman.

"Oh good, Doc's here, *Mommi*, now you'll be able to sleep better tonight again!"

"Yes, that's awfully nice," *Mommi* Katie said with a smile. "And then I can eat again, too!" she added, rubbing a very distended abdomen.

"What makes *Mommi* blow up like a big balloon all the time?" the young granddaughter wondered.

"Your grandma had rheumatic fever when she was a child," Dr. Lehman explained while Chris took the elderly woman's blood pressure. "She suffers from heart failure now, and her kidneys aren't functioning anymore. That causes fluid to build up inside her, which causes painful pressure, as you can tell," he went on, as he extracted a sterile needle and syringe from his bag.

"Do you do this often?" Katie's daughter wondered, handing Chris clean towels to place around the patient's stomach.

"We have several patients right now that we take fluid from," the doctor replied, holding the syringe while Chris took the stainless steel mixing bowl the granddaughter handed her. "There's a man not far from here who has lymphoma and keeps filling up with fluid, so every three weeks we go over to his home and draw it out. We perform paracentesis for patients with liver cancer, too."

The room fell silent as Dr. Lehman carefully poised the large needle. Concentration masked his face, as he was well aware that striking a vital organ could threaten Katie's life. After jabbing the needle into the abdomen, he detached the syringe and yellow fluid burst from the needle and flowed into the bowl Chris held. The abdomen gradually deflated like a leaking balloon. When the flow of liquid slowed, Dr. Lehman pressed on the abdomen, helping the last bit of liquid to drain.

Chris measured the yellowish fluid. "Fifteen hundred cc's!" she announced. "We got pretty much tonight, Katie. You should feel a lot better now!"

"*Vundahboah besser!*" the woman sighed, closing her eyes. "Now I'll be able to sleep again."

Katie's granddaughter was so grateful. "It's so nice for *Mommi* that she can stay here with us. I don't know how we'd manage if you wouldn't come out to the house. She's not well enough to go to your office."

They're always so grateful, the doctor thought, watching the horizon lighten to a slate blue. It's worth all the extra effort to make house calls just to see the happiness it brings to families.

And patients' homes were much easier to locate since a system of house numbers was introduced. Now, if the doctor needed to locate a John Miller, he could easily do so.

Alice's eyes popped open as the cell phone began to ring. "That was the Care Center," Dr. Lehman informed her after he ended the call. "They just wanted me to know that we've got a patient in labor. If we don't make it back in time, Byler said he can cover for me."

"How'd you manage before you had your cell phone, Doc?"

"How did we! You know, Dr. Eberly and I thought we had it made when we got those two-way radios, but now I can't imagine going out to the car and calling my wife, then waiting in the car while she called the hospital and called me back again. It's just great to be able to call anyone I need to wherever I am.

"I can still remember the first time I used a cell phone out on a house call," he continued. "Here I was in a second floor bedroom of a Swartzentruber Amish home talking to a doctor at Doctors Hospital, telling him I was sending him an appendicitis patient! I looked at that little gadget not connected to any wires and picking up signals in that Amish home and thought it was the best invention after the Jeep!" he declared.

"Rebecca would have missed out on delivering some babies while she waited for you if we had cell phones 20 years ago."

"Not that she would have minded!" the doctor agreed with a thoughtful smile. "Yes, Rebecca was one loyal nurse. I haven't seen much of her since she retired. I don't see her at church anymore either, since Phyllis and I started attending Kidron Mennonite Church."

"Then you must not have heard."

"Heard what?"

"About her wedding plans."

"*Rebecca*! Rebecca has wedding plans!"

"Yes, she and Albert—"

"*Albert*! Not Pastor Albert!"

"Yes, Pastor Albert! You know how lonely he was after his second wife died in the car accident. He asked Rebecca to have lunch with him at a restaurant, 'just as friends,' and a week or two later the same thing happened. Finally, he stopped adding the phrase 'just as friends.'"

"And now there's going to be a wedding?"

"And they're as happy as a couple of teenagers."

"Alice, it's ideal. Albert needs someone to help care for him with his Parkinson's disease and Rebecca was lonely and searching for purpose after retirement. Who would ever have thought," the doctor remarked.

As the rising sun tinted the skies with pink and lavender hues, Dr. Lehman slowed the Jeep to study the name on a mailbox in front of a small house next to a spacious farmhouse and barn. "Mullet," he read, turning the Jeep up the drive. "This is the place," he announced.

A balding man with a long, gray beard held the screen door open with one hand and leaned on a cane with the other.

"It's so good to see ya, Doc," the elderly man hobbled through the house, leaning on his cane as he led the way to the first floor *kammah*. The early morning sunlight streamed through the spotless windows past the violets blooming on the windowsills. The orderly home held a refreshing, cheery atmosphere.

In the bedroom, Melvin's cane clicked across the wood floor to the window where he pulled up the green window shade, letting the sunbeams bathe his frail wife. "Mattie, Doc's here to see you this morning," he said, tenderly tucking the patchwork quilt around his wife's feet.

When there was no visible response other than a restless shifting of the elderly woman's left limbs, the elderly man lifted his eyebrows questioningly toward the doctor. "This is how she's been the last couple of hours," he whispered.

Dr. Lehman studied the elderly woman as he listened to her breathing with his stethoscope. Every symptom—from the deep breathing to her paralyzed side—pointed to a full stroke. He ran his hand along the bottom of Mattie's wrinkled foot. When there was no response, he knew that Mrs. Mullet had suffered a stroke. Her condition was terminal. In fact, there was almost nothing the hospital could do for Mattie that could not be done in this home, except to empty Mr. Mullet's wallet.

With the cows milked, several of the Mullet family had returned to their mother's bedside and stood quietly along the wall waiting for the doctor's prognosis. He turned to face them, "I'm sorry, but she's had a stroke. It will only be a matter of hours."

The elderly man continued to stroke the pale, wrinkled hand lovingly for a moment, then he looked up with pain-filled eyes. "Could they do anything for her at the hospital?" he whispered hoarsely.

"Technically, no. They could do nothing, except to keep her comfortable."

"And she'll be more comfortable here at home."

"That's right."

"What can we do so we can keep her here?" one of the sons wondered.

"Alice will set up an I-V, then we'll show you how to monitor and regulate it."

"*Ach*, that would be *vundahboah*," the patriarch sighed. "I know Mattie would be much more content that way." Then, eyeing the I-V equipment warily, he added, "*Ei yi yi*, Doc, don't ask me to run that contraption."

"There's really nothing to it," the doctor assured him. "We'll hang this sack of fluid on the nail on the window frame, like this," Dr. Lehman explained to the family. "The fluid drips down the tube and through this needle, which we'll stick in a vein. We'll tape the needle fast so it will stay in place. When the liquid has drained out of the pouch, turn the drip off here, and exchange the bag for a new one," he finished.

"Doc," one of the sons began in an emotion-filled voice, "you don't know how much it means to our family that mother can stay here in her own bedroom to die surrounded with her children and grandchildren. If she were in a hospital, she'd be restless. They'd just prolong her discomfort and charge us a lot for the fuss. And there's no way we could all be with her, since the hospital's a good hour's drive away by car. You don't know what this means to us."

"I think I do know," Dr. Lehman said quietly. "You see, my mother lived in our home for 17 years, but finally, after a fall, it was impossible to keep her any longer because of her condition. She would have loved to stay on in our home to the end, surrounded by her family, but it wasn't possible. And now if I can help someone else's mother spend her last minutes in the comfort and privacy of her own home surrounded by her family, it will make me very happy."

"Well, Doc, you saved us a million dollar work-up, and we're mighty grateful," another of Melvin's husky, bearded sons acknowledged.

"I have one request yet before you leave, Doc," the elderly man said, leaning forward in his rocker.

"What's that, Melvin?" Dr. Lehman asked setting his satchel on the floor.

"Well, Doc, you're getting up there in years."

Dr. Lehman looked startled. "Well, I guess I am."

"One of these days," the elderly man continued, "you're going to think about hangin' that stethoscope on the hook. When that time comes, Doc, remember our folks. When you get another doctor to take your place, get one just like you, one who respects our customs, and goes the extra mile to help us, like you're doin' here today."

Melvin leaned back in his rocker and the squeaking chair filled the room for a moment. He adjusted his wire-rimmed glasses resting on his nose and continued. "You've been a blessing, and I thank God for the doctor you've been—comin' to our homes, and all. Settin' up traction for broken bones, helping cancer patients in their own houses, comin' in to the office after hours to stitch our grandchildren up, and starting the Care Center, and all. And now, Doc, please try and find another doctor just like you. We need another Doc Lehman when you retire."

Dr. Lehman kept thinking about Melvin's request as he drove the Jeep down the country roads toward Mount Eaton. Unfortunately, there wouldn't be another Dr. Lehman in Mount Eaton. He had never pressured his children to follow his footsteps. He always urged them to do what they enjoyed and what they were called to, and he didn't want them to feel obligated to carry on his vision unless it was their dream, too.

"I don't mind being a doctor," Brent had said when he was young, "but I don't want to do what you're doing."

But Melvin was right, Dr. Lehman realized. It was time to look into finding a doctor to take over the practice. But where could he find someone who would understand his patients and care for them in a way that would respect their convictions and way of life? He couldn't let his patients set, and yet those 80-hour work weeks were taking their toll.

As he approached Mount Eaton that morning, cows filed out of the barns and into the pastures. Colorful shirts and dresses flapped from wash lines. A plain-clad woman bent over a row of plants in a vegetable garden while her husband drove a team of horses through the rolling, dew-covered fields. But nothing about the peaceful, pastoral scene indicated that the media would soon descend on this small, two-stoplight village. Or, that Dr. Lehman's office was their destination.

30.

THE PIE TAKES THE PRIZE

When Dr. Lehman saw a car flying up the lane in a cloud of dust, he knew that trouble had arrived with the spewing gravel.

"I thought I told you never to set a foot on this property again!" a woman cursed, slamming the car door and charging across the yard, shaking her fist. "Now go! And if you don't know what that means, the sheriff can explain it when he arrests you for trespassing and harassment." She discharged the expletives like a volley of shots from an automatic rifle. "The nerve! Rezoning that property next to ours, making our land worthless, and then traipsing over here to try to influence Harry! You low-down, good-for-nothing—"

"That's no way to talk to the village mayor!" the doctor's colleague clenched his fists and red splotches speckled his neck. "Besides, our ruling didn't devalue your land in the least. Actually, your land will be worth more. . . ."

Dr. Lehman caught his colleague's eye. Don't bother arguing, his eyes signaled. You won't get anywhere with her.

Driving out the lane, the two men exchanged meaningful glances. "Well, did you ever see anything like that!" the board member from Public Affairs fumed. "Running us off the property when we were having a friendly chat with her father."

"No, thank God, I never ran into a case like that before," the doctor sighed. "Never. Honestly, the only complaint I've ever run into during my 14-year tenure as mayor of Mount Eaton was a man reporting a barking dog."

"A barking dog?"

"Yes, a barking dog. Soon after I became mayor I told my son, 'Brent, if anyone calls for the mayor while I'm out, take a message and a phone number, but don't argue with anyone.' The only call we ever got was an elderly man who complained to Brent that his neighbor's dog was barking too much, and would the mayor please make the owners shut him up."

"And that's the only problem you've had in 14 years until today?"

"Exactly. And my colleagues at the hospital kid me about it. Every time they see me, Drs. Ergun and Riether bark at me and say, 'Woof woof, Dr. Lehman, what big problems you have in your little town!'"

The doctor shook his head. "The woman's mad because she thinks the ruling lowered the value of her property. Mark my words, someday she'll see that rezoning the land actually increased its value."

As he walked into his darkened office, Dr. Lehman felt like the dirt on the bottom of his shoe. No one had ever called him such degrading names before. It hurt. Even if he didn't deserve them, the words stung worse than a slap across the face.

I can just see the headlines of the paper tomorrow: "Village Mayor and Board Member for Public Affairs Arrested on Charges of Trespassing." He gloomily switched on the office light.

"Hmmm, what do we have here?" he asked himself, picking up the white Federal Express envelope on his desk. One of Dr. Byler's nurses must have signed for it while I was out. Who's this from? he wondered, glancing at the return address.

"Staff Care Inc., Irving, Texas!" The room seemed to spin as Dr. Lehman sank into his chair. For several long moments, he studied the envelope, not daring to open it.

Four years earlier, Staff Care, a temporary placement firm for rural physicians, initiated the annual Country Doctor of the Year award to recognize outstanding rural doctors and to encourage young physicians to consider country practice. An awards committee, made up of Staff Care executives and a country doctor, judged the nominations on scope and continuity of care as well as dedication. To qualify as a candidate, a physician needed to give primary care to patients of all ages, serve a community of not more than 25,000 for a period of five years or more, and must have shown exceptional dedication.

The moment Thomas Cecconi, the chief executive from Doctors Hospital, heard about the award, he knew he had to nominate Dr. Lehman. But he didn't tell Dr. Lehman about the nomination until Staff Care notified Doctors Hospital that Dr. Lehman was one of the top three candidates out of 400 national nominees.

Dr. Lehman's cheeks reddened when his colleague told him of the nomination. "There are a lot of other physicians out there who have done a lot more for their patients than I have done for mine," Dr. Lehman protested.

"Describe a typical day," the Staff Care agent asked when he called to interview Dr. Lehman.

"My days often start in the wee hours of the morning with a phone call from a nurse at the Mount Eaton Care Center saying I'm needed to deliver a baby," he began. "Before office hours, I go to the hospital to make my rounds, seeing surgery or maternity cases there. Most of my day I spend in my office doing everything from examining a newborn's rash to cutting out a cyst on an elderly patient's head," he explained.

"I'll often treat emergencies during the day—perhaps stitching a hand mangled in farm equipment or casting a bone broken by a fall through a hay hole. If I don't have too many emergencies, I will go home just over the hill for lunch," he continued. "Then I'll see more patients in the afternoon. I may have to run to the Care Center two minutes away to deliver a baby. After office hours, I'll often make a house call or two, examining elderly or terminally ill patients. And, if I'm lucky, a call from a patient in labor will come at bedtime instead of the middle of the night, allowing me to have a solid night of sleep for once!"

"You mentioned going home for lunch. Are you married?" the representative asked.

"Yes, for 35 years."

"Thirty-five years! Surely not to the same woman?"

"That's right. The same one."

"Unbelievable. Absolutely unbelievable! Your wife must be an unusual woman."

"She is," Dr. Lehman replied, thinking of how flexible and supportive Phyllis had been through the years. They shared the same worldview and she helped wherever she was needed.

"What's up? Who's that distinguished-looking gentleman?" Dr. Lehman's nurses asked each other when Phil Miller arrived from Staff Care to meet the doctor, visit Mount Eaton, and to observe a typical day of office visits and house calls.

"Oh, that's the agent from Staff Care who came to see Doc, since he's one of the top candidates for the Country Doctor of the Year award. Didn't you know?" No, they hadn't heard. The doctor hadn't bothered to mention it.

"I could take Mr. Miller out to one of those wonderful Amish restaurants for dinner," Dr. Lehman told his wife. "But since your cooking is as tasty as any dish the local restaurants serve, I'd like to invite him to our house for one of your good home-cooked meals."

After a delightful meal with the Lehmans, Mr. Miller pushed back his chair with a satisfied sigh. "A wonderful meal, Mrs. Lehman," Mr. Miller remarked. "Your elderberry pie was fabulous. Absolutely marvelous."

Now, three days later, Dr. Lehman picked up the Federal Express package from his desk, still smarting from the names the angry woman had called him when she ran him off her property minutes before.

What's this all about? Dr. Lehman wondered. He shakily pulled the tab to open the cardboard packet. Not daring to breathe, he slipped the letter out of the envelope and scanned the words: "You have been selected as 1998 Country Doctor of the Year."

There's got to be a mistake! he thought, carefully reading each word again.

No matter what names that angry woman called me, I'm somebody after all! he sighed. But really, I didn't do anything all that great. I just did my job.

"Must have been your wonderful elderberry pie that won the award for me," he told Phyllis, showing her the letter that evening. "That's all I can figure out. Must have been that pie."

I'd rather stay out of the limelight, he thought. But if I can inspire a young man or woman to be of service to others, then it's worth it, I suppose.

Staff Care chose *Parade Magazine* to break the news. Two local papers, however, scooped the story the day before. The headlines of *Massillon Independent* and *Akron Beacon Journal* shouted: "Country 'Doc' the Country's Best Doctor."

The following day, *Parade Magazine* announced to its 36 million readers that Dr. Elton Lehman was named 1998 Country Doctor of the Year.

Photographers and reporters from *USA Today* drove into Mount Eaton nine days later, following the doctor for three days on house calls and office visits.

The staff at Doctors Hospital planned an award ceremony to honor Dr. Lehman and invited his relatives, friends, and associates. Local newspaper articles announced the public was welcome, as well. In the communities surrounding Mount Eaton, newspapers sold faster than they could be stocked. Area residents wanted to read for themselves about their beloved doctor's national recognition.

Dr. Lehman's acquaintances and patients marked April 24 on

their calendars as the whole community anticipated seeing their "Doc" receive his award.

On the afternoon of April 24, village police directed the lines of cars clogging Routes 250 and 241 coming into Mount Eaton. Music floated from the doors of the Paint Township fire hall as the crowds streamed into the building. Inside, the Lehmans greeted arriving guests. Phyllis greeted well-wishers with characteristic warmth. "How nice of you to come!"

A sense of unworthy awe swelled in the doctor's heart as he glanced across the growing crowd of statesmen, former professors, boyhood chums, patients, hospital executives, church friends, and all 11 siblings. There are more people here than the entire population of Mount Eaton! he realized. And quite a few of them have driven across the country to be here today.

An instrumental quartet from Central Christian High School played in the background while Amish and plain-clad Mennonites, as well as "English" friends, relatives, and patients, congratulated the doctor.

An air of expectation charged the building as guests filled the backless Amish church benches. Balloons, flowers, and music boosted the exuberant atmosphere. A banner stretching across the building proclaimed: "Doctors Hospital Salutes Mount Eaton—Home of Country Doctor of the Year."

As the benches filled, the last notes of music faded into the air. The chatter subsided expectantly as a tall, distinguished gentleman with thick, graying hair approached the lectern to welcome the crowd.

Thomas Cecconi, Chief Executive Officer of Doctors Hospital who had nominated Dr. Lehman for the award, addressed the expectant audience. "It is truly a pleasure to work with a physician who has demonstrated such extraordinary devotion to his patients," he declared. "Dr. Lehman has provided expert medical care as a valued staff member here since 1964. His dedication is further noted by his past willingness to serve as a distinguished member of the Doctors Hospital Board of Trustees."

After Cecconi introduced Phillip Miller, the audience listened intently as the tall, dark-haired executive from Staff Care explained why Dr. Lehman was chosen for the award. The choice was not an easy one, he said, but despite hundreds of nominations, Dr. Lehman stood out.

"It was apparent that in his 35 years of service to his community, he has had a tremendous positive impact in establishing the birthing center, delivering over 6,100 babies, volunteering at the free clinic in Canton, and in performing countless other services.

"There was another aspect of Dr. Lehman's work that impressed us, however," Mr. Miller continued in his solemn, dignified manner. "Medicine has changed dramatically. It is now a business, not an art. The personal connection has been lost. Dr. Lehman's practice is an exception.

"It is apparent that he still operates from the position of trust, compassion, and communication that is such an important part of the healing art. Dr. Lehman, I believe, practices medicine the way it is truly meant to be practiced—he puts patients first."

It was a style of practice, that was "as rare as the horse and buggy," he declared. And inevitably, he said, the physicians nominated for this award were referred to by their patients as "Doc."

As part of the award, Miller announced, Dr. Lehman would receive an interim physician for one week at no cost—a service valued at about $10,000—allowing the doctor to take some deserved time away from the office.

Flash bulbs popped as Mr. Miller handed Dr. Lehman the bronze plaque with the award's logo, a country doctor making a house call in a horse and buggy. With characteristic unpretentious dignity, Dr. Lehman graciously accepted the award and approached the lectern.

Scanning the faces of professors, legislators, colleagues, dignitaries, and media reporters with their huge cameras, note pads, and recorders, the doctor's chest tightened. *How am I going to talk to all these folks? What if I forget what I'm going to say and my words get twisted over one another?*

"Thank you," Dr. Lehman smiled, turning to the tall slender gentleman. "Thank you, Staff Care, thank you, Mr. Miller. In the spirit of humility, I accept your award. I hope that I can live up to Staff Care's expectations of the spirit the award is intended to represent. I will cherish my award, placing it in my office as a constant reminder. Again, thank you."

Facing the audience, the doctor continued. "In my high school and college public speaking classes, and later at a Dale Carnegie Course that I took, the instructors said, 'When you receive an award, stand up, thank them for it, state what you will do with it, thank them again, and then shut up and sit down.' Since my instructors are not here today, I will break the last two rules!" As the audience broke out into laughter, he felt some of the tension in his chest slip away.

"Because, as John Donne wrote in 1624, 'No man is an island, entire of itself,' I want to share this honor with others that have touched my life in a special way. These people themselves supported me, or represent institutions or organizations that supported me. *I could not* and *did not* do this alone."

With the warmth and humor that permeated his relationships, the doctor selflessly honored people who shared his life work. Dr. Lehman invited each honored guest to the platform. In turn, he introduced them and posed with each for a photograph. Then he related a humorous or touching incident about the person, giving a small window into his practice, after which the guest took a seat in the row of chairs flanking the podium.

Phyllis was the first person he honored.

"Phyllis," he said, addressing his wife at his side after the cameras stopped flashing. "Thank you for letting me do what I was called to do and wanted to do, and thanks for your love, support, and for keeping the home fires burning. Our marriage had a slow start. The first month after our honeymoon, I worked night shift in the emergency room. The second month, I was assigned to work as night house physician. Of the 35 years of our marriage, we have lived together only 28," the doctor acknowledged. "With over 6,100 deliveries, and knowing the average hours of labor per birth, I've figured that I spent seven years of my life with women in labor. Thanks for waiting, Phyllis. You deserve part of this reward!" With that, he kissed her tenderly.

"Thank you for your patience and understanding when I wasn't there and family plans were changed by the next phone call," Dr. Lehman said, thanking his three children he had invited to stand at his side after Phyllis was seated. "To spend quality time, I took each of you on house calls or nursing home visits.

"Brenda would sing to the residents at the nursing home, and that did more good than any medicine I had to offer," he said of the poised young woman at his side. "Thanks for singing to my nursing home patients—I am proud of you.

"Brent, you have been my best son, and I am proud of you," he told the clean-cut young man in a suit and tie standing next to his sisters. "Because of my frequent absences, I bought Brent a Honda 50 when he was very young, thinking when it wore out, he would be tired of motorcycles. Well, guess what? He is on his fifth one and still rides motorcycles today.

"Bev frequently went with me on house calls and to nursing homes," he said, turning to his youngest daughter, a slender young woman with the same sweet face and sparkling eyes of the preschooler that had accompanied him to the nursing home so many years before. "She also sang for the patients like Brenda; however, while Brenda sang songs from memory, Bev made up her own songs instead. She was creative then, and still is today. I'm proud of you! Thank you! You three deserve part of the award."

The Lehman children found chairs behind their father as he announced the next person he wished to honor.

"Phillip Miller, Staff Care. May I again thank you for the honor Staff Care has given me—and even more for the fact that you permitted me to receive the honor here in Mount Eaton, where it all happened.

"Thomas E. Cecconi, CEO Doctors Hospital," Dr. Lehman announced. Flash bulbs popped as he continued. "Today I want to publicly thank Doctors Hospital for supporting and assisting me when I saw a need and had a dream or an idea to meet that need," he said. "The medical staff and administration were very supportive and encouraged me to meet the needs of my patients."

Dr. Lehman shared his journey from a child fascinated with nature to becoming a country doctor. As he spun the story, he began to enjoy himself, relaxing even more.

"At home on the farm, I was always intrigued with the baby chicks we raised, wondering where the peeping sound came from. One day, my curiosity got the best of me, and I pulled out my little pen knife and exposed the tiny organs to find out what made the chick peep. I was so captivated with my first anatomy lesson that I didn't hear my dad coming up behind me. I won't say what happened next, except to mention that I never dissected another chick, and neither did I become a surgeon!" he chuckled.

Then he invited retired Eastern Mennonite University biology professor Kenton Brubaker to the platform and posed with him for a photo. "The University did well in preparing me for med school and preparing me for Christ's call to a life of witness, service, and peacemaking," Dr. Lehman praised. "Thank you.

"You well lived up to your motto, 'To Teach, to Heal, to Serve,'" Dr. Lehman told Thomas O. Adams, public relations director representing Midwestern University and Chicago College of Osteopathic Medicine, who, in turn, took a seat in the row behind the lectern.

Dr. Lehman spent the next hour graciously thanking and praising those who had helped him achieve the honor.

"Going to school didn't come without a price," Dr. Lehman remarked as he called his brother Merlin Lehman and cousin Bessie Nussbaum to the platform. The doctor shared with the audience how he had lost his financial support when his father died suddenly 10 days before the end of his first year at med school. Then his brother Merlin and Uncle Silas Lehman stepped in and helped to pay tuition bills and co-sign loans. Bessie's husband, the late Willis Nussbaum, gave Elton summer jobs when he was a student and became Dr. Lehman's first patient. After relating how he had knelt on the floor to treat Willis because his examining table had not arrived, Dr. Lehman remarked, "Now that was real country medicine!"

Dr. Lehman thought of Willis Nussbaum. He'd have loved to be here today to see that I made it in Mount Eaton in spite of what the old-timers said. Veterinarian John Reber and I both survived.

"Drs. Eberly, Byler, and Showalter, my fellow colleagues." The three doctors came to the platform and Dr. Lehman explained how Dr. Wain Eberly's invitation had prompted Dr. Lehman to come to Mount Eaton. Then 15 years later, when the Lehman children were entering their teens, Dr. Nolan Byler joined the team, giving Dr. Lehman more coverage and more time off. Dr. Anita Showalter, married to Eli Showalter, whose brothers were burned in the car accident, had joined the practice the previous August, further relieving Dr. Lehman's workload.

As the physicians took their seats on the stage with the other honored guests, Dr. Lehman called up Rebecca Byler Slabach and her husband Albert. The small nurse with her graying hair pulled back into a knot took the arm of the elderly man at her side as they climbed the steps to the platform.

"Rebecca worked in my office for 26 years," Dr. Lehman explained. "She was my right hand, helping with deliveries, repairing lacerations, and setting fractures—after hours and on Sundays.

"One of our patients, like many of the Amish, had a sense of humor. Every time we'd ask him what he was naming his newborn, he'd always ask: 'Well, did he come with a name?' Playing along with him, we'd examine the new baby, checking his feet, his body, and head, 'Well, I can't find any name,' I'd say, and Jake would laugh and name the child.

"'Let's be ready for that man next time,' I told my nurse. And we were. When his wife went into labor, I reminded Rebecca that this was Jake's wife, so she wrote a boy's name on one slip of paper and a girl's name on another, laying each on a separate piece of tape in a convenient, hidden place.

"As soon as the little boy was born and we had him suctioned out, my nurse dried one of the little feet and discreetly taped the name to the heel.

"I put on a serious face and said to the father, 'Do you have a name for this little guy?' wondering if he'd forget his line this time.

"'Well, did he come with a name?' Jake asked as usual.

"I picked up the baby and carefully examined his head, then his body, turning him over, checking his legs and finally his feet.

"'Here it is!' I announced. 'His name is Mose!' You should have seen that father's face. His jaw dropped a mile. But he must not have liked the name, because he gave him another name," Dr. Lehman laughed with his audience.

Hey, this isn't so bad after all. It's almost fun.

Rebecca stood beaming beside her husband, as Dr. Lehman continued after the chuckles faded into the rafters. "Albert was my pastor for 23 years. Your friendship and moral and spiritual support were unwavering, Albert. It was a privilege that you let me walk with you and minister to you during the many tragedies in your life: the loss of your first wife and infant son, the loss of your brother in a truck accident, the loss of your other son in a truck accident, and then the loss of your second wife in an auto accident. We wept together and laughed together, and then you turned around and stole my nurse of 26 years for your third wife! I'll forgive you for that, and I am happy for you. Thank you, Albert."

Barb Hostetler, too, was a big part of his story, Dr. Lehman said. He requested that out of respect to her religious convictions, no photographs be taken of the stately midwife in the wire-rimmed glasses, long black dress, and neatly-pleated *kapp* tied beneath her chin. What would he have done without Barb who so graciously opened her home to so many of his patients?

And then there was Nancy Spiker. "Nancy represents my office nurses through the years," he said. "I have had the best working for me in my office. In 34 years, I have had fewer than a dozen different nurses. They stay until they move or retire. Nancy has been working with me for 24 years. I have turned over so many responsibilities to her that I'm not sure who is working for whom. In fact, I think I'm working for Nancy! Thank you, Nancy, and all the nurses past and present."

As Dr. Lehman acknowledged Bonnie Neuenschwander, the Care Center administrator representing the dedicated staff, board, and nurses who made the center run so smoothly, he couldn't help but think of Jonas D. Yoder. The adventuresome Amishman, who had made it all possible, was not in attendance, because he was killed when he fell from a scaffold on a construction project several years before. Jonas' seat was empty.

"Dr. Questel, county coroner, has been a friend and mentor," Dr. Lehman continued, introducing the senior doctor. "His prompt response, thorough exam, and sensitivity to the survivors are something to model.

"Maxine Hewitt, village clerk and treasurer, and Rod Constable, president of the village council," Dr. Lehman announced with a smile. "I have been mayor for the past 14 years and could only do it because of the good and loyal help from the clerk–treasurer and president of the council.

"And now, I would like to introduce two of my oldest patients," Dr. Lehman said, inviting a spunky woman by the name of Lucille Torgler to the front, along with 94-year-old John Martin, a clean-shaven Mennonite man in a black suit. "When I called John Martin's daughter to see if he was in good enough health to come to the ceremony, she responded, 'I suppose he is. He's out chopping down a tree!'

"Brenda Hoover was one of my first deliveries," Dr. Lehman said, introducing a young Mennonite mother in a long dress and head veiling. "Her one-week-old niece, Sonya Trautwein, one of my youngest patients and my 6,145th delivery, is here today, as well.

"Waid Spidell is the local funeral director," the doctor presented the next honored guest. "And unfortunately, sometimes our work overlaps. If I have to notify him of a death after midnight or if he has to notify me to sign a death certificate, the standard saying is, 'If I can't sleep, you can't sleep either!'"

Not only did the jobs of the two men overlap, but their families were close friends, as well, the doctor said. "Our children have spent hours together," Dr. Lehman explained. "In fact, I once told my son Brent, 'You don't have brothers like I did when I grew up, but you have Scott Spidell, and when you get upset, you can send him home until you make up again. If I got upset at my brother, I still had to eat with him and sleep with him in the same room.'"

Thanking his pastor and church friends, he told Pastor Terry Shue the church had "been a moral and spiritual support to carry out my medical ministry. And I thank the Special Interests Sunday School Class for its lively discussions on Christian principles and how they apply today. I am also grateful for the small group and men's group to which I belong, for their inspiration to me, and for their prayers. Thank you, Terry."

Deafening applause shook the building as Dr. Lehman gathered his notes and took his seat with the semi-circle of friends and colleagues he had honored. He had survived the speech. Somehow, having others share the podium with him and telling their stories had made the speech seem less intimidating.

State Senator Ronald Amstutz rose to give a presentation, as did delegates representing Ohio Governor George Voinovich, Congressman Ralph Regula, and State Representative Grace Drake. Institutions and organizations including Chicago College of Osteopathic Medicine, Eastern Mennonite University, and Mennonite Medical Association acknowledged the doctor, as well.

Help! I didn't know about all these presentations, Dr. Lehman thought. I'd rather be seeing patients in my office!

When the mayor of Canton commended Dr. Lehman for the time he volunteered at a free clinic in one of the local cities, Dr.

Byler looked up with surprise. "I didn't know he did that!" he whispered to his wife. But that was Dr. Lehman. He went about serving the needs around him in his quiet way.

Toward the close of the ceremony, Thomas Cecconi presented the village with a plaque to hang in the town hall.

In a final proclamation, Albert Spector, owner of Spector's stores, announced in jest: "The mayor of Mount Eaton forgot to appoint someone from the community to honor the Country Doctor of the Year recipient. A $1,000 donation to the birthing center is being made on behalf of the Amish community and Mount Eaton for Dr. Lehman's many contributions to the area residents. Dr. Lehman," Spector finished, "you bring great honor to our village."

Pastor Terry Shue closed the ceremony with a prayer of thanksgiving to God, the Great Physician, who, too, deserved to be honored, he said. The pastor thanked God for Dr. Lehman's life of service, competency, compassion, and faith. He asked for "God's love and grace to rest on the family today and forever."

After the prayer, Dr. Byler and Tim Shue accompanied Bev and Phyllis in singing Dr. Lehman's's favorite song, "My God and I."

Last of all, Phyllis joined the Kidron Mennonite Church Choir as they lifted their voices with the song, "Praise God from Whom All Blessings Flow." The building rang with the words:

Praise God from whom all blessings flow.
Praise Him all creatures here below.
Praise Him above, ye heavenly host,
Praise Father, Son, and Holy Ghost.

The glow of excitement that hung over the audience flamed into a blaze of awe for the man who was willing to serve others so selflessly while serving God.

The next day, the front page of the *Wooster Daily Record* reported the honors ceremony with the headlines: "Big-Time Small

Town Honors: Mt. Eaton's Lehman Earns Nationwide Recognition."

"Because of his many Amish patients, Dr. Lehman has one of the most unique practices in the country," Joseph Caldwell, Staff Care's executive vice president told journalists. "His dedication to a unique patient population perfectly reflects the skill and caring of America's country doctors. While adapting to the Amish way of life, he has managed to elevate health care standards for them, yet still respects their beliefs," the story reported. "His idea to get his Amish patients out of the home and into a setting other than a hospital was typical of his sensitivity to his Amish patients."[16]

During his interviews, Dr. Lehman spoke respectfully of his Amish patients and their ways. He noted that in all the years he did home deliveries, he recalled one case of infection. He attributed the absence of infections in home deliveries to the cleanliness of his patients' homes and to their comfort in being in their own environment.

The reporters wrote about the 6,145 babies Dr. Lehman had delivered, including 72 sets of twins, one set of triplets, and the 18 babies he delivered to one Amish couple. "My mom had 10 children," an Amish patient was quoted as saying. "And they all came from Dr. Lehman!"[17]

Days after the awards ceremony, former Major League Baseball catcher Joe Garagiola of NBC's *Today Show* drove into Mount Eaton to interview Dr. Lehman. The baseball great spent two days with Dr. Lehman, trailing him with television cameras, interviewing office patients and hospital staff, accompanying the doctor on house calls, and visiting the Mount Eaton Care Center. On May 29, NBC aired the story to an audience of 10 million. A lengthy segment portrayed the doctor's practice, especially his relationships with his Amish patients.

But it wasn't what celebrities said that Dr. Lehman valued most. It was what his colleagues said after working with him for more than a quarter of a century. Dr. Lehman is "a community leader, neighbor, public servant, husband, father, and friend. In short, an exemplary citizen," Cecconi told the *Wooster Daily Record*. "He is held in very high regard by all the medical staff here."[18]

"Doc Lehman is a Bridge to Divergent Worlds," the June 9, 1998 *USA Today's* headlines proclaimed on over four million copies. "Doctor of the Year Operates Seamlessly in a World of Buggies, Plain Clothes, and Kerosene."

Like many of the articles, the story described house calls to care for elderly housebound patients and a visit to the Care Center. Of course, Dr. Lehman took the reporters to visit Barb in the *Dawdi haus* apartment of her farmhouse adjacent to the former birthing center wing her grandson's family now occupied.

"He was a God-send," Barb claimed. "Doc Lehman was a beginner when I got a hold of him," she told the *USA Today* reporter, adding, "He didn't let me down once."

"Having my picture in the paper is bad enough," the doctor told Phyllis when yet another publication arrived in the mail with an article about the Country Doctor of the Year. "But those parades," he sighed. "I'd rather be out on a house call any day."

"At least you can hide inside your '35 Ford in the Hall of Fame Parade in August," Phyllis tried to console her husband.

But two weeks before the special parade, the Ford gave out. Dr. Lehman was driving the car in a parade through Brewster when the old Ford groaned to a stop and couldn't be coaxed to start again. A group of firefighters pushed the antique car. It sputtered to a start, then a little way down the road it coasted to a stop and refused to start up again. A number of old-timers swarmed around the black '35. "Hey, we remember that one," they beamed. "You know what's wrong with it? It's vapor locked."

"You'd better find me another car," Dr. Lehman told the Hall of Fame committee, "the '35 Ford is out of commission right now."

Arriving on the parade grounds, Dr. Lehman discovered that he was expected to ride on the back of a convertible Corvette. "I should have arranged to ride in a horse and buggy!" he groaned to his wife.

Reporters kept finding their way to the two-stoplight town of Mount Eaton, and headlines continued to proclaim Dr. Lehman's work and his honors. *When will this end?* the doctor wondered when *People* magazine carried a four-page spread about him titled, "Care and Compassion."

A large photograph portrayed Dr. Lehman leaning forward on a rocking chair, his stethoscope in hand, listening to the heartbeat of a wrinkled, bonneted patient in her chair next to him. Other photos captured the doctor examining a two-week-old baby, standing next to a buggy, or leaning over his '35 Ford. Then there was the childhood photo of a young Dr. Lehman wearing a straw hat and posing next to his pony.

When asked about his hobbies, Dr. Lehman replied, "I do not fish. I do not hunt. I do not golf. That's addicting." Instead, he said, he used time to volunteer at health clinics. He relaxed by digging in a flower garden or tooling around with his antique cars. "You live here, therefore you support it," he said, explaining his involvement in community work. "Because if you don't, who will?"[19]

The news articles revealed how those closest to the doctor viewed him. Phyllis was quoted in *People* as saying, "He's a very giving person." The same publication quoted Brent: "Maybe he wasn't at every ball game. We still had our time together."[20]

"Does that mean working long hours?" reporters asked when Dr. Lehman talked of his office hours, deliveries, and house calls. "You bet! To the tune of 80 hours a week." But then he added, "It's not work, it's fun!"[21]

While Dr. Lehman received national coverage, it was the local acclaim that meant the most to him. The *Dalton Gazette and Kidron News*, the publication from Dr. Lehman's childhood home of Kidron reported: "If attitude and dedication separate good physicians from the best, Dr. Lehman is a premier caregiver. So say the people who know him best. His patients cannot find enough words of praise for their family physician, family friend."[22]

The article quoted a patient as saying: "He's an excellent physician who won't hesitate to have you call him anytime, day or night. I can't remember a time when Dr. Lehman was not there for me and my family." The people of Mt. Eaton feel fortunate to have such an extraordinary physician practicing in their neighborhood, the paper reported. "We have the best of both worlds, access to high quality medicine and the warmth of personal care we have come to trust . . . The doctor is like family to many, having grown up in the neighboring town of Kidron."[23]

"Do you think the woman who cussed you out and ran you off her property has seen your picture in the paper or saw you on NBC's *Today Show?*" Phyllis asked her husband.

"She must have," he replied. "But it doesn't really matter to me. I just hope someday she discovers that the secret to happiness comes from ministering to the needs of others."

"Do you think after four months that this is about the end of the publicity?" Phyllis wondered in September.

"Well, after the *Columbus Dispatch* carries the story on September 21, I've been told it'll be released to the Associated Press and it will begin all over."

"I thought it already was carried all over the place!" Phyllis declared.

Everywhere the doctor and Phyllis went, friends, relatives, and colleagues handed them newspaper clippings they had cut out of the *Canton Repository, The Budget, Das Botschaft, The Ohio Magazine, Mennonite Medical Messenger, Ohio Osteopathic Annual Report,* and the *Ohio Hospital Association News.*

"I saw the news while in the air," a United Airlines pilot and fellow student of Dr. Lehman's told him. "When I was on a flight on the way home from Germany, I heard about your award," another friend said. Phyllis' nephew spotted Dr. Lehman's face on the television in his classroom in North Carolina. "That's my uncle!" he cried, but, of course, his classmates didn't believe him.

By July, media coverage reached over 51,000,000 people with the equivalence of $600,000 worth of advertising, Cecconi told

Dr. Lehman. When all was said and done, it was calculated that exposure for the 1998 Country Doctor of the Year had reached close to 100 million people.

Six months after the award ceremony, the Ohio State Society of Osteopathic Physicians awarded Dr. Lehman the Family Physician of the Year award.

"I've almost had enough!" he joked when he was chosen as *Wooster Daily Record's* Citizen of the Year. "It's just about enough."

In spite of all the honors and headlines, Elton remained characteristically modest. He was still the country doctor who unabashedly drove his Jeep to black tie affairs, wearing a suit and tie while his associates arrived wearing tuxedos and driving BMWs and Mercedes. On trips and various excursions, he drove an old '75 four-door hardtop Cadillac he purchased for $1,800. Wherever he drove it, parking attendants ignored the luxury automobiles and fought to drive his unusual car.

Often he was asked what he'd do with the vacation time he received as part of the award. He and Phyllis planned to take in his fortieth college class reunion at Eastern Mennonite University and then travel to South Carolina to visit Dr. Finer and his wife at Hilton Head. In addition, they planned to see Phyllis' niece and family in North Carolina. At the end of the week, the Lehmans would return to Harrisonburg, Virginia, where he was scheduled to receive Eastern Mennonite University's Alumnus of the Year award.

CCOM also honored Dr. Lehman with its Alumnus of the Year award. The Mental Health and Recovery Board of Wayne and Holmes counties gave its Shining Light award, and the Ohio Osteopathic Association bestowed on him the Distinguished Service award.

Meanwhile, one subject weighed heavily on the minds of many of Dr. Lehman's patients. "I don't know how on earth I'll survive when he retires," they lamented. "I often wonder where I would go. I could never find somebody as good as he is."

But Dr. Lehman wasn't worrying about a replacement just yet.

Why would any healthy man who loved his work need a replacement?

"I could never have served my community in this capacity without my wife's support," he always said. "She made it all possible." After all the times she's canceled plans or entertained guests alone because I was called away, it's time I do something special for her, he decided.

"So, where would you like to go to celebrate our 35th anniversary?" he asked her.

"Oh, Elton, if there'd be anywhere I'd like to go, it would be on Goshen Alumni Choir's Mountains and Music Tour," she had said. "They'll be going to Switzerland and singing in the oldest Mennonite church in the world there in the Emmental region not far from your roots."

"So we're going back to my roots," Elton mused dreamily. "And you'd love to sing with the choir again, wouldn't you? Hey, if that's what you'd like to do, then let's go. You deserve a special trip. After all, it was your elderberry pie that won the award for me."

Epilogue

"Say, Doc, when are you going to retire?" a fellow tour member asked Dr. Lehman one afternoon as they drove through the Swiss countryside.

"Retire?" he had responded. "What's that? I've got good health and lots of energy. Why should I think about retiring? I'd rather be helping folks."

"Well, you can't punch out 80-hour weeks forever. Someday, you'll have to start slowing down."

"I've got a dozen good years ahead of me before I even need to start thinking of retiring," Elton countered, unaware of the medical crisis he'd soon face.

When Dr. Lehman felt the first troubling tinges of tightness in his chest several months later, he thought he'd take a round of medication, the symptoms would vanish, and he'd keep right on barreling through life. But the occasional sensation of pressure and heaviness in his chest didn't disappear as he had hoped.

"One coronary vessel is 100 percent blocked," the cardiologist explained after a heart catheterization at Cleveland Clinic. "And another is 85 percent closed."

Less than a year after the memorable awards ceremony, the doctor lay on an operating table at the Cleveland Clinic. Recuperating from the double-bypass surgery, he lay in the hospital bed thinking of his waiting room packed with patients. How will I ever have the strength to keep up with my demanding schedule? he wondered. And what about my patients who've become like family to me? Who's going to care for their lacerations, rashes, and broken bones, and wake in the middle of the night to deliver their babies? For the moment, the patients were under the capable care of Dr. Anita Showalter, who had just completed her residency. But what of the future? he kept wondering.

"God has a purpose," he remembered his patients saying during difficult times. "We just need to trust that he is in control, accept what he allows, and believe that someday we'll understand."

I never thought I'd see this day, Dr. Lehman mused, picking up the airline tickets lying on his desk and scanning his schedule once again. "Cleveland . . . Miami . . . Guatemala City." He slipped the tickets into his attaché, mentally checking off the duties he needed to complete in the next few short hours. First of all, I'd better wrap up the paper work at the Care Center, he decided. Then I've got some packing to do when I get back.

Walking up to the window of the nurses' station, Dr. Lehman spotted Brent, his face veiled in concentration as he listened to the tones the stethoscope picked up from the chest of a newborn infant. The scene seemed to blur until Dr. Lehman could see a two-year-old toddler wearing his father's stethoscope, searching for the heartbeat of his sister's doll.

How'd it ever happen that there's still a Dr. Lehman in town? he marveled as he thought back to the memorable telephone conversation he and his son shared after the heart surgery at Cleveland Clinic.

"You know, Dad," Brent had said. "I've finished my residency, and my year of teaching here at my alma mater is almost over. I've been praying about my future. I've checked into numerous foreign medical mission possibilities, but no door seems to be opening right now. I've been doing a lot of thinking since you were in the hospital, Dad. And I've decided that while you have a measure of health, I want to see you experience some of those things you always wanted to—like those short-term medical mission trips. And besides, Dad, I'd like to spend some time working with you and learning from you. Dad," Brent continued, "if you could use me, I'd be willing to come back and work with you this fall."

"If I could use you? Brent!" Dr. Lehman nearly shot out of his chair. "Let me tell you, there couldn't be a better answer to my prayers. You are like a light at the end of the tunnel, Brent! But Son," the doctor's voice lowered. "Son, listen, I want you to be where God wants you to be. I don't want any of my children to feel obligated to step into my shoes."

"Dad," there was a hint of resolved Lehman firmness in Brent's tone. "I've been doing a lot of thinking and praying about this, and I feel I'm supposed to come to Mount Eaton. I signed up for a stint with an orphanage in Nicaragua this summer, and I have the bicycle ride from Oregon to Ohio scheduled for August. After that, I'll be available to help you out."

After 36 years of practice, Dr. Lehman experienced the pleasure of introducing his patients to their new doctor, his son Brent. Nancy and nurses Alice and Elaine, who had known the ropes of the practice for years, worked for the young doctor as well. The patients found Brent to be a competent, careful, compassionate physician. When Brent shut his eyes in thoughtful contemplation, just like his father had, the patients knew they could trust the "chip off the old block."

"Can't you guys think with your eyes open?" Nancy would laugh.

"He's just like his dad," the patients remarked in relief.

"He sure is," Alice and Nancy agreed. "And he's a great doctor, too. After all, we helped raise him."

To distinguish between the two Dr. Lehmans, the young doctor became known as "Dr. Brent," while his father remained "Dr. Lehman," or occasionally "Dr. Elton."

Dr. Lehman wouldn't fade from the office immediately, he assured patients and staff. He'd work with his son for a time and continue to deliver babies for patients who requested his service. Frequently, he transported X-rays for Brent's patients to Doctors Hospital for Drs. Ergun and Riether to review. And, of course, when Dr. Brent went out of town, the father would cover for him, like the weeks the young doctor took off for his wedding trip with Claudia, a young dentist from El Salvador. They met on a medical team that went to an Albanian refugee camp.

Just because Dr. Lehman was easing out of the office didn't mean emergencies stopped coming in the front door. No, indeed. Brent often went to the office after hours to stitch a laceration or to X-ray and cast a fracture, saving his patients trips to the emergency room. The doctor happened to be in the office the day a baby was born in the treatment room. Alice and Nancy scrambled around searching for a suction syringe and cord clips, calling for Mary, the young Amish receptionist, to find a blanket for the infant. It was a moment to remember as Dr. Brent caught the baby and Dr. Elton gave an encouraging word and a suggestion or two in the background.

In many ways, the transition from father to son seemed flawless. One evening, Dr. Lehman walked into the nurses' station at the Mount Eaton Care Center and placed a hand on his son's shoulder. "Did you deliver this baby, Brent?"

"Oh, hi Dad!" his son looked up in surprise. "Yes, I delivered this one. And by the way, you might be interested to know that this is Barb's great-granddaughter."

"I see! A healthy youngster, from the looks of it. Everything went well, I suppose?"

"Quite well, Dad. It was the granddaughter's first delivery, and at every checkup she'd say, 'Oh I just hope the baby comes during the day, then I'll bring Grandma along." She said it would mean so much to have her grandmother along, but she didn't want to bother Barb during the night. And it all worked out, Dad. They came in today and brought Barb with them."

"Barb was here! Did she help with the delivery?"

"Actually, she stayed in the background, sitting on a chair, giving a suggestion now and then, but it seemed to be a moral support to the young mother, just knowing her experienced grandmother was in the room."

"Brent?" There was one question, the ultimate test of his son's competence and his acceptance into the practice. Dr. Lehman asked, "Brent, uh, did Barb have anything special to say?"

"Barb? Why?" Brent studied his father questioningly.

"I'll tell you if he won't," Susie put in as she wrapped the infant in a hand-quilted comforter. "Barb told me, 'Young Lehman handled that delivery very well—just like his dad!'"

With his patients in Brent's capable hands, Dr. Lehman flew to clinics in Honduras, the Dominican Republic, and Kenya. He and several colleagues treated as many as 750 patients in four days. Everywhere he traveled, he saw desperate needs and met scores of extremely grateful patients.

On one trip, Dr. Lehman and Phyllis flew to Honduras to join a team of doctors holding medical clinics across the country. There, in forgotten pockets of the rugged mountains, he treated malaria, dispensed worm medication, and cut out cysts and ingrown toenails for patients in remote villages without access to medical help. Without the makeshift clinic, they'd have a day's hike to a doctor's office, if they could afford the physician's fee.

On another occasion, Dr. Dan Miller invited Dr. Lehman to go to Kenya with him. "My son says they could use help at the hospital where he practices. The needs there are great, Elton. And if you'll go with me, I'll take you on wildlife safaris and fishing on Lake Victoria on the side," he promised.

So Dr. Lehman found himself spending a month treating AIDS, TB, malaria, meningitis, and rabies cases in the African hospital. "I've only seen one case of TB and one case of malaria in all my years of practice," he told Dr. Miller. "And here I see an unbelievable number. And I've never seen rabies before. The medical needs are incredible."

And so, he continued to pack his stethoscope and travel to far-off places, caring for folks who had no doctors to stitch their lacerations, make house calls, or diagnose their illnesses. Wherever he traveled, he found grateful patients that desperately needed his care, even on an airplane.

"Is there a doctor on board?" the pilot asked on a flight home from the Dominican Republic after a medical mission trip. Always one to stay out of the limelight, Dr. Lehman waited. I'll give another doctor the chance to respond, he thought.

Twice more the captain asked, "Is there a doctor on board?"

I must be the only one, he thought, pressing the button in response to the pilot's request.

A flight attendant hurried to his seat. "We've got a woman up front who's breathing really fast," she explained. "She tells me she had open heart surgery recently, and now she's sensing that her heart is beating faster than it should. Would you mind checking on her?"

Before she finished speaking, Dr. Lehman had already unbuckled his seatbelt and was rising from his seat. The flight attendant led the way to a wide-eyed woman with an oxygen mask covering her face.

"She'll be more comfortable lying on a blanket on the floor," the doctor suggested.

Quickly, the flight attendant grabbed several blankets from an overhead compartment and spread them on the floor just behind the cockpit.

"Do you have a stethoscope?" he asked the flight attendant after the patient was settled.

"We've got this," she replied. Dr. Lehman eyed the blood pressure cuff she extended to him and knew the flight attendant wouldn't be much help. He found a stethoscope himself in the first aid kit and, there at the front of the plane, he knelt at the woman's side, checking her blood pressure and pulse. Meanwhile, the flight attendant quietly reassured the patient and her husband in Spanish that the doctor would take care of her and everything would be okay.

"Her pulse is actually lower than normal, but her blood pressure is higher than it should be," Dr. Lehman reported to the flight attendant and the pilot, who stood in the door of the cockpit.

"It'll be 35 minutes until we land at Miami," the pilot informed him. "But we are approaching Nassau, Doctor. Where would you like us to land?"

"I'd like to get her into a hospital as soon as possible," the doctor replied. "But what kind of medical care can we expect to find on the island?"

"Nassau doesn't have the modern medical facilities that Miami does," the flight attendant put in.

"Then let's head for Miami," Dr. Lehman decided.

For the remainder of the flight, Dr. Lehman and the flight attendant stayed quietly at the couple's side, calmly reassuring them and monitoring the patient's pulse. Medics met the plane at the gate of the Miami Airport, where Dr. Lehman briefed them on the woman's condition.

"Please, I give you some dollars," the husband offered as the medics rolled the stretcher up the gangway. "You much help my *señora.*"

"Let's forget it," the doctor said with a smile, "I was glad to be of service. Now, all I want is to make my next flight."

"Wait. Let me get you a bottle of wine," the flight attendant offered. "Just having you on board was so reassuring for all of us."

"No, thanks," he declined politely, glancing down at his ticket.

"That's kind of you to offer it, but the only payment I'll accept is for someone to tell me the shortest route to my gate."

When the Jeep coasted into Mount Eaton after returning from one mission trip, Dr. Lehman glanced at the sign greeting them: "Welcome to Mount Eaton, Home of Elton Lehman, D.O., 1998 Country Doctor of the Year."

"If I could have seen this sign when we first drove into Mount Eaton almost 40 years ago, I would have never believed it," he sighed.

"As shy as you were, if you had seen that sign back then, you would have turned your Mercury around and headed north again, knowing you," Phyllis laughed.

"I could never have done it without you, Phyllis," he said tenderly as he drove up the drive to their stone home on the hill silhouetted in the sunset.

I've had a great life doing the work God called me to, the work I enjoyed, he thought looking back over the valley, suitcase in hand as he listened to the echoing chimes. But Mount Eaton isn't my permanent destination. Life's a journey and Mount Eaton is a hitching place—a place to come back to, a place of rest and refreshment before the next journey.

I've handed over the clinic keys to my son, he thought, but I can't hang up my stethoscope. There are too many patients who have no doctor to make house calls, to stitch their lacerations, or to bandage their wounds. After all, that is Christ's call—to live a life of service, witness, and ministry.

ENDNOTES

1. *The Sugarcreek Budget* is a weekly newspaper published in Sugarcreek, Ohio, that provides news from Amish and Mennonite communities across the country.
2. Known as Eastern Mennonite College when Dr. Lehman attended.
3. Romans 12:2; King James Version.
4. Amish peanut butter is a sweet spread made of corn syrup mixed with peanut butter.
5. "A Psalm of David, Praise to the Lord."
6. Psalm 103:1-3; King James Version.
7. Hurt, Henry, "Little Boy Blue of Chester, Nebraska," *Reader's Digest* (December 1987): 73-74.
8. Ibid., 77.
9. Caniglia, John, "Local Authorities Re-examining," *Wooster (Ohio) Daily Record,* 16 December 1987.
10. Dougherty, Margot and Civia Tamarkin, "The Riddle of Little Boy Blue," *People,* 22 February 1988: 26-31.
11. Norris, Kelleye, "Stutzman Given 40 Years in Killing of Albert Pritchett, a Former Employee and Roommate," *The Canton (Ohio) Repository,* 2 August 1989.
12. Ibid.
13. Matthew 25:40; King James Version.
14. Lange, Tami and Molly Callahan, "Thousands Mourn Deaths of Five Accident Victims Sunday," *Wooster (Ohio) Daily Record,* 17 May 1993.
15. Lewellen, David, "We're Not Angry at the Guy; We Feel Sorry for Him," *Wooster (Ohio) Daily Record,* 26 May 1993.
16. Dottavio, Peg, "Country Doctor Extraordinaire," *The Massillon (Ohio) Independent,* 4-5 April 1998.
17. Kelly, Katie, "'Doc Lehman' is a Bridge to Divergent Worlds," *USA Today,* 9 June 1998.
18. Hall, Linda, "Big-Time Small Town Honors," *Wooster (Ohio) Daily Record,* 26 April, 1998.
19. Wellman, Jennifer, "Lehman's Motto: You Live Here, Therefore Support It," *Wooster (Ohio) Daily Record,* 30 December 1998.
20. Foege, Alec and Giovanna Breu, "Care and Compassion," *People,* 14 September 1998.
21. "Doctor Elton Lehman Named Country Doctor of the Year," *Dalton (Ohio) Gazette and Kidron (Ohio) News,* 8 April 1998.
22. Ibid.
23. Ibid.

GLOSSARY

Ach—oh!

Ach mei zeit—oh how awful!

Ach yammah—oh bother! Or, oh trouble!

Adonai—a Hebrew name for God

Bohnesupp—bean soup

Brit Milah—Jewish rite of circumcision

Buppeli—baby

Chuppah—a wedding canopy

Dabbah schpring—Run quick.

Daett—Dad

Dawdi—grandfather

Dawdi haus—an extension built on to the main house for grandparents' quarters

Die doch is doah—The doc is here.

Du muscht—You must.

Dummheit—foolish or stupid

Ei yi yi—an expression of displeasure or surprise

Englischer—a non-Amish person

Frau—wife or woman

Gmay—church

Grohs dank—thanks a lot

Grohs Dawdi—grandfather

Grohs Mommi—grandmother

Gut—good

Hand—hand

Hend—hands

Hoi loch—hay hole

Hoimacher—hay mower

Ich kahn net ferschtay—I can't understand.

Ich saag—I'd say.

Kammah—bedroom

Kapp—prayer veiling worn by Amish women

Kibbutz—a communal farm or settlement in Israel

Kippah—a skull cap

Kumm rei—Come in.

Kumm uscht rei—Come on in.

L' Chaim—To Life!

Lebt Friedsam—"Live Peaceably," a parting song

Liebe—a term of affection meaning "dear"

Lobe—praise

Lobleid—a praise song

Maam—Mom

Maam, die Doc is doah—Mom, the doc is here.

Mach schnell—hurry

Maut—maid or hired girl

Mazel-tov—congratulations

Mei zeit—oh my!

Mommi—grandmother

O du yammah—oh how strange!

Rumshpringa—running around

Schechinah—presence of God
Schick dich—Behave yourself.
Schnitzboi—pie made from dried
   apples
Schnuck buppelin—cute babies
Schpring—run
Schtiffel—boots
Schuslich—careless
Sei shiah—pig barn
Sella kall—that guy
Shabbat—the Jewish Sabbath
Shiah—barn
Shul—synagogue
Sis gahns fer schrecklich—It's just
   frightful!
Sitzschtupp—living room

Tanakh—the Old Testament

Un naggle—a nail
Unfahgleichlich—how weird! Or,
   how strange!

Vas danksht—What do you think?
Vas in die velt—What in the world?
Veah ist es—Who is it?
Veah ist sella kall—Who is that guy?
Veck uff—Wake up!
Vundahboah—wonderful
Vundahboah besser—much better
Vee gehts—How's it going?

Yah—yes
Yah vell, so gehts—Yes well, that's
   the way it is.
Yammah—trouble
Yammahlich—something to wonder about; gross, lamentable,
   wretched

ABOUT THE AUTHOR

Dorcas Sharp Hoover, a former schoolteacher, lives with her family in Dover, Ohio, a short drive from what is known as "Amish Country."

Dorcas is married to Jerry, pastor and businessman. They have six children, ages five to 19.

Dr. Elton Lehman delivered four of their six children in the birthing center he designed. At every delivery, he always had a new story to tell. Jerry would say, "Dr. Lehman, you need to write a book!" Dr. Lehman would reply, "Yes, but I'm not a writer." And then, Dr. Lehman asked Dorcas if she would write his story.

House Calls and Hitching Posts is Dorcas' fourth book.